D0184755

ON A WING AND
A PRAYER

ON A WING
AND
A PRAYER

Joshua Levine

Collins

Collins
A division of HarperCollins Publishers
77–85 Fulham Palace Road
London W6 8JB
www.collins.co.uk

Published by Collins in 2008.

Copyright © Joshua Levine, 2008

1

Joshua Levine asserts the moral right to
be identified as the author of this work

A catalogue record for this book is
available from the British Library

ISBN 978-0-00-726945-7

Set in PostScript Giovanni Book with Photina display by
Rowland Phototypesetting Ltd, Bury St Edmunds, Suffolk

Printed and bound in Great Britain by
Clays Ltd, St Ives plc

Mixed Sources
Product group from well-managed
forests and other controlled sources
www.fsc.org Cert no. SW-COC-1806
© 1996 Forest Stewardship Council
FSC

FSC is a non-profit international organisation established to promote the
responsible management of the world's forests. Products carrying the FSC
label are independently certified to assure consumers that they come
from forests that are managed to meet the social, economic and
ecological needs of present and future generations.

Find out more about HarperCollins and the environment at
www.harpercollins.co.uk/green

For Dorothy Sahm

Contents

Introduction   ix
Prologue: December 1917   1

1   Emulating the Birds   7
2   The Combatants   27
3   A Flying Start   63
4   And so to War   91
5   An Office Job   124
6   Fighters and the Fokker Scourge   149
7   Life and Death   183
8   Over the Top   226
9   Bombing and the Royal Air Force   269
10 A Fight to the End   308

Epilogue   346
Acknowledgements   352
Index   355

Introduction

There are certain historical subjects which can always be counted on to capture the public imagination. One of these is infantry fighting on the Western Front, with its vivid evocations of suffering and wasted life. Yet taking place above the very same Western Front was a conflict that is less well known, but which deserves to become just as embedded in the public consciousness – the Great War in the Air.

Most people will have heard of Baron von Richthofen, but they will have little idea of why he was flying or who he was flying against. Yet the story of air fighting is one of intense human emotion, of young men growing up quickly in an exciting and terrible world, of chivalry and fear and danger, of the creation of modern warfare, of the development of modern sensibilities. Such an extraordinary story deserves a wider audience, and an acknowledgment of its place in history.

In 1976, it began to reach that wider audience when the BBC broadcast a television drama called *Wings*. Set in a Royal Flying Corps squadron in 1915, its central character is a young blacksmith who becomes a sergeant pilot on the Western Front. It is a moving series, which portrays the lives of young men attempting to make sense of a strange and terrifying world – and that is exactly what this book tries to do; to place individuals in the foreground who can paint detailed pictures, whilst never losing sight of the chaos erupting in the background.

Whilst writing this book, I have discovered how vivid and evocative a world it can be; I have found myself immersed in it – in its diaries, novels, letters, memoirs, aircraft, people, and sensibilities – only returning to the twenty-first century to pay the occasional bill. I hope that you, the reader, find yourself similarly engaged (not perhaps to the detriment of your household finances) so that the exploits of Mannock, Ball, James, Powell, and many others, become important to you. It is easy to identify with these recognizably modern men, carrying out a modern activity, with surprisingly modern attitudes, from a time long gone.

Whilst the time may have gone, one of its inhabitants is still with us. Henry Allingham, 111 years old as I write, served with the Royal Naval Air Service on the Western Front and at Jutland. He is a Victorian by birth, who has watched troops return from both the Boer War and the Second Gulf War. He has outlived many comrades by over ninety years, and he is the sole founder member of the Royal Air Force still alive. In the year of its ninetieth anniversary, it is fitting that we should remember the men who came together, some willingly, others less so, to form the Royal Air Force, and equally fitting that we should remember the thousands of airmen who died as it came into being.

In the pages that follow, the thoughts, feelings, fears and sensations of long ago are aired. Listen to them, and enter a world quite different to our own – inhabited by people not so very different at all.

JOSHUA LEVINE

PROLOGUE

December 1917

"Some time after the Cambrai attack in 1917, my scout squadron, No. 3 RFC, which was equipped with single-seater Sopwith Camels, each carrying two Vickers guns firing through the propeller, was stationed near Bapaume, and was manned by comparatively new pilots with no combat experience to speak of, as the squadron losses in the Cambrai battle had been complete, with the exception of two pilots – myself and a Captain Babington.

One day after the two flights, 'A' and 'B', the latter under my command, had been detailed to carry out a routine patrol over the enemy lines, I remember walking across the worn grass on a bright sunny morning towards our eight machines lined up in front of the hangars. The air mechanics were standing by as usual after having very carefully checked over guns and engines. They helped us into our cockpits and saw us settled in our seats and safety belts fastened, then they climbed down with a quiet, 'Good luck, sir.'

It was only then that the tension that was always present just before taking off on a patrol left us and we were able to think of our immediate duties. After having repeated the mechanics' 'Contact!', our engines roared into life and we all revved them up against the chocks with the mechanics holding down the tail to check that we were getting full revolutions. Then I throttled down and after a glance round the flight to see that all were ready, I taxied into the wind and took off, closely followed by the whole patrol.

We climbed to cross the trenches a few miles away at 12,000 to 13,000 feet, and while doing so, fired a few rounds from both of our guns to make sure there was no jamming as this was very difficult to clear while in action. Our Camels being tail heavy, the stick had to be held between our knees to free both hands to clear the stoppage, otherwise the planes immediately shot up into a loop. The trenches beneath us wound like long scars meandering across the seemingly lifeless dun-coloured countryside, pitted with thousands of shell craters, not a single tree or building left standing anywhere near the lines.

Very soon, we heard and saw our usual welcome from 'Archie', bursting in black puffs all around us, but carried on, only varying our height to spoil his aim. After crossing the lines without further incident, we found that the fresh wind, which always seemed to blow to the east, was drifting us too far into enemy territory, and it would have been unwise to penetrate, our limit of flying time being only two hours: a return slow flight against the wind under possible attack might have exhausted our petrol before it was possible to reach our landing field. I therefore gave the signal to turn north, parallel with the trenches, and we continued our patrol.

Just then, several thousand feet above us and right in the sun, I saw a formation of sixteen enemy aircraft (we were always outnumbered) and in a few seconds they were diving on our formation from all directions, and the air was full of tracer, and twisting and turning machines, engaged in a general dogfight. One of ours was soon in difficulties and was seen to go down, out of control, at the same time as two of the Huns also broke off, apparently badly damaged. We closed formation again with 'B' Flight still intact, followed by two of 'A' Flight, and waited for the next assault, as the Germans had dived past us after their first attack, and were now gaining height again. They were a squadron of Richthofen's Circus, and they were painted in all sorts of colours and patterns, and one, I noticed, had a wavy red snake painted along the fuselage. But there was not much time to wonder at them, as part of their squadron had been kept in reserve a few thousand feet above: their Albatroses could always out-climb and out-dive our Camels, as they had beautifully streamlined plywood fuselages and powerful engines, while our machines were still at the fabric-covered wooden-framed stage, with rotary engines.

These Huns came down at us and one of 'A' Flight was soon in difficulties, being surrounded by at least three of the enemy, and fighting hard against such odds. To go to his assistance was, of course, the only thing to do, and by waggling my wings from side to side, I gave the one signal we could use in those days in an emergency, for the rest of the flight to follow. But in all the excitement and tension, my turn to the right was not noticed, and I realised that I was single-handed in the rescue attempt, and would have to deal with four Huns, as by the time I reached the scene, our machine was already going down practically out of control, and I was quickly in a dogfight with three highly coloured Albatroses.

I picked on the one which seemed to be piloted by the leader as it had a small triangular black flag attached to the vertical fin of his rudder, besides being vividly coloured. We engaged in the usual circling tactics, each trying to out-turn the other and keep on the inside, and in this manoeuvre, I was successful owing to the remarkable turning property of the Camel, and I held the inside position with my guns aimed at the front of the Hun machine. We were so close that I could clearly see the pilot's white face with his goggles and black flying helmet, looking over the side at my machine, and although I fired several short bursts, I could

3

see all my tracers swinging to just miss his tail. My Camel was very near to the limit of its turning circle, but I realised that I had to turn just that little extra in order to rake his fuselage with my fire.

We had been circling for what seemed like hours but must have been only minutes, when I pulled the Camel still further round on its left hand turn, and loosed off a long burst which hit just behind the pilot, and put his machine out of control. We both fell away, myself in a fast full-power spin. By this time, three other enemy aircraft had climbed above us, waiting their chance, and I realised that as I came out of my spin, I would present a good target on straightening out in a vertical dive.

After falling about a thousand feet, I stopped the spin, and immediately did a fast turn and climb to face two of the diving enemies as they came at me, their tracers crackling past and my guns replying, but all without apparent effect. The two Huns had dived past as I turned to meet the third machine which was following the first two, and I noticed his painted red nose and blue fuselage, and realised too late, that he had a bead on me. A frantic pull over on the joystick was also too late, and the next thing I knew was a stunning sledgehammer blow as a bullet sunk into my right thigh.

Recovering from the shock, and finding the Camel in a vertical climb through the instinctive pulling back of the stick after being hit, I pulled over hard into a quick roll, just in time to miss a burst from a diving Hun, who was waiting above. It must have been about this time that my feed pipe was partly shot through, and the escaping petrol started spraying over my right leg, making it numb and cold, but my worry now was how to get out of the fight alive, and reach our lines again.

Three Huns were now following me down in a steep dive, firing as they came, but when any of them approached too close, I pulled the Camel into a vertical climb, and fired bursts at the nearest, then turned and dived again towards our lines, still some miles away. These manoeuvres continued in a running fight for a long time, and I began to feel a little sick through loss of blood, especially when my leg felt hot and warm instead of cold, through blood running down from my wound overcoming the previous numbness.

With all these odds against me, there suddenly came the realization that these Huns were out to kill me without mercy or hesitation, crippled as I was, and the enormity of it momentarily created the thought that just by turning towards enemy territory, this fate could be avoided, and I should be saved from further suffering. Perhaps some feeling of pride overcoming the indignity of the suggestion enabled me to regain my self-control, and to continue the running fight towards our trenches, losing height and turning every now and then to face and drive off my attackers.

Down to about a thousand feet, and feeling pretty weak, I managed to find a stick of chewing gum in my flying coat breast pocket, and I ate that, paper and all. The Huns followed down to 500 feet, just above their trenches, and then turned away as I crossed our lines at 200 feet, making for one of our emergency landing fields, containing a hut and one air mechanic on duty.

With some difficulty, as I could not see very well, and my Camel was badly shot up, with most of the flying wires cut and dangling, I made a fair landing, and was helped out by the airman. In getting out, I could not help noticing a neat group of four bullet holes in the cowling behind my seat, and about two inches behind where my head had been; an inch or two further to the rear and this burst would have hit my petrol tank, and what we all fear most – to be set on fire in the air – would have happened. And there would have been no escape, parachutes for pilots not having been issued.

Why those bullets should have missed me is one of the

unsolved mysteries of my life; some lasted a few weeks, others months, one never knew. So often had I packed up my roommates' belongings, always left ready in case, and forwarded them to relatives, wondering when my own turn would come. Now it had – and more fortunately for me than for most of these young pilots.

The airman soon had a stretcher party along which took me to an advanced dressing station, where my wound was dressed, and a day or two later, I was on my way to Rouen, then back to London. After some two months in hospital, convalescing, I was posted to a training squadron as flying instructor, and only returned to active service just before the end of the war."

Howard Brokensha

1

Emulating the Birds

If you happen to be reading this book on board a commercial flight, take a look around you. You are sitting in a pressurized cabin. You have no real sense of movement and you probably have no view. Your fellow passengers are eating and drinking, reading and sleeping. Unless they are nervous flyers, they are unlikely to be reflecting that they are breaking the laws of nature and defying common sense. The 'wonder of flight' is in short supply on the trans-atlantic run – but it has not always been so. In 1915, Duncan Grinnell-Milne was a young officer serving in the Royal Flying Corps. On a BE2c reconnaissance flight over the German lines in that year, in the midst of the bloodiest war ever fought, he experienced an overwhelming sensation:

> I must be asleep, dreaming. The war was an illusion of my own. Surely the immense and placid world upon which I gazed could not be troubled by human storms such as I had been imagining. In that quiet land human beings could never have become so furiously enraged that they must fly at each other's throats. At 10,000 feet, on a sunny afternoon, with only the keen wind upon one's face and the hum of an aero-engine in one's ears, it is hard not to feel godlike and judicial.

In flight, the normal yardsticks that apply on the ground are suspended. Perceptions of speed and distance are altered. Mountains, rivers, urban sprawls, even battlegrounds lose their significance. This is why man has always dreamt of flying: to distance himself from his human frailty and place himself closer to the mysteries of the universe. Yet the godlike sensation felt by Grinnell-Milne also encourages a sense of power. The desire to fly has long been accompanied by the urge to dominate. In 1737, almost 200 years before powered flight, the poet Thomas Gray imagined the sky as a battlefield on which England could affirm her superiority:

> The day will come when thou shalt lift thine eyes
> To watch a long drawn battle of the skies,
> And aged peasants too amazed for words,
> stare at the flying fleets of wondrous birds.
>
> And England, so long mistress of the seas,
> Where winds and waves confess her sovereignty,
> Her ancient triumphs yet on high shall bear
> And reign the sovereign of the conquered air.

In 1907, before a truly reliable aircraft had even been constructed, H. G. Wells was already predicting how the new technology would be used to wage war. In *The War in the Air*, described by Wells as a 'fantasia of possibility', he imagines a future conflict in which New York is destroyed by bombs dropped from German airships. The city becomes a 'furnace of crimson flames, from which there was no escape'. The central character, a young British civilian, witnesses the devastation, recognizes that national boundaries no longer exist and awaits the collapse of civilization. We still await the collapse of civilization, but Wells' predictions have proved more than mere fantasias of possibility.

On 17 December 1903, however, no such thoughts

were in the minds of Orville and Wilbur Wright, bicycle shop owners from Dayton, Ohio. On that morning, at Kitty Hawk, North Carolina, a site chosen for its forgiving sands and coastal breezes, Orville flew the first aircraft, powered by a tiny petrol engine. The *Wright Flyer* harnessed the wind and struggled into the air. It flew a distance of 120 feet at a height of ten feet. The brothers believed that the key to successful flight was control of an inherently unstable machine and that the key to control was to copy a bird in flight by warping (or twisting) the machine's wings. As the wings were warped, the end of one wing would receive more lift than the other and that wing would rise, banking the machine and turning it in the direction of the other. In this way, the machine could be guided onto a particular course, as well as returned to stable flight when tipped by a gust of wind.

Over time, the Wrights improved their machine until, on 5 October 1905, Orville flew twenty-four miles at a speed of thirty-eight miles per hour. The brothers remained quiet about their achievements, commenting that of all the birds, the parrot talks the most but flies the worst. In fact, they were nervous of competitors discovering their secrets. They carried out no flights in 1906 and 1907, on the advice of their attorney, as they attempted to sell the machine to military authorities across the world. They were charging $250,000, but refusing to give a demonstration until a contract was signed. Unsurprisingly, nobody took up their offer.

In September 1906, the first machine took to the air outside the United States, flown by Alberto Santos-Dumont at Bagatelle, near Paris. French aircraft designers began to make impressive progress and they were soon claiming world records for flight duration and distance. They were unaware of the advances made by the Wrights, however, so when, in August 1908, Wilbur demonstrated the *Wright Flyer* at Hunaudières, near Le Mans, his audience was astounded. Not only had he complete control of the machine, but he was even able to carry a passenger. French claims were quietly dropped. In July 1909, the Wrights finally sold their aircraft to the U.S. Army but in the years that followed they became mired in patent litigation, and their creative drive petered out. In 1946, James Goodson, a colonel in the U.S. Air Force, persuaded the elderly Orville Wright to attend a military conference in New York. The two men flew together. Goodson remembers:

> The hostess on the aeroplane saw this elderly gentleman and she approached him and asked, 'Are you enjoying the flight?' and Orville said, 'Yeah, very much.' She said, 'Have you flown before?' He said, 'Yeah, I've flown before.' She said, 'That's great! Do you enjoy it?' He said, 'I enjoyed the first flight and I'm enjoying this one too . . .'

Once at the conference, Orville was keen to distance himself from the world of modern aviation:

> In introducing Orville to the conference, Eddie Rickenbacker, the First World War ace, said in his usual flamboyant manner, 'Today, we have fleets of aircraft flying to all corners of the world. We've brought the world together. We've just finished a war in which fleets of aircraft have destroyed the industrial potential of entire nations. Fifty years ago, no one would have believed this but two men – and two men alone – had a magnificent vision and we're fortunate to have one of them here today. I give you Mr. Orville Wright!' There was a standing ovation, and little Orville stood up. He said, 'My name is Orville Wright.' There was a blast of applause. 'But that's about the only true thing that Eddie Rickenbacker has said. Wilbur and I had no idea that aviation would take off the way it has. As a matter

of fact, we were convinced that the aeroplane could never carry more than one passenger. We had no idea that there'd be thousands of aircraft flying around the world. We had no idea that aircraft would be dropping bombs. We were just a couple of kids with a bike shop who wanted to get this contraption up in the air. It was a hobby. *We had no idea . . .'*

Given the strenuous efforts of the brothers to sell their machine to a military bidder, Orville's words might appear slightly disingenuous, but in their wake, designers across the world competed to produce faster and more reliable aircraft. In Germany, research was focused not on aeroplanes but on dirigible airships. The first Zeppelin had flown in July 1900 but it was not until 1907, prompted by the military authorities, that work began on a large-scale airship.

In 1908, the first flying machine took to the air in Britain. It was flown by an American, Samuel Cody. Cody, cowboy, actor, kite inventor, balloonist, aviator and eccentric, had arrived in Britain in 1901, bringing his Wild West stage show with him. Dolly Shepherd, a pre-war balloonist and parachutist, remembers being drafted in to act as his assistant:

Cody was a sharpshooter with long hair, pointed beard, great big hat and white trousers. He was quite a showman. When I met him, he was frustrated because he used to shoot an egg off his wife's head and the night before, he had grazed her skull. 'Don't despair!' I said, 'I'll take her place!' I'd never even seen the show, but that night, I went up on stage, and he put an egg on my head and took aim. What I hadn't reckoned for – his son came up and blindfolded him. I didn't dare move but he shot the egg and all was well. The next day, Cody invited me to see his kites. He had to do the sharpshooting business and theatrical things to make money. But he was making his big kites in the great hall at Alexandra Palace.

These were man-lifting Boxkites, which Cody intended to sell to the military authorities for use as observation posts. Over the years, Cody progressed from kites to airships to aircraft, and in October 1908, his flying machine, powered by an Antoinette engine, flew for a distance of 1390 feet. One of his first flights is remembered by Edward Bolt, an NCO with the Royal Engineers Balloon Section at Farnborough:

> He was doing practice flights for a long time before he got off the ground. I remember one of his flights when I was one of the markers. He circled for a mile and there were twelve of us stood there with flags until he'd completed his circuit and landed. We all came towards the machine and Cody said to our corporal, 'Here's a pound! Take these men to the Queen's Hotel and buy them a drink! That's the only pound I've got left . . .'

In May 1909, John Moore-Brabazon (who later proved an old adage by flying a pig in his passenger seat) became the first British man to fly an aircraft in Britain. Five months later, he collected a prize of £1000 offered by the *Daily Mail* to the first person to fly a circular mile in a British aircraft. Recalling this event, Moore-Brabazon describes it as 'the real start of the British aeroplane industry'. Despite his achievements, there were many in Britain, including Lord Northcliffe, owner of the *Daily Mail*, who were worried that the country was falling dangerously behind its rivals. The newspaper attempted to rouse public concerns, by announcing that Britain was 'no longer an island', and it offered a new prize to the first pilot to fly across the English Channel. On 25 July 1909, the prize was won – but not by a Briton. Louis Blériot, a Frenchman, flying his own monoplane, flew from Calais to Dover in thirty-seven minutes. Northcliffe's fears concerning British vulnerability appeared justified. 'The British people have hitherto dwelt secure in their islands . . . but locomotion is now being transferred to an element where sea power is no shield against attack,' warned the *Daily Mail*. Describing Blériot's achievement with barely a hint of sour grapes, Moore-Brabazon comments:

> He rather gallantly and very luckily crossed the Channel in a monoplane tractor with a three cylinder air-cooled engine that never before or after – even when copied – ever ran so long. His success was due to running into a very big shower of rain that cooled his engine when in sight of our shores.

Lucky or not, Blériot's achievement hastened British aircraft development. Across the country, engineers and mechanics began to adapt their skills to the design and construction of flying machines. Frederick Handley-Page was eventually to become a celebrated aeronautical designer, responsible for the first heavy British bombers which flew towards the end of the Great War, as well as the Second World War Halifax bomber. At first, however, he was working out of a shed in Barking, with a coppersmith, Charles Tye, as his sole assistant. Tye recalls meeting Handley-Page in a pub:

> One Friday night, the barmaid said to me, 'Charlie, the gentleman sitting down there with a beer is looking for a coppersmith who can use a blowlamp.' So I looked round and saw Handley-Page. I went across to him and he told me he was opening up a workshop and was building a 'machine'. I didn't know he meant an aircraft. But I went down to his workshop, where he only had a little coke brazier. There were two benches with wing spars that would take the wings of the mono-plane that he was building, but apart from that, the shop was bare. He had no tools whatever – only a plane and some chisels. So we started to build the machine

together. I was making all the fittings. I was brazing pieces of tube onto plates that would take the struts. As we went on, we took on a carpenter called Cyril who made the ribs and the longerons. By the time the aircraft was finished, there were a dozen of us working on it. We called it *Yellow Peril* because the wings were covered in fabric and doped in a yellow cellulose material.

Other great aeronautical companies were also setting up. The Avro company was formed by A. V. Roe, a marine engineer from Manchester, who had made detailed observations of birds while at sea. In June 1908, four months before Cody's maiden flight, Roe almost took to the air in a machine of his own design, but he never quite made it off the ground. Geoffrey de Havilland – who would one day design the Mosquito, the Second World War fighter-bomber, and the Comet, the world's first jet airliner – began work on his first aircraft in the same year, in a shed off the Fulham Road in London. He flew the machine, eighteen months later, from a hilltop on the Hampshire Downs. It took off, flew for thirty-five yards, and crashed. De Havilland suffered only cuts and bruises, but the machine was wrecked.

A crucial boost to designers arrived in 1909 with the introduction of the French Gnôme rotary engine. Rotary engines had a better power-to-weight ratio than conventional engines, they reduced vibration and they were far more efficiently cooled, due to the rotation of the cylinder block around the crankshaft. Copies of the Gnôme engine were soon produced, and powered flight became a far more practical proposition.

It was not long before flying gripped the British public's imagination. In 1910, Claude Grahame-White, a motorcar dealer, established an aerodrome at Hendon in north London – nowadays the site of the Royal Air Force Museum. 'London Aerodrome', as Grahame-White called it, quickly became a venue for aerial displays and joyrides for day-trippers. Eric Furlong was a young man, living in Hendon, whose interest in flying was sparked by visits to the aerodrome. He remembers:

> Clarence Winchester was a freelance pilot with his own aeroplane giving joyrides to people for something like £1 a time. He used to put the passenger in the aeroplane and then start frightening them by telling them that they mustn't touch *this*, that whatever they do, they were not to lean against *that*, *that* wire was absolute death if they got tangled up in it. By the time they took off, the passenger was jelly. When we asked him why he did this, he said, 'Well, they think they're getting their money's worth if they're really frightened . . .'

On Sundays, Frederick Handley-Page would send his aircraft, *Yellow Peril*, down to London Aerodrome, where its pilot would give joyrides. There was one man who refused to take a 'flip', however, as Charles Tye recalls:

> Every Sunday, we used to take people up for trips. From Hendon, round Hyde Park and back. I don't suppose the trip lasted more than ten minutes and we used to charge a guinea. One particular Sunday, Handley-Page was there himself and I saw him talking to the actress Gladys Cooper. We hadn't had a customer for a while, and the pilot, a man named Whitehead, said to me, 'I wonder if Miss Gladys Cooper wants a trip? Go and ask! And if she doesn't want a flip, ask Mr. Page if he'd like one. I don't think he's ever been in the air before!' So I went over and just stood aside Mr. Page while he was talking to Gladys Cooper. 'What do you want, Charlie?' he asked. I said, 'Mr. Whitehead is sitting up there and he's getting fed up. Is anybody coming up?' He said, 'No!' So I said, 'Well, he says he'd like to take *you* up as he doesn't think you've been in the air before!' He looked at Miss Gladys Cooper and he took

me aside and whispered in my ear, 'You go back and tell Whitehead – I build them. I don't bloody well fly them!'

For a number of years, the military authorities in Britain had financed the development of airships while leaving aircraft production to private enterprise. However shortsighted this may now seem, the fact was that early aircraft could not reach high altitudes, they could not carry great weights and they could not fly at night or in high winds. Airships could do all of these things. They were also considered rather more genteel than aeroplanes. Robert Pigot recalls an agreeable morning spent aboard an airship, while serving with the Royal Flying Corps in 1913:

> I was living about fourteen miles from Farnborough, where I was stationed, and one morning, I thought I'd go home for breakfast so I flew my airship over and circled round my house until the butler came out. He fetched the gardener. The two of them pulled me down and tied the airship to a tree at one end and a garden roller at the other. And I went in and had breakfast.

Over time, as aircraft became sturdier and more reliable, the military authorities began to take them more seriously. A 1911 report of the Committee of Imperial Defence declared that aeroplanes could 'keep army commanders in the field as fully informed as possible of the movements of the enemy'. The idea of entrusting the role of military reconnaissance to a fleet of flying birdcages was unsettling to the armed forces. It was particularly unsettling to the cavalry, whose job reconnaissance had always been, and who still dominated the War Office. There was not yet any official expectation that aircraft could contribute to military operations, drop bombs, or engage in air-to-air combat, but there was now the prospect of a role.

The new thinking was reinforced in April 1911, with the establishment of the Army Aircraft Factory (later renamed the Royal Aircraft Factory) at Farnborough. Under its Superintendent, Mervyn O'Gorman, the Factory assembled a team of designers, who were immediately hampered by the limitations placed on the Factory by its charter, which stated that it could not manufacture new types of aircraft, merely produce conversions from existing aircraft. Geoffrey de Havilland joined the Factory as a designer. He describes how it was possible to circumvent the Factory's restrictive charter:

> We weren't supposed to design new aeroplanes but we could reconstruct them from a landing wheel or a few old bolts from a crashed machine. In this way, during my time at Farnborough, we designed and built several new aeroplanes. When I'd been at Farnborough for about a year, we designed the BE1. We did it by taking a small part of a broken-down French Voisin and reconstructing it into something totally different. The BE1 was quite a successful aeroplane but it was unstable – meaning that you had to control it all the time. I was not very interested in stability until Edward Busk, who had studied the theory of stability, joined the Factory. He took the BE1 and applied his knowledge to modifying it in order to get stability. He moved the lower plane back about three feet, which was equivalent to moving the centre of gravity forward, he fitted a bigger span tailplane, he fitted a fin in front of the rudder and we ended up with a really stable aeroplane. It was quite astonishing to be able to get into this machine, after the unstable machines of the early days, and fly around with hands and feet off indefinitely. That machine eventually became the BE2c and it was really the start of practical, stable aeroplanes.

The Factory produced a series of aircraft, each classified by type. The first type, designated BE (Blériot Experimental) was a 'tractor' biplane, with the propeller at the front of the aircraft. This is the type described by de Havilland. The second type, designated FE (Farman Experimental), was a 'pusher' biplane, with the propeller behind the fuselage. A third type, with the elevators at the front, was named SE (Santos-Dumont Experimental). The final type produced by the Factory was the RE (Reconnaissance Experimental). Different versions of these types constituted the Factory's output throughout the Great War.

As the Army Aircraft Factory came into being, a body of men was needed to fly the new machines. On 1 April 1911, the Air Battalion, Royal Engineers was created. Consisting initially of 14 officers and 150 other ranks, it was decided that officers could join the battalion from any arm or branch of the army but that the other ranks must come from within the Royal Engineers. Pilots would not be trained *ab initio*, however. Prior to joining, they would have to learn to fly at their own expense, before being reimbursed on acceptance by the Air Battalion.

While the British High Command could not see beyond the possibilities of aerial reconnaissance, Germany was proposing a far more aggressive function for its airborne fleet. The Germans considered the Zeppelin airships superior to any weapon possessed by any other nation. General von Moltke, the Chief of the German General Staff, announced to his War Ministry that 'its speediest development is required to enable us at the beginning of a war to strike a first and telling blow, whose practical and moral effect could be quite extraordinary'.

On 13 April 1912, the Air Battalion was superseded by a larger organization: the Royal Flying Corps. This was intended to join together, under a single umbrella, the army aviators of the Air Battalion with a group of naval aviators who had been running their own flying school at Eastchurch, on the Isle of Sheppey. The Royal Flying Corps comprised a military wing, a naval wing and a Central Flying School at Upavon, on Salisbury Plain.

Doubts were expressed about the location of the Central Flying School. The area around Upavon was prone to dangerous air currents, which had brought down many aircraft over the previous few years, causing the area to become known as 'The Valley of Death'. Another issue was the status of The Royal Flying Corps. As a corps, its leaders would be subordinate to those in the established services, guaranteeing it little say in its own destiny. Nevertheless, it appeared that unity had been imposed on the world of British military aviation.

That unity did not last very long. The Admiralty was not keen to hand control of its flying matters over to an army corps. It therefore rejected the idea of a 'naval wing' and announced the formation of the Royal Naval Air Service, under the command of Murray Sueter. This unilateral decision went entirely unchallenged, leaving the Royal Flying Corps to represent the army alone – although, officially, the Royal Naval Air Service did not come into being until July 1914. Philip Joubert de la Ferté, an early member of the Royal Flying Corps, who was to fly one of the first two 'shows' of the war in August 1914, remembers the divide between army and navy:

> The Admiralty never really accepted the recommendations of the Committee of Imperial Defence. They didn't want to be organized by the War Office in any way. They paid lip service to the royal warrant for a period of years, but they went along in their own way. When the Royal Flying Corps was formed, Brigadier General David Henderson took the military and naval wings under his charge. He was an authority on

reconnaissance – he'd written a book on reconnaissance. He was a soldier, not an airman. Looking at an aeroplane, he could only imagine flying over an enemy force at low speed so that you could literally count the men on the ground. He believed that there should be no aeroplane with an engine more powerful than it should have a speed of more than 100 miles per hour in the air. The Admiralty, on the other hand, was looking into the problem of fighting and offensive operations in the air. It was fully alive to all the possibilities and it wanted bigger and faster aeroplanes than were thought necessary for the army. The navy took a much broader view.

The intention of the War Office was that all military aircraft would be built by the Royal Aircraft Factory but the Admiralty began to turn to private enterprise to design and build its machines. While it was hardly satisfactory that the infant British flying service should consist of two rival organizations, it at least meant that, eventually, a greater choice of aircraft and engines would be available to both branches. Once the war had begun, this would prove crucial.

At the date of its formation, the Royal Flying Corps had only eleven aircraft in active use. An up-to-date, reliable machine was needed that could be produced by the Royal Aircraft Factory. To this end, Military Aeroplane Trials were held on Salisbury Plain in August 1912. The machine which most impressed the judges was designed and built by Samuel Cody. Handley-Page's assistant, Charles Tye, was present:

> I was in the next shed to Cody. All the hangars were built by the government and they wanted a machine for the Royal Flying Corps. There was about fifteen sheds. A. V. Roe had one, Martinsyde had one, we had one, Samuel Cody had one. I used to do a bit of work

on Cody's machine – I used to true it up for him now and again. When I had trips with him, I sat on a bicycle seat behind him with my hands on his shoulders. His machine was a pusher type with the prop behind. We used to call it the 'Cathedral' because it was so huge.

The trials were that you landed on a ploughed field and you got off again. The only thing was that every machine that landed on that ploughed field couldn't get off again. Cody was the last one to land on this ploughed field and it had been raked up so much by the time he landed. He had a son with him and I was there too. Cody was sitting up at the top of this machine while the inspector was testing his tank and testing all his controls. When Cody had word to get off, his son called out 'Look!' What he'd seen was that there was a space in that field that was nearly bare. The machines that had been trying to take off previously had flattened down the ground. It was like a steamroller had been over it. I believe that if Cody had landed first, he wouldn't have got off that ploughed field.

Although he won, Cody's machine was never taken up by the Royal Flying Corps. N. V. Piper remembers why:

In 1912, I was lent to Cody and I worked with him, building a replica of the machine that had won the military trials, the sale of which was part of the prize of those trials. Major Raleigh smashed the replica on a very short flight. He'd been flying an aircraft that had been sluggish on the controls but the Cody was hypersensitive, particularly on the fore and aft control. So he crashed it. We rebuilt it and brought it back, but in the meantime the machine that had won the military trials crashed, and it was decided to drop the Cody machine.

Instead of Cody's machine, the Royal Flying Corps adopted the BE2, the machine worked on by Geoffrey de Havilland at the Royal Aircraft Factory. A year after the Trials, Cody crashed his machine on Laffan's Plain. Edward Bolt was present:

> Cody took up a passenger, a man that came from Reading. Leon Cody and I were watching and all of a sudden, the machine started wobbling and we could quite clearly see that the passenger was grabbing hold of Cody's shoulders, which I am sure caused the crash.

Frederick Laws, an NCO with the Royal Flying Corps, ran over to the crumpled aircraft, where he found both Cody and his passenger lying dead. Cody was fifty-one years old. Remembering him, Laws comments, 'I wouldn't say he was unbalanced – but he was erratic.' Erratic he may have been, but with his tireless enthusiasm and air of self-invention, Cody embodies the age of the pioneers. At his funeral, his importance as an aircraft designer was recognized. James Gascoyne, a Royal Flying Corps mechanic, was a wreath bearer:

> Cody's funeral was a very, very ceremonial affair. It lasted about two hours, I suppose. It was an enormous gathering of civilians and soldiers.

Shortly after the Military Trials, in September 1912, the British army held its annual manoeuvres, in East Anglia. During the exercise, a red army, commanded by Sir Douglas Haig was soundly beaten by a blue army, commanded by Sir James Grierson. The deciding factor in Grierson's victory was his use of aerial reconnaissance. One of Grierson's aircraft, piloted by Lieutenant Arthur Longmore, with Major Hugh Trenchard (a name to remember) as his observer, spotted the advance of Haig's troops and immediately reported its findings. Grierson, meanwhile, had hidden his troops from observation, remarking afterwards that he had ordered them 'to look as like toadstools as they could and to make noises like oysters'. The blue army's victory, apparently inspired by Lewis Carroll, ensured a role for aviation in a future war.

While the 'military wing' concentrated on preparing for the role of reconnaissance, the 'naval wing' trod a more experimental path, prompted by Winston Churchill, First Lord of the Admiralty. Churchill, always open to novel ideas, had been an early supporter of flying. Philip Joubert de la Ferté remembers:

> Churchill had become First Lord of the Admiralty in 1911. He got to hear of the activities at Eastchurch and he decided that he should take some interest. Not only did he take an interest, but he learnt to fly. He was a perishing pilot, most dangerous, but he did it and he got to know something about the air, and it was his authority and his enthusiasm which got the Royal Naval Air Service off to a tremendous start.

The Admiralty began investigating the most effective methods of bombing ships and submarines, although not always with sufficient flexibility. In 1912, Victor Goddard, a cadet at Dartmouth Naval College, witnessed the invention of a fellow cadet:

> Cadet Robinson had devised a bombsight which allowed for the drift of the aeroplane in the air, and also for its forward speed of flight. This was something which was new to me, and I think it was new to the whole world. At any rate, he was almost certainly the first person to submit a bombsight to a government department. The reply from the Admiralty was that their Lordships saw no application for this invention.

Nevertheless, their Lordships examined other interesting possibilities, including the bombing of longer-range targets such as German airship bases. The navy felt vulnerable to Zeppelin bombing, as their own bases were to be found along the coast, and so a chain of air stations was constructed from which naval airships and aircraft could strike out against enemy raiders. As a result, the Royal Naval Air Service was to become responsible for the defence of the mainland from aerial attack in the forthcoming war.

As the prospect of a European war became more real, it was very clear that aviation would have a part to play, if, at first, only in an observational role. Nevertheless, that prospect ought to have been sufficient for the politicians and generals to predict an aerial escalation. To send an aircraft up to spy on the enemy is to invite preventative measures, and the simplest way to prevent an aircraft from spying is to send another aircraft up to shoot it down. Every aircraft would therefore need the means to defend itself. This had all been foreseen in a Royal Flying Corps training manual, produced a few months before the outbreak of war:

> It is probable that one phase of the struggle for the command of the air will resolve itself into a series of combats between individual aeroplanes or pairs of aeroplanes. If the pilots of one side can succeed in obtaining victory in a succession of such combats, they will establish a moral ascendancy over the surviving pilots of the enemy, and be left free to carry out their duties of reconnaissance.

Taken a stage further, if an aircraft is capable of observing the enemy in its activities, it is surely capable of disrupting those very activities by dropping bombs. Yet every aircraft that went to war in the summer of 1914 was completely unarmed and unprepared to carry arms of any kind. When asking why, it should be remembered that at the outbreak of war aeroplanes had been flying for less than eleven years. They were not yet sturdy platforms for guns or bombs. They were flimsy contraptions, liable to tear themselves to pieces if handled roughly or landed steeply. And they were deliberately flimsy in order to minimize the weight of a craft that was breaking the laws of nature by taking to the air in the first place. Aeroplanes were still mistrusted for their very novelty. It was to take a war to demonstrate the extraordinary potential of the flying machine.

If there were still military doubts about the machines, there were also doubts about the men flying them. Many of the early flyers had been daredevils and risk-takers, nonconforming young men who valued adventure above duty, individuality above discipline. Edward Peter was such a man. Charles Tye remembers how, in 1912, Peter had jumped into Handley-Page's precious machine and made off:

> Edward Peter got up and he got into *Yellow Peril*. And all of a sudden, he was trying the controls – he was working the empennage and working the rudder. Then, he opened up the engine full. I shouted out, 'What are you up to, Edward? What the devil are you up to? Come you out! Come you out! This machine has never been up before!' But Edward didn't take no notice. He simply revved up and went over the chocks and away he went. He ran about 200 yards and he was in the air. He flew that machine as an experienced man. He turned it round and climbed and away he went. Next thing we heard, he'd landed at Brooklands Aerodrome. When he landed, he was interviewed by an official at Brooklands and he got severely reprimanded and they were going to charge him with flying a machine without a licence. Because he had no licence – and this was his first time in an aeroplane!

This was the sort of person who might well progress from civilian flying into the Royal Flying Corps or Royal Naval Air Service and it frightened the conservative majority within the armed forces. Claude Grahame-White, the pioneer and founder of the London Aerodrome, was something of a dandy. This ensured him a dry reception on his arrival in the Royal Naval Air Service, by whom he had been granted a commission. Lance Sieveking tells the tale:

> Grahame-White had been given the rank of flight commander and we heard that on his first day, he had presented himself at the admiralty in his beautiful new uniform, a diamond tiepin and white spats. He was a very handsome man. 'Well, old boy,' he said jauntily to Lord Edward Grosvenor, in his office over the Admiralty Arch, 'How will I do? Is it all right?' Lord Edward looked at him critically and said in a tone of reproach, 'I think you've forgotten one thing. The gold earrings, dear fellow . . .'

With aviation came a new breed of soldier and sailor, irreverent, questioning, likely to appreciate the 'wonder of flight' with which we began this chapter. Despite the best efforts of Hugh Trenchard, the man who was to take command of the Royal Flying Corps in 1915, the First World War flying services were never as regimented as the older services. Standards of dress and mess-room behaviour often fell short of accepted standards. Yet, these were men who were living on their nerves and putting all their energies into an undertaking that they were not likely to survive. These are the men whose voices will be heard in the pages that follow.

2

The Combatants

The following letter was written by a young man to his parents in 1916:

> Last night I was just getting into my bed when a sponge full of water came along the room. At once the place was in a fine mess. I threw a jug of water, but the same was returned with interest. Next the place got so full of water that I ran into the garden, falling into a big hole full of mud. I managed to obtain two onions on my way back, and with these attacked the mob. All our beds are wet through. However, at last all got right again and we got our sleep. It was great sport.

The young man was not a schoolboy but a fighter pilot. His name was Albert Ball, and within a year he would earn a Victoria Cross, a Military Cross and three Distinguished Service Orders as arguably the greatest British fighter ace of the war. His letter describes the adolescent horseplay common in the squadrons. Situated in comfortable chateaux and farmhouses behind the lines, these squadrons served as a refuge from the realities of life in the air. When a man was killed, the custom was to carry on as though nothing had happened, to drink and sing, to shed no tears. With their outward confidence, emotional reserve and 'great sport', these squadrons brought the world of the English public school to France. It is not surprising that so many letters home were childlike. Albert Ball again:

> Am feeling very poo-poo today. Five of my best pals were done in yesterday, and I think it is so rotten.

In terms of background, if not of achievement, Ball was a typical British Great War pilot. Middle class, public school educated, and keen, the squadrons were full of men like him. Frederick Winterbotham was one:

> I was born in the reign of Queen Victoria, in 1897, and I always remember my annoyance at the age of three, when I was given a prayer book with Queen Victoria on it, and she died, and I felt that I had been done down because I no longer had a queen. I grew up in a normal household in Stroud in Gloucestershire, where my father had a law business. I suppose my great love was always ponies and horses. It went on throughout my life. I went to an excellent school in Eastbourne and then I went on to Charterhouse, in that hot summer of 1911. I loved Charterhouse. It was the most gorgeous place and we played every sort of sport and game. My only trouble was that I was growing rather too fast and after I'd been there for a couple of years, I was well over six feet and I'd outgrown my strength. I was no longer fit to play games properly – so the medical people said that I should go for a sea voyage. I persuaded my father and mother to send me round the world and I was fortunate in that I had relations and friends in various places.
>
> So it was that I set off in 1913, to Canada, where I helped a man to build a house and clear his land up in the Rockies. Then I went to Vancouver, during the Canadian real estate boom, where I was pestered to buy land. Strange gentlemen would ring me up and say, 'I see you've come from Gloucestershire, you must know

the Duke of Beaufort, I'd like to come and see you and sell you some land.' Actually, I did know the Duke of Beaufort, but I didn't tell them that.

Having seen Canada, I crossed the Pacific to China in a big new ship that was full of dead Chinese, going home to be buried, and American missionaries, going out to China. I loved Japan, I had a marvellous time. In those days, the Japanese loved the English, and all the women wore kimonos and walked in wooden sandals. The drains in the villages were all open, you rode in a rickshaw and you drank green tea.

Leaving Japan, I went down to Shanghai, to see the British colony down there. Unfortunately, a man came aboard the boat, and took the next cabin to myself, and he had a rash all over him. I mentioned this, and a doctor was brought, and of course, it was smallpox. I was rather lucky. I'd had measles before I left England, and I was well vaccinated, and I didn't catch it. Then I went on to Hong Kong, where I had friends, and then down to Australia. And in Australia, I went to live on a sheep station that belonged to a friend of ours from Gloucestershire. I was a jackaroo, 180 miles north of the nearest railway line, right out in the desert. I loved it. If it hadn't been for the coming war, I might have stayed there. I adored the life.

However, I did come home. I stopped in New Zealand to see where my grandfather had once owned what is now the great suburb of Remuera, outside Auckland. Unfortunately, he sold it a bit too soon. Then, I came home, via India, and on the way, I remember hearing news that the Kaiser had taken a very large percentage out of all the fortunes of the rich Germans. It was a wealth tax, and I remember discussing it with people on board the ship, asking why he wanted all this money, and we all came to the conclusion that there was trouble coming.

Back home, in England, in 1914, I went back to Charterhouse for a term, and took my entrance exam to Trinity, Cambridge. But then, of course, came the outbreak of war. I was in camp with the Charterhouse Officer Training Corps, in Staffordshire, at the time. I went back home in my uniform to Gloucestershire, and people were making a fuss of anybody in uniform, and a woman came up to me at Gloucester Station, and she asked me to hold her baby for a minute, while she went and got something, but she didn't come back . . .

I wanted to join up. I'd always been keen on horses, and I thought I'd join the local Gloucestershire Yeomanry, which was one of the very good yeomanry regiments. So, at the age of seventeen, I became a subaltern in the Yeomanry, where I had a glorious two years, training men and horses. I was given a hundred butchers' boys and grocers' boys from Gloucester who'd ridden nothing but a bicycle, and a hundred Canadian horses that had never been ridden at all, and I had to put them together and make them into a squadron of cavalry. Which was quite an interesting job, actually. But before long, cavalry weren't wanted any more and we had to get rid of our horses. I suppose it was one of the most traumatic days that I ever remember, because we all loved our horses, and we had to take them away and load them onto a train and send them off, goodness knows where, after having trained them up for two years. They then said that they were going to give us bicycles but I didn't really fancy that very much.

I'd met a man quite recently, who'd been flying and he'd been explaining to me how he was co-operating with a new, very secret weapon, called a 'tank' and it was the greatest fun. So I went back and told my colonel that I was going to go flying. He was a little bit cross, but I said, no, it's the thing for me, so off I went. I went to see some people in London, in the War Office.

There was a very nice young cavalry officer who was interviewing possible candidates for the Royal Flying Corps. He noted my shoulder straps, and he said, 'Ah, you're Gloucester Yeomanry. You ride a horse?' 'Yes,' I said, 'I do.' 'Do you know where the pole star is?' he asked. 'Yes,' I said, 'I think I could find it.' 'You'll do,' he said.

British society in 1914, patriotic and obedient, was firmly ordered by class. Frederick Winterbotham represented the next generation of officers and empire builders. Young men like him, and those from every social class for that matter, knew their place. They were born with a role to fulfil, and, when war came, a new and appropriate role was assigned, and carried out unhesitatingly. For all that the new flying services attracted men of originality and disregard for military custom, their originality usually only extended to their immediate world. Larger moral and political conventions remained unchallenged. The structure of the flying services neatly reflected the social order; officers came from one background, the rank and file from another. In general, pilots were officers, while the riggers who tended the airframes, and the fitters who looked after the engines, were in the ranks. Occasionally, however, the social order blurred. Within the squadrons there were a number of sergeant pilots, from humble backgrounds, who lived and messed separately to the officers, but who experienced precisely the same dangers. Among these were men who had learnt to fly in the pre-war pioneering days. Donald Clappen was one of them:

I was always interested in flying. I used to take the aviation journals, *Flight* and *Aeroplane*. Then in July 1911, the Gordon Bennett Cup took place at Eastchurch. I was living at Westcliff-on-Sea at the time, and I took an excursion boat across to Sheerness and I saw all the famous pilots flying. The Gordon Bennett Cup was an international affair. Pilots represented their countries. I saw not only my first flying, but also my first crash.

It appears that Gustav Hamel, a famous British pilot, was flying practice laps in a Blériot, but found that his time was slightly slower than that of a rival Nieuport machine. Blériot himself was present, and he decided to cut about a foot off of each wing. This went well. Hamel was faster in his next practice circuit. But in the actual race, he got to the first pylon, overbanked and flew straight into the ground, with the engine running full on. He was thrown twenty-five or thirty yards, rolling over and over. The machine was a total wreck, but Hamel was only badly bruised, and didn't even break a bone.

It was as big a crash as one could ever wish to see – yet he got up almost unhurt. That made me think that aviation was not quite as dangerous as I had believed. However, everyone thought I was quite mad to want to learn to fly. In fact, so much so, that I hardly told anyone of my interest – not even my own parents. That's why I started off by getting myself apprenticed to the Chanter School of Flying at Hendon, just as a start. They had an advertisement in one of the aviation journals.

The Chanter School was rather a ropey concern. It had two Blériots and a machine which they were building themselves. They ceased to exist in October or November 1911, by which time I'd learnt to sweep the floor and push the machines about. I then got in touch with the Blériot Aviation Company, also at Hendon, and asked if I could join them as an apprentice, with a view to becoming a flying pupil at a later date.

I joined Blériot in November 1911, and I was just a general dogsbody at first, but I was allowed to fly.

Learning was entirely a solo effort. There were no dual-control machines, nor were there any machines that could take up a passenger. At first, the aircraft was raised onto a pedestal, showing what it was like, and the view one would get as a pilot in the flying position. Then one was put into the machine, told to keep straight ahead, towards a tree or something like that on the other side of the aerodrome. One learnt to roll across the ground. From thence, one started by doing short hops, followed by longer hops, until one could fly straight across the other side of the aerodrome. After that, one was able to do half circuits, one to the left and then to the right, and so forth, until one was able to fly in a complete circuit around the aerodrome.

The first time I flew was quite by accident. I was in a machine which was not supposed to fly. It had been detuned. I was rolling across the ground, doing a straight, as I thought, when suddenly I found the ground receding under me. Of course, this was so un-expected that I pushed my stick down and landed with a bit of a crash and found myself with the undercarriage spread all around me and the prop broken. My in-structor – Monsieur Salmet – came rushing up to me, 'Why you fly? Why you fly?' I had no answer. I didn't know.

What had happened was that a gust of wind had caught my plane and it had taken off without my ex-pecting it to. In those days, no one ever flew unless it was dead calm. My punishment was that I was not allowed to practise on an aircraft until I had participated in the repair of the machine, which took some months. That put me back quite a lot, but I still qualified for my pilot's certificate when I turned eighteen. After that, I was made a sort of assistant instructor, but I was also expected to do absolutely everything connected with the running, repairing and mending of the aircraft, tuning up of the engines. I did everything concerned with the maintenance of the machines.

In general, the majority of pupils were army officers, who were learning to fly with a view to joining the Royal Flying Corps, which had started in 1912. There were a few others – some rich people who went on to buy their own aircraft. And most weekends, at Hendon, there were competitions and flying displays. It was quite a fashionable affair, almost like Ascot, with people flocking down to see the flying.

I was assistant instructor until April 1914, but then Blériot moved to Brooklands, and I became an instructor at the Hall School of Flying at Hendon, which consisted of two Blériots, a Deperdussin, a Caudron and an Avro. I received a pound a week, and we taught a few pupils.

I was on holiday in Scotland when the war broke out. It didn't upset my holiday. I was thinking this war would be of the nature of the Boer War. But when I got back to Hendon, I found that the cry had gone out for pilots for the Flying Corps, and that a few of the instructors had actually become sergeant pilots. So I promptly put my name down. I signed the papers and waited. I continued instructing with the Hall School – but nothing happened. A lot of my friends were joining up, anxious to get into the war as quickly as possible, as everyone thought the war would be finished by Christmas. I found they were joining the London Scottish, so I spent all day queuing and found myself a perfectly good private in the London Scottish territorial battalion.

By April 1915, I was looking up with great envy from the trenches at the aircraft flying above, so I put in another application to join the Royal Flying Corps. I said that I'd already applied, but had had no reply. My colonel was not very keen because he was losing a lot of his personnel. So he instructed that he would pass on any application if the applicant could get somebody to apply for him from whatever regiment he wished to join. In my case, I knew nobody in the Royal Flying Corps.

Just a week before the Battle of Loos – we were resting behind the trenches – I went up to Auchel where I was watching the aircraft with envy. As I stood, watching the machines landing, a general emerged from the office. As he stepped into his car, acting on the spur of the moment, I said, 'Please sir, may I speak?' He looked round, astonished, and didn't say anything. I pulled out my application papers and told him my story, the fact that I was a qualified pilot, that I wanted to join the Royal Flying Corps but had some difficulty getting anyone to apply for me, that I had replied and had heard nothing more about it. In a very deep voice, he told another officer, also a brass hat, 'Make a note of that; make a note of that' . . . and so on. He said, 'I'll see what we can do.' In the meantime, he called to an airman and said 'Is there a transport going back towards the trenches, to Béthune? If so, make sure this soldier gets a lift back.' With that I saluted smartly and off he went. In the tender which took me back to Béthune, I asked the driver, 'Who was I speaking to?' 'Blimey,' he said, 'You've got a nerve! That was General Trenchard. He's in charge of the Royal Flying Corps!'

After that, I went through the Battle of Loos, twice over the top. We had a pretty bad time. Each time, I was lucky to get away with it. At one point, there was only one other fellow left in my section. On 9 October, as I was coming out of the trenches, I was greeted by a telegram which said, 'Report at once to the War Office.' That night, not having slept for days, dirty and filthy, I was given a first-class warrant and I found myself back in London on a Sunday morning. I wasn't feeling too good, and I was sent to a specialist, who pronounced that I needed three weeks' rest. After that, I was in the Royal Flying Corps.

Cecil King was a working-class boy who joined the Royal Flying Corps in 1913. He was to become a rigger and, ultimately, a flight sergeant:

Originally, I was an apprentice to a wheelwright and coach builder in the country, but after I'd come through my apprenticeship, I came to London. I did roughly a year's work in a London workshop, which was partially underground, and very depressing, and I wanted to get into a more open-air life. I cast about to see what I would do and one day, when I was walking in Kingston, I met two soldiers. They had an unusual badge, with the letters RFC, on their shoulders. I got into a conversation with them and they told me they were members of a new unit called the Royal Flying Corps, which had just started – and why didn't I join?

I'd never heard of the Royal Flying Corps, and I didn't know there was a military regiment concerned with flying. Actually, I wasn't bothered about that – I just knew it would be out in the open air and on big open fields. That's what I wanted. I was interested in flying, though. In 1911, I'd seen Gustav Hamel flying at Hendon. I remember the announcer said, 'This is Gustav Hamel on an aeroplane with a Gnome engine.' The crowd thought he'd said, 'No engine' and there was quite a stir.

But after I'd met these two members of the Royal Flying Corps, I went to a Recruiting Sergeant and asked him about it, and he said, 'Yes, I think something like that has started, and if you'd like to join, I'll find out for you.' I decided I would go a bit further with it. I went to Kingston Barracks and made my final decision. I was sworn into the army there, and I expressed a desire to go in the RFC, so I was given a railway warrant and sent down to Aldershot. When I got there, I asked the first serviceman I saw, 'Where are the barracks of the Royal Flying Corps?' and he said, 'Never heard of it.'

But by inquiring once or twice more I finally found that the Royal Flying Corps shared barracks with the Black Watch so I reported there, and I was sent up to a small building on the aerodrome at Farnborough where all the further particulars of my enlistment were taken down. I was sent back to the barracks for my first night. And when I woke up in the morning I heard the trumpets from the South Camp – that was the cavalry – and the bugles from the North Camp; and I was delighted. I thought, 'I'm really and truly in the army.'

When war was declared on 4 August 1914, many of the men who were to fly were scattered across the globe. Charles Chabot was living in Bangkok:

The European population of Bangkok at this time was absolutely minimal. A hundred would cover the entire European population of Siam. Nevertheless we had enough English people to rake up a rugby football team. The Germans had a rugby team as well. As the final game of the season, the Germans challenged us and this match was to be followed by dinner at the German club. So we played the game and we were beaten by the Germans and we congregated for the party after the match. We were all mixed up around the table – a German here, an Englishman here, next to him a German, next to him a Frenchman and so on. It began and it was like every other rugby football dinner since time immemorial. And then came a bang at the door and a runner came in from the French Embassy with the extraordinary news of the outbreak of war and he was quickly followed by another runner from the German Embassy. We'd never thought of other chaps in terms of war and we didn't know what we ought to do, whether we ought to seize a knife off the table and plunge it into the next chap, or what. After a little bit of discussion, we decided that as far as we were concerned, the war was going to start tomorrow. The party proceeded and that was that.

In Britain, the prevailing mood in August 1914 was euphoric. Leslie Kemp remembers:

The war came and threw everything and everybody out of balance. The enthusiasm for the war was really fantastic. There were actresses singing, there were concerts in Trafalgar Square and, if you enlisted, you were given the 'King's Shilling'. It was entirely different to the atmosphere that prevailed at the start of the Second World War.

Young men with romantic dreams of flying seized their opportunity. Charles Burne:

When I went home and told my father that I wanted to join the Royal Naval Air Service, he signed the papers but he said, 'Don't start flying. It's only damn fools and birds that fly.'

At the beginning of the war, a man with specialist knowledge was a welcome addition to the flying services. William Richards, self-taught and highly motivated, was such a man:

My father and my mother emigrated separately in the eighties, around 1884. My father was from Cornwall, at a time when the Cornish tin mines were in difficulty and closing down. And people concerned with that sort of work, at that time, were emigrating. At the age of twenty-one, he went to New Zealand. My mother's was an agricultural family in Essex. When she was about fourteen, they moved to New Zealand. She was that much younger than my father.

They met at Dougville, eight or nine years after arrival in New Zealand, and they fell in love, married, and there's no doubt about it, it was a very happy and romantic marriage. She was a lovely person. I was born a year after their marriage on St George's Day in 1893. They'd set up home in Auckland, in Queen Street, at that time, scarcely developed. They set up home in a kind of colonial style, and there's no question that they were very happy. I have the photographs of myself as a baby, and they go to show that's what it was – a happy home.

My mother contracted some sort of tropical fever at the age of twenty-five, and when I was a year and ten months old, she was taken from us, leaving my father with me, more or less in arms, to cope with a tragic situation. Friends came to his help, and I was looked after for a time, but it was quite clear to him that he couldn't carry on. It so happened that a relative in Cornwall had lost her first baby, and been told that she couldn't have another, and she, knowing my father's predicament, wrote to him, suggesting that if he cared to bring me to England, she would take care of me.

So she became, in a way, my foster mother. We lived on a farm, very isolated. I had no contact with any other children excepting when I later went to a village school at St Neot. So I was mixing very freely with grown-ups, all of them occupied in agricultural work. My only playmate, as a matter of fact, was a sporting dog. And I became rather self contained, independent, perhaps a little bit difficult, being alone in that way. I developed into rather an interesting child, in that I insisted that I would set my own way of life, and form my own ideas. I had quite strong ideas as a child. When I reached the age of ten, the dear lady who had been looking after me decided to go to America with her husband, and my father felt it necessary that a home should be provided for me, so he decided to marry. And he did. He just married, not for any romantic reason. Just to make a home.

I was independent minded and I refused to accept my stepmother. And it wasn't long before, on the excuse of going to spend a holiday with some friends in another part of Cornwall, I left home and refused to return. And from then on, I continued from one thing to another, living in different places, lodging with different persons, being employed in different things. I worked in the tin mines, and because I'd developed an interest in machinery, I was given some responsibility, even at a very young age. I was looking after power equipment, and doing survey work along the valleys for tin.

In the meantime, I took an interest in politics. At the age of eighteen, I stood with Isaac Foot, the father of Michael Foot, on his platform in Bolventor. I wrote letters for people in the farms who were scarcely literate. I had educated myself entirely – I was never coached, assisted or guided. I don't think I was helped at any time. I just pursued my own way. I was good tempered, bright, inquisitive and well inclined to learn anything and everything from observation and experience. I gained a lot of experience.

It started to appear to me that I had a purpose in life. I was at that age, in my later teens, when a teenager develops this disposition. And I thought that my purpose could well be served if I were to adopt a religious career. I came under the influence of a book that was published at that time by the minister of the City Temple, Archie Campbell, *The New Theology*, which suited my ideas of religion. I was old enough to draw certain conclusions about the difference between fundamental religion, evangelical religion, and the more liberal attitude to religious dogma and doctrine. In that connection, I spoke in public on many occasions. And the local stewards of the Church nominated me for the ministry.

I accepted the nomination and acted on it. I went to London, where I was examined by a committee with the purpose of going to theological college, but I was turned down because my self-education had only equipped me for certain things. For example, they asked what books I had read. I couldn't answer. I just hadn't had books, the classics, and that kind of thing. I was just so completely self-educated, in a rag-tag fashion, quite uncontrolled, without direction. The committee put me back for a year, as a result of my inability to quote Shakespeare. My attitude of mind was, whilst religious to a degree, critical of a number of things that I could not accept, and I decided that my future would be secular and not religious. I turned immediately to earning my living in a commercial or engineering way, and dropped any idea of pursuing a religious life.

So I went to London with £5 in my pocket, knowing nothing more than that the streets of London were paved with gold, and my future was what I could make of it. I booked in at the YMCA in Tottenham Court Road, and within twenty-four hours I had a job at the London County Council as a temporary assistant.

By then, I had studied electricity and magnetism in books, and I'd given myself a fairly good grounding. And at the time, the big trans-continental wireless stations, Poldhu, Eiffel Tower and Nauen, were operating, and it was possible with a simple piece of apparatus – a crystal and a pair of headphones – to pick up those signals, and if you knew Morse code, you could read what they were saying. So I learnt the Morse code, and followed these transmissions as a kind of hobby. And in that way, wireless became my forte.

At the outbreak of war, I was fired with the idea,

and I walked into a recruiting station and offered myself. They examined me as to who I was, and what I could do, and it came out that I knew Morse, and I was booked as one of the very, very few wireless operators for the Royal Flying Corps. One thing followed another. I was sent to study under Professor Price at the London Polytechnic for two months, and then I was handed a New Testament, a revolver, and I was told to proceed to 4 Squadron in France.

Archibald James began the war as a well-connected young subaltern in the 3rd Hussars:

My primary recollection of the first winter of the war is of mud, Flanders clay, our wretched horses standing on long picket lines, hock-deep in mud, misery, living on bully beef and biscuit, and great discomfort. We were employed as dismounted cavalry to take over trench lines, usually for a short time before infantry became available. The British front had been extended to the north. And the line in the north of Flanders was held mainly by old French Territorials. The trenches were very sketchy. And we were quite ill-adapted to this sort of work and quite unsuitably clothed for it, as indeed, at that stage of the war, were the infantry for trench warfare.

The worst episode of this period was three miserable days when we stood to in the afternoon, then rode about ten miles. On the way it came on to pour with rain. And by the time we got to about a mile and a half from the trenches we were to take over, we were all absolutely soaked to the skin. My trench was an isolated length, with no idea how far away the German trenches were. In the night, it stopped raining and started to freeze hard. We had three days in these wretched little trenches, frozen miserable. And we had the greatest difficulty getting rations up because, from one flank, the Germans overlooked our rear. And when we got back to billets after three nights in these trenches, we had without exception what became known as trench feet. We had one-third of the regiment out of action for a week while their wretched feet thawed out. My feet were throbbing with pain for at least a week.

We were then sent to take over from another cavalry regiment who had been occupying a trench line in Sanctuary Wood for three days. Our period was to be three days also. The wood was still composed of young larch trees which had been fairly heavily knocked about by rifle fire. The trench had been constructed shortly before by French Territorials. It had been too wet to dig down and the parapet consisted largely of dead French bodies covered over with a superficial covering of earth. There was no wire in front of us. And the German trenches were about thirty yards away. It was here that I received my first utterly trivial wound.

Opposite my troop front – as I say at thirty yards' range – were the German trenches. And I quickly noticed, looking through a loophole, that opposite me was a place where the German trenches, for some reason, were shallower. And when a man walked along them, he appeared up to about the middle of his upper arm. This seemed to me to offer an opportunity. So I took a rifle from one of my troopers and posted myself at a loophole waiting for the next German to come along.

In due course, the German appeared. I'm a good rifle shot and it was no question that I'd got him. But what I hadn't realized was that a German was watching the end of my rifle and had a shot at me. And as our trench wall was in no way bulletproof, the bullet hit me under my left arm and merely grazed the skin. But it certainly discouraged me from any further sniping.

We were relieved by the 16th Lancers. I had been convinced from what I'd heard while I was listening in the watches of the night, that the Germans were sapping under our trenches and so I reported to my commanding officer. He reported to brigade and nothing happened. The night after we left, the Germans blew a mine under the very trenches we had been in. And it cost the lives of five or six 16th Lancer officers and about twenty men, partly in a futile counter-attack which ensued from this episode.

Shortly after this, a circular came round all cavalry divisions asking for lightweight – specified lightweight – officers to become observers in the Royal Flying Corps. It came at a very opportune moment for me.

For Walter Ostler, the flying services offered an alternative to the trenches:

I well remember, one night, I was in a very crowded tramcar, going home from Finsbury Park to Wood Green. This lady – if I may call her so – simply pushed up alongside me and stuck this white feather in my buttonhole, much to my embarrassment. It was time to think about service in one of the Forces. For me, it was the Royal Flying Corps because the thing I wanted to avoid most of all was the Army and trench life in France. I'd spoken to soldiers returning from France during the winter of 1914 and they had two words for life out there: 'Bloody awful.'

T. E. Rogers was an officer who had spent too long in the trenches:

I knew what war was like. I had seen death – too much of it. When I left the trenches, my brother officers said 'Good heavens, haven't you seen enough planes come down in flames?' I said, 'Yes, but haven't you seen enough death in trenches?' With flying, it would soon be over if you'd come to the end of your life. You didn't have to sleep in mud, night after night, day after day, in mud and water.

When R. J. Duce's wounds prevented him from continuing in the infantry, he saw the Flying Corps as an opportunity to continue the fight. The path that led him to the RFC began many thousands of miles from France:

I had been in India with one of the merchant banks before the war, and during my five years there, I had joined the equivalent of the territorial force. We were fully trained, to the extent that we were better armed with the Lee Enfields rifle than the British army in England. When the war started, after a little while, a notice came in the clubs, from the Inns of Court Officers Training Corps, asking if we would come home and join, and be commissioned into the British army. I asked the bank if I could go, and they told me that there were other people, senior to me, who should have the choice before me. I pointed out that these people weren't going. They said that I couldn't go, but I was going to go, anyway.

I didn't expect to come out of the war alive. I had been living on the North-West Frontier, up near the Khyber Pass, and I had a lot of nice books and various other things, and I gave them all away, I had the idea, as did a lot of my friends, that I shouldn't come through it, but I was of a very religious turn of mind, so it didn't bother me.

I went down to Karachi, and I shipped on board a Japanese boat as a purser. There were forty-nine Chinese crew, six Japanese officers, and an English captain. I paid the captain six shillings a day for my food, and I got one shilling pay when I got to England. The bank sent my resignation after me. Just after I arrived in England, I was stopped, and asked, 'What about joining up, young man?' I said, 'I've just come six thousand miles! Give me a chance!'

In the end, I didn't join the Inns of Court, I joined the Artists Rifles. I was fully trained, so myself and three others, one from India and two from South Africa, were put on as orderlies in the sergeants' mess. We waited so well on the sergeants that they were delighted. But we wouldn't take that on permanently. Next, I was made an officer's servant. Considering that I'd come from India where I'd had eleven servants, it was rather amusing. But then, I was commissioned into the 20th London, Royal West Kent Regiment. In due course, I went out to France.

On my first day in the line, I was on duty – and I remember looking over and seeing that the Germans were shelling from an armoured train that ran along a track. I was so interested to watch the shells suddenly appear like a panther approaching. You could see the shells coming over the last five yards. There was a young fellow there, named Atkins, and I chatted to him for some time. He said to me, 'Yes, sir, this is my first time in the line.' And then I walked about twenty yards away from him, to our company dugout, and I looked round, and in that second, a shell came over right on top of him, and the blast blew me down into the dugout. It was quite a first experience.

A while later, we sent over a party of twenty men, their faces blacked, to do a raid. A couple were officers, a few were NCOs and the rest were Tommies. I was in the front line, and a heavy barrage opened up, from behind our second line. We had to keep our heads down in the trench. Then, suddenly the Germans started shelling as well, for all they were worth. Something came down and hit my tin helmet, knocking it off. I picked up the helmet, put it back on, and one second later, something else hit it, and knocked it off again. It showed the value of these helmets. Once the shelling had stopped, we found a strange thing in the back of the trench: one of our own shells had hit a German shell in mid-air, and come down straight behind us in the trench. It should have burst – but it hadn't.

I don't know that I ever felt frightened – because I was too dedicated a patriot. And the finest patriot you can get is the Englishman living abroad. Having said that, I remember one incident – we were in France and I was in billets. I had a room by myself, and I woke up in the night to find that I was half hanging out of a dormer window. In my sleep, with the nerves that I must have had, I had thought that I'd been climbing out of the dugout.

At the end of June 1916, we marched down to the Somme. We were detailed to go over the top, in an attack on High Wood. I had No. 5 Platoon, B Company, and we were detailed to go all the way through. I was darned annoyed because I was going over first. We were to go over at 3.15 on Sunday afternoon, and while I was waiting, there was nothing to do but go to sleep, and I found that I was able to sleep at the side of the trench. When we went over, I was quite fortunate. Of the three officers of my company, two were killed and I was only wounded. Out of 480 men, 160 were killed, 160 were wounded and 160 got through. It was rather extraordinary. As I was stepping over the wire, I was shot straight through the foot, which knocked me down. If I'd put my foot down before, I'd have got it right through the knee. I laid out there for some hours, and then as I started to crawl back, parallel to the German line, a German came over the top, and stood, looking out, holding his machine gun. I just had to freeze. I can tell you, it's quite a nervous tension to lie there for ten minutes, without moving, so that he thinks you're a dead body. Gradually, I turned my head round to look, and saw that he had gone, and I crawled back. As I was crawling back, I followed a small trench, in which I came across a dead man. All I could do was crawl straight over him. It wasn't a pleasant thing.

When I got back to the UK, I was on crutches, and I realized that I would be lame for a while, so I went into the Royal Flying Corps headquarters, and saw them. I said that I wanted to transfer to the Royal Flying Corps, and I was abruptly told to clear off, and come back when I hadn't got crutches. I was then offered a job with Motor Transport, but I said no. I'd come all the way from India, and I didn't want to take on a non-combatant role. So I put in again for the Royal Flying Corps and this time, I was accepted pretty quickly. I was given instructions to report to Edin, near St Pol, and I was sent to 98 Squadron.

William Berry, some way down the social order, was so keen to join the Flying Corps, that he accepted the only job available:

I didn't think about volunteering straight away when war broke out. I rather fancy my parents were against it. They didn't want me going out and getting killed. There were lots of posters up. Kitchener with a finger pointing, Kitchener wants *you*. There were all the recruiting meetings in Trafalgar Square with Horatio Bottomley very much to the fore. There were also recruiting sergeants who stopped you in the street and I was quite frequently stopped: 'A young fellow like you, why aren't you in the army?' sort of thing. That was the general line, which was quite true, and I resented it very much because I really wanted to volunteer, but my parents weren't very amenable. They were very patriotic, but in those days you obeyed what your parents told you, and I wasn't twenty-one years old.

Then one day, I happened to go to the cinema in

Croydon, and one of the newsreels showed a house in Belgium. There were German soldiers knocking in all the windows with the butts of their rifles. They then set the house on fire because it was in the way of their guns. I was very upset at this. I sympathized, and I thought, 'Right! I am going to do something about it!' So I wrote to the Royal Flying Corps at Farnborough.

I had had a pre-war interest in going to Hendon and seeing all the early pioneers. If you saw an aeroplane in those days, it was quite something. Flying, I thought, was the coming thing, and the RFC was open again for recruits. Directly the Flying Corps was opened, in about five minutes, it was full up, as they'd got all the recruits they wanted. They had no difficulty getting recruits of a good calibre who knew their trades and knew what they were doing. I wrote and said I wanted to enlist and I got a letter back immediately, saying that they would welcome me as a wireless operator, and would I go to the recruiting centre in Farnborough?

So I went to the recruiting centre and they said, 'I'm sorry, you can't join the Royal Flying Corps, it's closed.' I said, 'That's impossible, I've got this letter from them!' and they said, 'It closed this morning! You're too late! Why don't you join the local regiment, the Seventh King's Royal Rifles?' As my father had been in the 'Shiny 7th', I thought, 'Well, that's an idea.' So I got the recruiting form and got three-quarters of the way through it when I thought, 'No! I'm going to join the Flying Corps!' I tore up the form and put it in the wastepaper basket.

I told the Recruiting Major that I was very disappointed that I'd got his letter but that now I couldn't join, and he was very much impressed with the trouble I'd taken to get all that way from London to Farnborough. He said, 'We are short of cooks. Have you ever done any cooking?' I said, 'I really can't say I'm a cook, but to get into the Flying Corps, I'm willing to take it on.' He said, 'Right! Hold up your hand!' I was sworn in, and I was a recruit and I spent that night at the recruits' barracks at Farnborough.

Leslie Murton joined out of a desire to exact revenge:

I was born in Magdalen Street, Norwich, in my grand-father's shop. My father was one of the finest turned shoemakers there ever was. One of the fastest. My eldest brother was a printer at the *Eastern Daily Press*. The next brother to him, Bertie, was training to be a hotel manager in London. Another brother, Sidney, was a motor mechanic.

I left school at fourteen, in the year that war broke out. At the time, it didn't mean much to me. But one day I came home from school, and my mum told me to read this letter. She could never read or write. It was from my brother in London. He said the girls were putting white feathers in his cap as he walked through the streets. He said he couldn't stand it, so he'd enlisted in the King's Royal Rifles. At the same time, my eldest brother had enlisted in the 7th Norfolks. Well, after a period, my brother in London said he couldn't stand the London people, they were rough to him, and in those days, you could transfer from one regiment to another, provided you had relations in the new regiment. So he transferred to the 7th Norfolks to be with his brother.

A little later, Sidney was sent straight to France as a transport driver. When he was there, he was sent down to the docks, where he met the regiments coming in, and he ran into my two brothers in the 7th Norfolks. He told me later that he'd said to them, 'Thing is, I won't see either of you two again.' And he was true to his word. On 13 October 1915, the two of them were killed side by side.

When we got the news from the War Office, I had to go to my father's place of business. I told him. He took his apron off, threw it down. I can see him now. He'd been a teetotaller for years but he said, 'I'll never come back till I've spent every penny.' And my dad never came back to work again, until he'd drank his money away. And after that, my poor old mother tried to do something to herself, but she was saved. You can understand it, can't you, when you lose two young boys of that age? It affected me as well. When I was old enough, I was going to get my own back.

From the time my brothers died, my mother put a memorial, every year, in the *Eastern Evening News*, where my brother had been a printer. One day, a man came to my office, where I was working, and said, 'Excuse me, Mr Murton. Could I ask you a question?' 'Certainly,' I said. 'I see in the paper, last night, there was a memorial to the Murton brothers.' 'Yes,' I said. 'I would like to know whether you're a relation,' he asked. 'Matter of fact,' I said, 'they're my two brothers, who were killed.' 'What I want you to know,' he said, 'is that I buried one of them. I was a stretcher bearer at the time, in France, in the 7th Norfolks, and I buried him, but the other one, his brother, was blown to pieces.' And that's the tragedy of my two brothers.

In the later part of 1915, the Royal Flying Corps formed a boys' section. I was sixteen, and I forged my mother's signature, and went up to Britannia barracks, where I was sworn in, and they told me that a month before I was seventeen, I would hear from them. And I did.

When I got called up, one evening, two military policemen came to my house with a warrant and said, 'Leslie Murton?' and my mother said, 'Yes!' because I was out with the boys. They said that I had to catch such and such a train tomorrow to London and then another to Aldershot, for the Royal Flying Corps. Next day, I took the train to Liverpool Street Station. I'd never been further than Yarmouth in my lifetime!

So at Liverpool Street, I got off the train and there was a policeman, and I said, 'Excuse me, old chap, how do I get on the Underground?' So he told me where to go. I followed his directions, until I saw a dustman, who was sweeping up the horse manure. I said to him, 'Excuse me, where's the Underground?' 'Down there!' he said, pointing down some steps. 'Look, old chap,' I said, 'I may have just come from the country, but I'm not daft enough to go down there! You're trying to send me down the toilet!' I thought he was. I'd never seen the Underground before. So he took me down and I got the train and went off to Aldershot. When I got there, I was really hungry, so I went out into the street, to a fried fish shop. I got some fish and chips, and just as I opened the paper to eat some, I saw my fish and chips going up in the air. Two military police had kicked it out of my hands. 'You don't do that here!' one of them said. I was in the services now.

Those who joined the other ranks of the Royal Flying Corps often considered themselves a cut above the humble infantryman. Cecil King:

Everyone who joined the Royal Flying Corps in the other ranks held some trade or other, whereas the men in the general regiments – they might be anyone. All us recruits in the RFC had some kind of training or apprenticeship; we actually had to pass a trade test before we got in. And therefore we considered ourselves a bit superior to the infantry and cavalry who may have come from any walk of life. We also got more pay than they did and when they found that out, they were a little bit jealous.

George Eddington was not a born soldier:

> The Flying Corps interested me because the army was
> rather a brutal affair full of big hefty Irishmen and that
> type of person. I was neither that way disposed nor that
> way built. It didn't attract me a bit. I was a tradesman
> rather than a soldier, so the Flying Corps sounded
> attractive.

The Great War was a time of intense patriotism in the British
colonies. Frank Burslem was born and raised in Trinidad,
but he considered himself as British as any man born in the
British Isles:

> I thought that any enemy of England was an enemy of
> mine and I wanted to be in the war. When I was sixteen
> years old in 1917, I was six foot two tall, and I knew
> that there was a ship going from Trinidad to England
> with eight vacant berths. Local merchants paid for the
> berths and sent eight young fellows who wanted to join
> the army over to England. My father allowed me to go,
> but when he gave me my birth certificate, he told me I
> was to do some kind of war work like munitions or
> working the land. But when I got to England, I never
> showed my birth certificate to anybody. I told them
> that I was three years older than I really was, and I
> joined the army. I had no difficulty going against my
> father's wishes – I was a patriotic youth and I wanted to
> be in it.
>
> When we arrived in England, the eight of us went to
> New Scotland Yard, where we saw a fatherly sergeant
> and told him we wanted to join the army – and he put
> us in. Being volunteers, we had a choice of what service
> or regiment to go for. As the other fellows were going
> into the Artists Rifles, that's what I chose too.
>
> I went to the basic training camp at Gidea Park,
> but I didn't like it very much. The marching was so

strenuous and I found it numbed and cramped the muscles in my thighs and calves. I stood it for a week, but after that I reported ill, and went before the doctor. He expected somebody 'swinging the lead'. He asked what the matter was, and I said, 'Anchhylostomiasis, sir.' 'Good God, what's that?' he asked. It was hookworm. I told him that just before leaving Trinidad, the Rockefeller Foundation had tested me and discovered that I had hookworm. I knew that I still had it. It meant that I wasn't strong enough to do the strenuous work in the infantry. So they sent me to hospital and gave me the remedy. After that I was cured, and I went back to the regiment, where I could stand the drill. But by now, I'd seen what life in the infantry was like, and I thought it would be better for me if I didn't do that kind of work. As they didn't form fours, or anything like that, I changed my papers for a commission in the RFC.

Stanley Walters had problems reaching Britain from Rhodesia:

I did my damnedest to join the Royal Flying Corps, but I hadn't got any money to get to England. Eventually, I persuaded somebody to let me go in and see the manager of the Union Castle Company. He asked what I wanted to see him about. I said, 'I want to join the Royal Flying Corps!' 'How praiseworthy,' he said, 'how commendable, what have I got to do with that?' 'I can't get to England!' I said. 'How disappointed you must be,' he said. I slid off the chair and went away. Six weeks later, at three o'clock in the afternoon, I got a message. The *Land Steffen Castle* sails at six o'clock. I could go in her as an assistant purser. He didn't call my bluff. I made it. I got to England with one golden sovereign so I was compelled to join the Royal Flying Corps immediately on my arrival.

Frederick Powell was stuck in an infantry regiment with no immediate prospect of joining the fight. He knew nothing of flying. He merely saw the Royal Flying Corps as a passport to France:

In November 1914, a circular came round to our battalion asking for volunteers to be an observer for the Royal Flying Corps. I didn't know what I was volunteering for; my only interest was to get out to France. There was no sense of my wanting to fly, but my regiment seemed to have no chance of getting out to France before Christmas. One point is that, at the time, an observer's weight had to be ten stone or less, so when I got down to ten stone, I was transferred to the Royal Flying Corps.

They had asked for one officer from each battalion, and there were two of us who wanted to volunteer; a man named Knowles was top of the list, and I was second. They only wanted one, but Knowles told me that he didn't really want to volunteer because he was engaged to a girl. So if we were asked for one from each battalion, he would stand down. In point of fact, when the moment arrived, he did not stand down; he went. But by great good luck, they asked for another officer from our battalion, so I went too.

Even though I went as an observer, after I had been there two days, I was put down as an orderly officer, which meant that I had to go and report to the adjutant at six o'clock in the evening, and sleep in his office all night, in case the telephone went.

As I reported to the adjutant, the colonel called him into his office. The adjutant went, leaving the door ajar. I didn't want to eavesdrop but I heard the adjutant say, 'We've got another officer called Knowles, who's been posted to us.' The colonel said, 'Is he an observer or a pilot?' The adjutant said, 'An observer.' The colonel said, 'Oh, we don't want any more observers! We've got nothing but observers!' The adjutant said, 'Well, what shall I do with him?' The colonel said, 'Send him back to his regiment!' And that was the end of Knowles. It frightened me, so that first thing in the morning, I reported to the adjutant and said, 'Is there any chance, sir, of me being able to learn to fly, to become a pilot?' I thought he was going to say, 'Oh no, certainly not!' but to my astonishment, he said, 'Really? Do you want to become a pilot?' 'Yes sir,' I said. 'Oh, good lad! Then start away. We'll put you down as a pilot!'

Arthur Harris, a man who was to achieve notoriety as commander-in-chief of Bomber Command during the Second World War, used his connections to jump the queue into the oversubscribed Royal Flying Corps:

I went round to the War Office where I was interviewed by a rather supercilious young man. When I said I would like to fly, he said, 'So would six thousand other people. Would you like to be six thousand and one on the waiting list?' So I retired rather disgruntled and when I got back, my father had just returned from India. When I told him what had happened, he said, 'Why didn't you go and see your Uncle Charlie?' I had many uncles. I didn't know who or what or where Uncle Charlie was but my father gave me a note and I went back to the War Office. When I handed the note addressed to Uncle Charlie to the same supercilious young fellow, he said, 'Oh, please sit down a minute, sir!' which was rather a change from the day before. He came back about ten minutes later and he said, 'Colonel Elliot is in conference and unable to see you at the moment but if you will report to Number 2 Reserve Squadron at Brooklands this evening you can start flying.'

Ernest Tomkins, from a humble background, demonstrated that ambition and enthusiasm could defeat social disadvantage:

> I asked how I could get into the Flying Corps. I was mad on flying. 'Not a hope!' said my brother, 'You'd have to apply for a commission.' 'That'll do' I said. 'Don't be stupid,' he said. 'You haven't got a certificate of education.' But he had a word with our CO, who agreed to get in touch with a schoolmaster who'd give me a test. So I took this test – I did some arithmetic and I wrote an essay on a subject I liked. About a month afterwards, I was sent in front of an Air Commodore. I was only eighteen – no age – and he had his staff with him and he said, 'You're applying to become an officer. Do you think you're old enough to become an officer and a gentleman of the British army?' I said, 'Yes, sir,' and I was marched outside. After everyone had been interviewed, the sergeant called out, '3659 Private Tomkins'. I took three paces forward and the Air Commodore was very friendly. He said, 'You're very interested in flying?' I said, 'Yes, sir.' He had the essay that I'd written in front of him, called 'The use of aircraft in modern warfare'. He complimented me on it and asked me questions about flying and engines. He said, 'What makes an aeroplane fly?' I said, 'Air has weight. It will resist motion. Flight is secured by driving through the air a plane inclined upwards and forwards of the direction of motion.' He was surprised and started asking me about combustion engines. Then he asked me questions about my school and family. I knew what I was in for because there were a lot of public schoolboys going in for commissions. So I withdrew while they deliberated. And when I went back, they all agreed that my papers should be forwarded to the War Office.

The Royal Naval Air Service, as befitted the flying branch of the senior service, took a rather high-handed attitude to its entrants. Donald Bremner remembers:

I went up to London once a fortnight to sit on the selection board for candidates for the Royal Naval Air Service. The officer in charge was Commander Samson, known as Sammy. He was a well-known character. He said what he thought to anybody. If you got on well with him – as I did – you got on very well. If you didn't, you got out. Sammy instituted a procedure where we each had a pencil and paper and all the time we were asking questions of the wretched candidate, we fiddled with our pencils. When we'd asked enough questions, we laid our pencils down. If we were satisfied with him, we held the pencil point upwards. If we wouldn't have him at any price, we held it point downwards. If there was anyone who was reasonable but we didn't like him enough, Sammy advised him to try the Royal Flying Corps. Our decision was really based on whether we liked the fellow. We wanted young people, about nineteen was the best. We always felt that someone who rode horses had the right kind of hands for flying and that somebody who rowed on the river could be useful. Social class counted because we were choosing officer pilots. I don't think people from a working-class background came before us – they were filtered out at an earlier stage. We wouldn't have turned down a really good candidate just because he didn't come from the right school but the organization of the RNAS was very similar to the organization of the navy – there was a bit of snobbishness.

Once the interview was passed, the medical examination posed fresh challenges. Vernon Coombs was fortunate to meet a friendly fellow candidate:

I was shortsighted and when no one was looking I wore glasses. I worried how I was going to get through the eyesight test. So I asked one chap what I should do and he said, 'It's easy! The bottom two lines of the eye-test chart are UBHDN, HRDNA.' So I passed with flying colours – and I've never forgotten those letters. When I was flying, I always slipped glasses on underneath my goggles. No one ever noticed and I never found it any disadvantage at all. I never wore my glasses on the ground. When my goggles came off, so did my glasses.

George Eddington took a gamble which paid off:

At Warley Barracks, I saw a medical officer who stripped me and gave me a very thorough examination. I was rather deaf in the right ear but I was fairly sharp-witted. In one of the tests, he whispered into each ear whilst plugging up the other one. First he plugged up my right ear and asked me my brother's name. I answered him. Then, he went to the other side and whispered something I couldn't hear. I took a guess and said, 'I haven't a sister.' He gave me the all-clear.

The Royal Flying Corps was not a male preserve. Women served with the RFC in a variety of roles. The Zeppelin raids inspired Florence Parrott to join up:

I never knew my own mother. I was brought up by an uncle. He was an engine driver. I went to school in Bletchley, and I was very happy there. We used to have lovely little operettas – I loved singing and dancing. I left school when I turned fourteen, and the next day, I was in London, in service. As quickly as that. Lady Leon lived at Bletchley Park, and she always took Bletchley girls when they left school. I was in her London home. I wanted to be a children's nurse, but I wasn't old enough.

I had to get up first thing in the morning, get the

stoves going, and wash the steps outside. I was lucky, really, because I received a good insight into cooking, because I'm sorry to say that our cook liked the bottle more than anything else. She'd get halfway through a dinner and then she'd hand it over to me to finish. I was only fifteen, but I managed. The family never knew I was doing the cooking. The family was only Sir Herbert and Lady Leon, and their son, but they used to give big parties. All the beautiful fresh stuff, fruit, vegetables, flowers, used to come from Bletchley to the London residence, by road every day.

I got on all right with Lady Leon, but there was one French maid, and she apparently didn't like me from the first, and I certainly didn't like her. But at the finish, I ran away because I wanted to be a children's nurse. I ran away and I got myself a job with a Japanese family. He'd been the Japanese ambassador to London, and they were returning to Japan, and they wanted to take an English girl with them. I got the job – but somehow my aunt got to hear about it and she fetched me back. I was packed up and ready to go, but my aunt wouldn't let me. In those days, people didn't trust the foreigners like they do today.

So I went back to Lady Leon and tried to settle down again, but I couldn't. I ran away again. This time, I got with an extremely nice family. He was a captain in the army, and she was a tall, beautiful lady, and they had a lovely little boy. That little boy idolized me, and I idolized him. The mother always used to go in to say goodnight to the little boy, before going in to dinner, and one night, she fell, from top of stairs to bottom. And it killed her. It was terrible. The captain asked me if I would carry on with the child. One Sunday night, the head nurse left me to see to the bathing of the boy, and to put him to bed. She told me how to do my sleeves, and what to do. I did everything as nanny told me, but the old Victorian grandmother came in, walked to one side of me, discovered I hadn't been vaccinated, and she sacked me there and then.

So I came back to Bletchley, where my uncle, being on the railway, got me a job in the refreshment rooms at Euston Station. Then some of the girls from Liverpool Street Station came to see me, and they said that they were getting a pound more than I was, so I went off there, and was taken on as a wine waitress in the dining room. I lived in a hostel, with a housekeeper, and that was very nice.

On a particular day, in 1917, while I was working at Liverpool Street, we had to serve a troop train. We gave each soldier a little box, with sandwiches, cake, cigarettes and an apple. When we'd served them, we let the guard know, and they started pushing all the boys onto the train. When they were all in, there was a shrill whistle and a blast of steam, and the train was ready to move out. The wheels were just turning, when three or four Zeppelin bombs came down. One after the other. Before we knew where we were, the corner of the station was blown apart. I got hit in my arm, by glass from the roof overhead. I was taken to St Bartholomew's Hospital, where they got the glass out of me. There weren't enough beds and we had to lie on the floor, and I said to the girl next to me, 'When I get out of here, I'm going to join up! If I'm going to get knocked about, I'll go where I expect it!' I'd never thought about joining up before. It was the air raid that did it. When I was out of the hospital, I went along Oxford Street, to the Connaught Club, and went in and joined the Women's Auxiliary Army Corps. I was interviewed by several officers, who asked me what I'd been doing, and when I said wine waitress, they said they didn't have anything like that, but they put me down as a cook. And they sent me to Denham, to the

Royal Flying Corps, where the boys were training to be pilots.

Raynor Taylor served with the Glamorgan Yeomanry. He cared nothing for aeroplanes, or for class:

William Spencer was a member of a very well-to-do family. We did our infantry training together and after a week or two, when we'd found out how to form fours and march in step, we were sent on a route march. Coming back into camp, we felt just like soldiers, with our full pack, and we watched a motor car drive through the gate. It was William Spencer's mother and father. They'd come to visit him. I can see the mother now – a big blousy woman, very arrogant. She stood there and Billy was in the same four as I was, and he couldn't say hello to them because he was marching at attention, so he acknowledged them as best he could and marched on. Well, his mother wasn't having that, at all! Her Willy, carrying a pack! Unheard of! He became embarrassed because she started ranting and raving, playing hell. Anyway, she made such a noise that he got transferred to the Royal Flying Corps as a pilot and an officer. He was shot down and killed on his first flight over the lines in France. His memorial's in the cemetery, and every time I pass it, I think, 'Eh, Billy. Your mother put you there. Because she couldn't abide to see you carrying a pack.'

3

A Flying Start

It is an extraordinary fact that, of the 14,166 pilots who lost their lives during the Great War, well over half were killed in training. Even without the obvious perils of combat, flying was a dangerous activity. In the years before the war, it had been even more so. Aircraft had been underpowered and slow. They were too fragile to risk being thrown around the sky, and flying – even for the thrill-seekers who pursued it – was usually more of a struggle to remain in control, than a dynamic effort to push the aircraft's limits. Simply maintaining straight and level flight placed considerable strain on flying wires. When coming in to land, early pilots would push the nose of the aircraft down and lose height with the engine running. Their turns would be made flat, with the minimum of bank. Flying was hazardous enough, without seeking to add to the dangers.

There were those, of course, who sought greater thrills. Intrepid individuals competed in circuit races, where they would fly close to the ground and race around pylons, attempting to overtake each other. It was only on 25 September 1913, however, that British aviators were shown the true potential of their craft. On that day, a French airman named Adolphe Pégoud came to Brooklands Aerodrome to give a flying demonstration. Placing terrible strain on his Blériot monoplane, he performed a vertical dive, a tail slide and a loop. The public was inspired and so were fellow pilots. Gustav Hamel, the first man to carry airmail, wrote that 'Pégoud's flights have given us all a new confidence'. Confidence might have been misplaced, however. Eleven months later, Hamel died in a flying accident, and less than two years after that, Pégoud was killed in combat – by a German pilot whom he had taught to fly before the war.

For men entering the infant flying services, loops and tail slides lay in the future. First, they would have to master the basics of flight. Very few of them ever forgot their first trip in a heavier-than-air machine. Ronald Sykes, who was taught to fly by the Royal Naval Air Service in 1917, might speak for thousands:

> I remember every minute of my first flight. Going round, feeling as though the world was whizzing – it was a terrific thrill. The great surprise was the effect of centrifugal force. When we were doing a sharp turn and the aeroplane was on its side, there was a pressure on me that pushed my head into the seat. That was a shock – I wasn't expecting it. On another turn, I couldn't lift my feet off the bottom of the aeroplane. After that, I did nothing but think about flying.

Nowadays, we are blasé about flying. The idea of looking down on the earth from a great height holds little wonder for the package tourist. During the Great War, however, for men such as Ernest Tomkins it was an unimaginable novelty:

> It's a very funny thing. Say you look down over the Clifton Suspension Bridge, you're a little bit scared of the height. But when you get up high in an aircraft, you're detached from the earth and you don't realize you're so high. You don't feel a bit 'windy' about being up that high. Even getting on top of a house and

looking down gives you more sense of height than if you're up at 20,000 feet. It's like you're looking at a map.

Until late 1914, men joining the Royal Flying Corps had to pay for their own tuition. They attended the civilian flying schools where they trained on some very primitive machines. In October 1914, Graham Donald trained on the *most* primitive:

> I got started training on a genuine American Wright Biplane with twin propellers, chain driven – one of them with a cross chain which makes most engineers shudder. It was completely, inherently unstable and a lot of people said that if you could fly a Wright Biplane you could fly anything. Well the fact remains that it flew. The speed range was about three knots: it flew level at 43 knots, began diving at 42 and stalled at 39 or 40. So you hadn't got very much to play with. The instrumentation was simple – there was a length of fine cord about eighteen inches long tied to one of the struts in front of you. You kept your eye on these cords, the idea being that if they went sideways you were side-slipping. If the chord went limp, the only thing to do was to start singing 'Nearer My God To Thee' . . .

In these basic machines, there was room for only one pilot. The instructor might give the novice some guidance, but essentially he was on his own. This method of training, known as the 'French School', was used to teach Eric Furlong to fly a Caudron, at the same school at which Donald Clappen, from the last chapter, was an instructor:

> I learnt to fly at Hendon in 1914 at the Hall School of Flying. I learnt on Caudrons. The Caudron was a small aeroplane with a nacelle rather than a cockpit. A nacelle was rather like a wooden bath that you sat in and the

engine was stuck in front of you. There were open booms to the tail rather than a fuselage. It only had 35 horse-power and we used to say that if one horse died, you did, too. In fact the stall point and the maximum speed were very nearly the same. The engine was going flat out all the time you were flying and if it stopped for a fraction of a second, the machine came down as though you were falling down stairs. One thing I remember – the Caudron burnt neat castor oil and the pupil inhaled a good deal of it with the result that we all needed to go to the lavatory constantly.

At first, you were strapped into the nacelle and told about the engine and the rudder and told to keep the control stick in the centre. At Hendon, there was a white patch on the fence at the far side. I was told to taxi the Caudron over to the fence. The Caudron was extremely difficult to steer. The two booms at the tail made it want to run in one direction only and the only way to steer it was to give a burst of throttle, which lifted the tail and allowed you to swing it a bit with the rudder. Invariably you swung it too far and you made your way across the aerodrome in a shocking series of S turns. Eventually you got the hang of it until one day – to your great surprise and consternation – you kept the engine on longer than you were expected to and suddenly you were in the air. You felt as though you were fifty feet up – in fact you were probably three feet up. So you stopped the engine until you were on the ground again. After that, the instructor would tear you to ribbons but he didn't mean it because you'd done a fairly straight flight and you'd landed all right. So then he'd tell you to go and do the same thing again. And as you got used to flying at five or six feet high, you gradually kept the engine on a bit longer and pulled the stick back a bit further and you got up higher until you were up to about fifty feet. And you'd go up and down the airfield, straight down the middle.

When you got that comfortably wrapped up, you'd try a turn. You would start off on the ground with the aeroplane at forty-five degrees to the white patch on the fence and you'd take off and when you'd levelled out at fifty to a hundred feet, you kicked on the rudder, which spoiled the aerodynamic state of the aeroplane and it dropped its nose and turned. It came as a shock because it felt like putting a brake on. The machine did a right-angled turn and down you went and landed. And you kept doing this, turning to one side and then the other, until you'd got it wrapped up. Nowadays, of course, one would be told to put on bank when turning, but at that time, the instructors knew nothing about aerodynamics. There was never any banking taught. So we were told to keep our turns absolutely flat, suicidal as it sounds. And after that you were allowed to struggle around the circuit. You sort of flew around the outside of the airfield and when you came back to where you started, you shut off the engine and landed. That was a circuit. And that's how I learned to fly.

Another very basic machine used for training was the Boxkite. In this aircraft, the pupil was able to wrap his body around that of the instructor. Donald Bremner flew a Boxkite from Chingford in September 1915:

Boxkites were very queer old machines with a 50-horse-power Gnome engine. They had practically no instruments – just a rev counter. There was a petrol tap and a joystick and a rudder bar. The joystick was along-side the pilot and came up from the right, across in front at a bit of an angle. There was a little wicker seat, bolted to the lower wing. The instructor sat in that and you sat behind him – not strapped in at all – you just put your legs round his waist and hung on round his shoulders. When he took the machine up, you leant your right arm round his shoulder, and caught hold of the joystick. You both had your hands on it and that's how you learnt to use it. After he'd taken you round a bit, you were then allowed to taxi the machine around the aerodrome using the rudder bar. Without taking off. Then the most heroic thing happened. You changed places with the instructor. He couldn't reach the rudder bar. All he could do was put his hand on the joystick round your shoulder. And together you flew off. When he thought you were ready – or perhaps when he'd had enough – you were allowed to do hops. You took the machine up on your own and flew about ten or fifteen yards and then put the machine down again. When you'd done enough of that, you started doing circuits.

The Boxkite might have been basic, but its slow speed and limited climb allowed Humphrey Leigh to perform a feat quite beyond any modern aircraft:

My Boxkite was on the far side of Hendon Aerodrome. A mechanic started up the engine and said 'Give me a lift to the other end of the aerodrome.' I said, 'All right,' and he stood on one of the skids and held onto the frame. I started taxiing across the field. 'No!' he said, 'Let her go!' So I told him to hold on tight and I took off and landed on the other side of the aerodrome. He was a very brave chap – stood firm, held on and didn't falter at all.

As the Royal Flying Corps began to justify its presence on the Western Front in the autumn of 1914, it increased the scope of its flying training. The Central Flying School at Upavon was expanded and several civilian flying schools (including Brooklands) were purchased. Most importantly, the Royal

Flying Corps began to teach pilots to fly from scratch. Young men no longer had to pay for their own tuition – although those that joined the reserve squadrons continued to do so. The training aircraft of choice, remembered by Donald Bremner, was the relatively advanced Maurice Farman Biplane:

> The Maurice Farman Longhorn was a big, clumsy aeroplane but rather pleasant to fly. It was a pusher, so you were sitting out in front of the engine in a nice comfortable seat and you weren't looking straight down onto the ground like you were in a Boxkite. And it had an airspeed indicator.

Gerald Livock also preferred the Maurice Farman to the Boxkite:

> I flew a Maurice Farman at Hendon. Oh, it was terrific. Magnificent. We didn't have altimeters so I don't know what height we went to, probably 2000 feet, and circled round Hendon. I'd only ever been up about 300 feet in my Boxkite. One felt like a God, looking down on these poor mortals below. One almost forgot to be frightened.

The Maurice Farman came in two versions – the Longhorn and the Shorthorn. The Longhorn was so called because of its pronounced outriggers to a forward elevator, giving it the appearance of a breed of cattle. Both aircraft were ungainly structures. Sixteen wooden struts joined the upper and lower wings together and they were interwoven with such a tangle of piano wires that it was said you could safely cage a canary inside. Nevertheless, they constituted a great leap forward for pupils as they were capable of dual-control flying – in other words the pupil and the instructor sat one in front of the other, each with his own set of controls. This meant, in theory, that pupils were able to learn in far greater safety.

Although, as Eric Furlong discovered, theory and practice did not always overlap:

> My application to join the Royal Flying Corps was finally accepted in the middle of 1917. I was posted to the flying training station at Harlaxton in Lincolnshire. I didn't tell them at first that I'd already learned to fly in 1914. I thought that I would learn more if I kept quiet. Whereas in 1914, all my training had been done on solo machines, in 1917, the system was dual training with the instructor in the other seat. Well, the instructor realized on my first flight that I knew something about flying so he told me to take control. He didn't like the way I turned using the rudder only, as I'd been taught. By 1917, training had progressed to proper banked turns. So he wrenched the controls out of my hand and said, 'This is what I want! Do it like this, you see?' and when we got to the next corner, he wrenched it out of my hands again and when we got to the last corner, I left it to him again. And then I just sat there and watched as we came gliding in. Wallop. We slapped into the ground and smashed the machine to smithers. He looked at me and said, 'What did you do that for?' I said, 'I didn't touch it!' He said, 'Neither did I!' He thought I had control of the aeroplane and I thought he had control. That was my first landing in a Maurice Farman Longhorn.

In the early days, as Frederick Powell remembers, communication between instructor and pupil was difficult:

> The instructor sat behind me in a dual-control Maurice Farman and he flew the machine while I lightly put my hands on the controls. We had no intercom in those days – so the conversation was shouting over the noise of a rattling engine. It was difficult to hear. Sign language came in handy. The sign I used most was the two-fingered salute.

Take-off and landing both presented difficulties for the pupil. Landing, argues Laurie Field, posed the greater challenge:

> Landing was the most difficult thing of all because it's the one thing that mattered! If you made a mistake in the air it didn't matter – if you made a mistake in landing, you were in trouble. The knack of the landing is that when you come down, you've got your gliding height, your engine is off. You gradually pull your nose up as you lose flying speed, it stalls your aeroplane and the perfect landing is to have the wheels and the tail skid hit the ground together. This happened once in every twenty times. A bad landing is when you pull your nose up too early and you're too far off the ground and your plane drops. If it drops sufficiently badly, your undercarriage is gone.

Reginald Fulljames was wary of taking off:

> I was more anxious about taking off than landing because you were entirely dependent upon your engine and if the engine coughed or spluttered as you took off, you had very little chance of avoiding a crash. Whereas if the engine failed at two or three thousand feet, I had every confidence that I could land the aircraft somewhere. And in those days – according to my logbook – one in every five or six flights ended up in some sort of engine failure which necessitated a forced landing.

If a pilot did have to carry out a forced landing shortly after take off, then Brooklands was not the place to do it, as S. S. Saunders recalls:

> One corner of Brooklands happened to be a sewage farm. This caused quite a lot of trouble with some of the boys because if they hadn't climbed up sufficiently high and then had engine failure, they just came down

in it. Everyone was warned to avoid it because if they didn't . . . well . . . everyone avoided them . . .

Once dual-control training had become the accepted method of training, the first 'solo' flight became a critical event for every pupil. Vernon Coombs made his first solo by accident:

> I was terribly anxious to fly solo and after I'd done one hour and thirty-five minutes dual, my instructor jumped out of the machine and shouted something at me. I thought he'd said, 'Take it up!' so I turned the machine round and I took it up. After I'd landed, he tore strips off me. 'What the hell do you mean doing that?' 'You told me to take it up,' I said. 'No, I didn't, he said, 'I told you to take it in!'

F. D. Silwood failed to make it off the ground:

> When the day came for my first solo, my instructor said, 'Now look, if you treat it very carefully you can do your first solo on my aeroplane.' So I got out into the middle of the aerodrome and my prop stopped. Well, of course, the normal thing to do is to call for a mechanic to start your prop but with the impetuosity of youth I thought I'd start the prop myself. As I swung it, the aeroplane started moving forwards. So I dashed under the plane, tried to get in the seat but I couldn't and I fell over. The tailplane hit my head and knocked me to the ground. I watched my instructor's beautiful aeroplane run away from me. It swerved to the left and I ran after it but it gradually gained speed until it started to turn towards me. I fell over which was just as well because the aeroplane took off over my head and flew at about fifty feet until it crashed. In the meantime, my instructor was going absolutely mad. I had to go in front of my commanding officer who told me, 'Pilots are cheap but aeroplanes are very, very expensive. You

made an awful mess of things today.' I thought I was going to be dismissed from the service and I held my head very low and said I was sorry. But he had a half smile on his face as he told me, 'Well, all right. We'll forget it this time!'

Stanley Walters learnt an important lesson during his first solo:

> The instructor said, 'See the nose?' I looked at it. 'See that little cap on the top of the nose? Remember to hold that on the horizon!' Then he hopped out of the aeroplane and said, 'She's all yours! Take it off and fly yourself! But wait a minute! There's another fellow there, he's going off solo from another instructor. Let him do his circuit and landing first. As soon as he's in the air, you take off. Just do one circuit and landing!' 'OK,' I said.
>
> The other fellow was a man called Day. He took off. I was thinking that a hell of a lot of pupils and instructors would be watching me because it was my first solo. 'One circuit and landing be damned!' I thought. 'I'll do a couple of loops, but they're all watching Day now, so I'll wait till he's landed.' So I took off and followed Day round to watch his landing – and I saw him stall from about fifteen feet, hit the ground, and burst into flames. He was killed on his first solo. All arrogance in me also died. I did exactly what I was told. I completed my circuit and landed.

Charles Chabot's first solo went according to plan:

> When I went solo for the first time – it seems completely ridiculous in present-day terms – I had had fifty minutes of instruction. But off I went. At one end of Brooklands Aerodrome was a pub – the Blue Boar. We knew that if we came in at 100 feet over the Blue Boar, we were in the right position to land. The sun was just

rising above the horizon and, as I came in, the shadow of the Longhorn was away on the left and, as I came down, it began creeping in under the plane, so when the shadow was properly comfortable under the wings, I yanked my stick back and sat down with a perfect landing on the aerodrome. My instructor was delighted. 'Right,' he said. 'Off you go, Chabot. Take your ticket.'

'Taking your ticket' meant taking the pilot certificate test conducted by the Royal Aero Club. Donald Clappen recalls the examination:

So far as the Aero Club certificate was concerned, one had to do five figures of eight observed by two qualified pilots who acted as observers. These observers were usually two of the instructors from one of the other flying schools. At the end of each flight of five figures of eight, one had to land within fifty metres of a specified spot, which was where the observers were standing. Then, came the height test. One had to fly up to a height of fifty metres, cut off one's engine and land again within fifty metres of the spot where the observers were standing. Often, if it looked as though the pupil was going to land too far away, the observers would walk to where they thought he would land. They wanted the pupil to pass, so that they could get back to their own job of teaching people to fly. I do not recall a single pupil failing to land within the specified distance.

Humphrey Leigh confirms that the pupils were not always rigorously examined:

There was one old boy, a captain, who was terribly ham-fisted. He smashed pretty well every aeroplane he got into. Eventually the time came for him to take his ticket. I remember the CO of the station seeing me standing on the tarmac, beckoning me over, and saying,

'Leigh, go and watch Captain X get his ticket, And what's more, see that he gets it!' So I said, 'Aye, aye, sir', and went off. In due course, the old boy had to land near the mark – and I was the mark. I could see that he was going to be miles away, so I ran like a stag. And as his aeroplane came to a grinding halt, the old boy said, 'Have I got it? Was it all right?' 'Yes, sir! Yes, sir! Yes, sir!' I said, clapping like anything.

Once the pupil had taken his ticket, he usually went to an advanced training school, to prepare for flying in action. Reginald Fulljames followed this path:

I was selected for fighter pilot training and I was sent to the Advanced School of Flying at Gosport. One morn-ing, I was surprised to hear that the commanding officer wanted to take me up. This shook me because you seldom had any dual control after you'd gone solo. The commanding officer was the famous Smith-Barry and I suppose he was using me as one of his early guinea pigs, trying out his new ideas.

Major Robert Smith-Barry revolutionized flying training from late 1916 onwards. He had noticed that flyers who arrived on the Western Front were often hesitant and diffi-dent in their approach to flying. This approach, he reasoned, must have been learnt from the instructors, who viewed instructing as a dead-end job. Smith-Barry aimed to revitalize teaching. He insisted that all pupils under dual training should sit in the pilot's seat in front of the full set of controls. He developed the 'Gosport tube', which enabled the in-structor to communicate with the pupil during the flight. He believed that a pilot, having flown solo, needed to learn advanced manoeuvres such as sudden turns and the correct way to recover from a spin. Of all the dilemmas that a pilot could face, the spin was the most feared. If the airflow over the wings decreased to the point where the machine could no longer sustain flight, it would fall out of the air. No longer an aircraft, cheating the laws of nature, it became a spinning hulk of wood, metal, wires and cloth. Until 1916, there was no known method of recovering from a spin. Some pilots who spun their aircraft managed to recover by chance, but they could not explain what they had done. Reginald Fulljames:

> Smith-Barry showed me, above all else, how to get out of a spin. Smith-Barry was undoubtedly a genius and his methods are the basis for modern flying training. He had been injured in France at the beginning of the war, when he had spun into the ground. After that, he intended to find a proper way of getting out of a spin, and when he had discovered the answer, he pressed the Air Ministry very hard to be allowed to teach this in the Royal Flying Corps. The confidence that I could get out of a spin saved my life when I was being chased by Baron von Richthofen. I went into a deliberate spin and I got away.

Ronald Sykes remembers the feeling of a spin:

> It was the most sickening sensation. You were thrown violently to one side of the cockpit with a fierce blast of wind on one cheek. You had to switch off the engine and straighten everything – the control stick and the rudder. You usually didn't come out of the spin quickly. You just had to put everything central and wait. Eventually you entered a nosedive and you pulled the stick back slightly and you were all right.

Smith-Barry argued that, in order for pupils to be able to practise manoeuvres such as these, the training schools needed a standard type of dual-training machine that was capable of performing them. In December 1916, he was placed in charge of the Gosport School of Flying. The aircraft that he chose as his advanced trainer was the Avro 504K. Frank Burslem encountered great difficulty flying an Avro:

> I was a very slow pupil. I suppose I was a little bit dense. I took eight hours to go solo whereas the average was about three hours. My problem was psychological. I went up in an Avro and was put into a spin by the instructor. He told me what to do and how to get out of the spin but when I saw the world turning round on an axis directly below me, I absolutely froze on the controls and I couldn't do anything. I was so fascinated watching the ground, getting lower and lower, that I couldn't do anything at all. The instructor was swearing and cursing and he overcame the pressure I was putting on the controls and he got us out of the spin about 500 feet off the ground. The instructors thought I wasn't fit to fly the faster machines – the single-seater fighters – so I was sent to fly heavier machines – two-seaters.

Smith-Barry's teaching methods prepared pupils for the realities of combat flying. They also allowed slower pupils – like Burslem – to learn their limits before it was too late. For the pilots such as James Gascoyne who relished the possibilities that flying offered, the sky was the limit:

> A loop comprises racing your engine, opening your engine full out, putting it into a slight dive to get full speed, then all you do is pull back the joystick, right back into your stomach, and the machine goes up, over, and then drops. As it drops, you switch off the engine and come smoothly out into a glide. They are usually done at a height of a thousand feet or more to give you time to recover in case you lose too much engine speed and the machine comes straight down.

Ronald Sykes remembers the thrill of the vertical bank:

It was the most delightful manoeuvre. You could just move your stick an inch or two over to the side and she would immediately turn over onto a wingtip. At the same time, you pulled the stick back into your stomach and the nose began to whip round the horizon. You also had to put on full left rudder because the engine tended to make the nose climb into the sky on a left turn and the left rudder kept it down.

Pilots took pleasure in trying to outdo each other and achieve what had not been achieved before. Frederick Powell came up with an idea that was very nearly his last:

One night I was lying in bed and I thought, 'I'll do something nobody else has ever done – tomorrow morning I will loop off the ground!' My Bristol Bullet had a maximum speed of about seventy miles an hour but I thought that if I held it down just over the top of the grass until I was going flat out, then I could go up in a very big loop and when I got to the top I could pull the joystick into my tummy, whip the tail over and gravity plus the engine would pull me round. So next morning, I went off and tried it. I pulled up in the loop, flipped it – and realized I hadn't enough room. I have a feeling that my life was saved by some sheep grazing at the far end of the airfield. They all started to run out star fashion away from me and I was so interested in watching them that I didn't stiffen myself up. I went straight into the ground at about 150 mph. I shot through the front of the aircraft, my belt broke, I hit my head on the instrument board and was knocked out. My legs shot through the rotary engine. Another quarter of a turn and I would have lost both my legs. As it was, I finished with the engine in my crotch. The ground was hard and nothing had sunk more than a few inches into the earth. Everything was flattened like a pancake. My CO stopped everyone from running out because he thought I was going to be a nasty mess. So he strolled slowly across to the crash. When he got there, he found me singing. I was quite out of it but I was singing the latest song:

> Sprinkle me with kisses,
> A lot of lovely kisses,
> If you want my love to grow . . .

While practising something new in his Sopwith Camel, Graham Donald cheated death in a manner that might make a believer of the sternest atheist:

As I was approaching the airfield at 6000 feet, I decided to try a new manoeuvre which might prove useful in combat. It was to be a half loop and then I would roll at the top and fly off in the opposite direction. I pulled her up into a neat half loop but I was going rather slowly and I was hanging upside down in the air. With an efficient safety belt that would have been no trouble at all – but our standard belts were a hundred per cent unsafe. Mine stretched a little and suddenly I dived clean through it and fell out of the cockpit. There was nothing between me and the ground. The first 2000 feet passed very quickly and terra firma looked damnably 'firma'. As I fell, I began to hear my faithful little Camel somewhere nearby. Suddenly I fell back onto her. I was able to grip onto her top plane and that saved me from slithering straight through the propeller which was glistening beautifully in the evening sunshine. She was now diving noisily at about 140 mph. I was hanging onto her with my left hand and with one foot hooked into the cockpit, I managed to reach down with my other hand and I pulled the control stick backwards to pull her gently out of her dive. This was a mistake – she immediately went into the most appalling inverted spin. Even with two hands on the top plane, I was slipping. I had about 2500 feet left. Remembering that everything was inverted, I managed to put my right foot on the control stick and I pushed it forwards. The Camel stopped spinning in half a turn and went into a smooth glide but upside down. It was now easy to reach my hand down (or up) and pull her gently down and round into a normal glide. I grabbed the seat cushion which was obstructing the cockpit, chucked it over the side and sat back down. I was now at about 800 feet but in spite of the extraordinary battering she had received, my little Camel was flying perfectly. One or two of the wings were a bit loose but nothing was broken. I turned the engine off in case of strains so my approach was made in silence. I made an unusually good landing but there was no one there to applaud – every man-jack of the squadron had mysteriously disappeared. After a minute or so, heads began to appear all over the place – popping up like bunny rabbits from every hole. Apparently, when I had pressed my foot on the control stick, I'd also pressed both triggers and the entire airfield had been sprinkled with bullets. Very wisely, the ground crew dived as one man for the nearest ditch.

As well as learning how to fall back into an aircraft from a height of several thousand feet, pilots had to learn to make cross-country flights. Charles Chabot remembers a particularly popular method of navigation:

One wasn't particularly instructed in the use of a compass and our map-reading technique was not very good. When we had to get from A to B, most of us used to fly by 'Bradshaw'. That was the name of the railway guide. One simply followed the railway lines. It was the recognized way of getting about.

A pilot who 'Bradshawed' his way down to a seaside resort, like Archibald Yuille, might have an enjoyable day out:

We used to go to Brighton and fly along the seafront and very often below the level of the pier. Then we'd zoom up over the West Pier, down again, zoom up over the Palace Pier and down again. We'd swing round and fly inland looking as if we were going to fly in the windows of the hotels then we'd zoom up over the roofs. That gave us great amusement but the people of Brighton didn't like it very much.

As the war progressed, pilots began to learn to fly at night. Archibald Yuille recalls the difficulties:

It's very funny, night flying. You get a good horizon to fly against and you can see water clearly underneath you but of course you can't pick out roads or railway lines. The main thing is to keep your eye on the horizon and not find yourself getting into a dive when you don't mean to. You had no aids – you were up there all by yourself in the dark for two hours. Not everybody has the mentality to do that. One of the things one did was sing – quite unconsciously. You'd come down absolutely hoarse.

Once a pilot had received his training, he was assigned to a squadron on active service. He was immediately confronted by his greatest challenge. He had to adapt to the reality of aerial warfare – and he had to adapt quickly. Some pilots were simply inept and no amount of training could make a difference. Harold Wyllie, an observer with 6 Squadron, was enraged by such a man in April 1915. His diary records:

Clarke was dreadfully smashed here today. Ross Hume was pilot and somehow managed to side slip and nose dive to the ground. This is wrong. Ross Hume stalled his machine turning. He was a rotten pilot and should never have been allowed to carry a passenger. Clarke died at 11.50 pm without regaining consciousness, thank God. He was one of the best fellows that ever lived and a valuable life has been thrown away by sheer bad flying.

By 1916, so many pilots were being lost that their replacements were barely trained when they arrived at the front. Cecil Lewis, arriving at 3 Squadron, was one of these replacements:

> When I got to France, I only had about twenty hours flying and I was posted to a BE2c squadron down on the Somme. The CO took one look at my logbook and said, 'My God, it's murder sending you chaps out with nothing on the logbook. You'd better put in a bit of time!' So he gave me an aircraft and I walloped off to have a look at the lines, to get used to the French maps, all the things that were different. One had always heard, 'Behind the lines, this side of the lines, the lines, the lines, the lines . . .' But I hadn't a clue as to what the lines looked like – really from the air – looked like . . .

John Boon was aware of the fate that awaited many of these schoolboys, like Lewis, who arrived to do a man's job:

> We used to see the young men coming in to the orderly office to receive their instructions as to where they had to go. Then the tenders from the squadrons came to the headquarters to pick up them up. You used to see these young fellows with their brand-new wings, brand-new uniform, brand-new Sam Browne belt. Everything was new and smart. Some of these boys didn't last twenty-four hours.

On joining the Royal Flying Corps or Royal Naval Air Service, the men of the rank and file were treated very differently from the officers. These were the men – the riggers and fitters and other technicians – who would be responsible for keeping the aeroplanes flying. They joined as tradesmen, but they were trained as raw recruits. William Berry made an inauspicious start:

> At my very first parade, the man next to me stood there with his boots all dusty. The sergeant said, 'Man left and right of him, escort him to the guardroom!' When we got him there, they made him turn out his pockets and I've never seen anything like it. He had nails sticking into bits of toffee, stubs of pencils – it was so funny that I burst out laughing. The corporal in charge of the guard looked at me and said, 'Laughing on escort – worse crime than the prisoner's! Get in there along with him!' So by ten past two on my first day, I was confined to barracks.

The discipline meted out to the recruits was of a traditional military variety. Cecil King:

> If we were such a superior corps we had to show it in discipline, especially when walking out. We were expected to set an example to everyone. That's why all our instructors came from the Brigade of Guards. Our discipline had to be second to none.

George Eddington remembers how the discipline was imposed:

> What struck me most was the absolute domination of the routine. From your feeding, to your sport, it was all routine. You were made to realize that you were there to do as you were told and not to ask questions. Even a simple thing like turning right or left had to be done just so. Squads were formed in fours, which meant a complicated movement of the feet. The food was not too good at all. You were only allowed out of camp with a pass and you were allowed once a week, until eleven o'clock. You were made to feel that you were nobody at all. You were a soldier first and last. The

instructors were, without exception, warrant officers, Guardsmen. They felt that a new-fangled thing like the Flying Corps was a lot of poppycock, and a waste of good men, and they didn't forget to let us know. We weren't made to feel that we were technicians. We were soldiers in the King's army: 'You are not a superior breed! Get rid of that idea as quick as you like!'

William Berry had a favourite NCO:

I remember Corporal Newbolt. He could have been acting unpaid for all I know. He was six foot odd of brute strength and he would come and put his face by your cheek, within two or three inches – and he would yell at you, 'Do you know Mrs Newbolt?' 'No, Corporal.' 'Well, you'll jolly well know her son!' He didn't say 'jolly' . . .

Cecil King discovered that the smallest act could breach army regulations:

I remember walking through Aldershot and it came on to rain. I was wearing an overcoat, and I turned the collar up. All of a sudden, I heard a man shouting behind me, 'That man!' and I looked round. It was a military policeman on a horse and he said, 'Do you know you're improperly dressed?' I said, 'No.' He said, 'How long have you been in the service?' 'Two months.' 'Well,' he said, 'you've turned your collar up without orders. You'll put it down in the proper manner.' I didn't argue the point. I turned it down. But it made me wonder why we had to have an order to be permitted to stay dry.

For some of the men the discipline proved unbearable. Edgar Wooley remembers an uprising in the ranks:

Amongst ourselves we decided we just could not stand the methods our military tutors were adopting. They were acting as a brake on our ability to do our technical training. They were preventing us from making progress as wireless operators. So we rebelled. We refused to carry on our technical training whilst the military training and discipline were so exacting. Word soon got round to those higher up and officers came along to find out what the trouble was. These officers picked out six men of our section – the assumed ringleaders. They were sent to Headquarters at Farnborough and sentenced to twenty-eight days' confinement. During their confinement, they were visited by a military parson who, on questioning one of them, was surprised by his intelligence and his desire to be a good soldier and a good wireless operator. The parson asked him why he was there. The soldier told him of the recruits' dissatisfaction at the treatment they had received at the hands of their military trainers. As a result of this discussion, the parson made a report to certain officers and the matter was brought up in Parliament – why was the Royal Flying Corps attempting to institute Prussian military methods into the British army?

Ultimately the six prisoners were released and the sergeant major in charge of training was relieved. He was replaced by another sergeant who found us to be a very satisfactory, efficient body of recruits – much to his surprise – and he couldn't understand why we had acted as we did unless there were justified reasons for it. He said, 'I want you now to be good soldiers and if you do as you're told and you continue to do your work properly, we shall get on very well together.' And that's exactly what we did. When he reluctantly left us, we made him a presentation. We found out that this hefty, jovial, soldierly sergeant was a big pipe smoker so we were only too pleased to give him a couple of pipes in a case. He was clearly very pleased – and surprised.

Irish charm made S. S. Saunders' life a little easier:

Sergeant Major Waddington from the Guards was a gentleman off parade, but a bastard on parade. I found that I could say things to him which he took in a good way because I was the only Irishman, and he sort of took things from me. One day, he put me on the Awkward Squad, because I wasn't properly shaved. The Awkward Squad was a squad which Sergeant Major Waddington took himself after lunch. We had to get on parade with our full kit including rifles and full pack. And he'd drill us like hell up and down there for about an hour. And then he'd dismiss us.

Well, we were issued with rifles which the Infantry had had for some time, and some of them had been lying in the mud for ages and practically rusted through. They were cleaned up and issued to us. Well, I had a rifle one day on the Awkward Squad and we were doing a drill where you pull back the bolt and hold the rifle in a certain position so that the inspecting officer can look down the barrel, and see that it's properly clean. We had done this four or five times but Sergeant Major Waddington wasn't satisfied. He said we weren't all together and we weren't making enough noise. So he shouted, 'Pull the bloody thing back till you break it!'

So I pulled the bolt, and when I did, it came away in my hand and left the head in the rifle. I just remained in the same position I was in, with my right forearm parallel with the ground and the bolt in my hand. He looked at me and he said, 'What the bloody hell's wrong with you Saunders?' And I said, 'Nothing sir. I've obeyed the last order. I've broken the bloody thing.' The other chaps were getting a side glance in and he chewed them up. He shouted, 'Look to your front!'

He came over and he looked at me and I could just

see a slight suspicion of a twinkle in his eye and he turned round to me and he said, 'Get off this squad immediately. You're too bloody awkward for the Awkward Squad. Dismiss!' So I hadn't to go on any more on the Awkward Squad, but the other fellows had to make up for it.

For William Hawkins of the Royal Naval Air Service, the end of a day's basic training brought a soothing recreation:

When I was training at the Crystal Palace Depot, square bashing, route marching and rifle training finished at about 5.00 pm and then, in the evening, we had dancing. There was no one of the opposite sex so we had to dance with each other. We waltzed and we did the Boston two-step – the old-fashioned dances. It was quite a lot of fun, actually.

As basic training progressed, the men began to spend their afternoons engaged in practical training. Cecil King:

The men were broadly divided into riggers and fitters. But every man had the same training on engines and airframes. To start with – on airframes. We had an aeroplane – which was old and broken – and we all stood round it with an instructor and he would tell us what the different parts were. And then we'd take it to pieces or we'd take a wing off and put it back again or take a wheel off and see how it was built. And he'd tell us what the different functions were on the airframe – which wire took which strain and so on. Then we'd go into the engine shop and they would teach us the engine. The engines there were the 80-horse-power Gnôme and the 70-horse-power Renault and they used to take them to pieces and tell us all the different parts and what its functions were. We would make rough notes so everyone learned this whatever their function was – rigger or fitter.

ON A WING AND A PRAYER

After three months, basic training was completed and the recruits passed out. Cecil King was posted to 5 Squadron, where he was gradually introduced to the squadron work of aircraft maintenance. After a few weeks, he was sent to the Central Flying School at Upavon for three months' intensive training as a rigger:

> Every day was spent on the aircraft in the sheds and in the workshops. We learnt to make simple parts out of any wood that was available. We learnt that, when filling up an aircraft with petrol, you must always pour the petrol through chamois leather. We learnt how to splice a wire cable, because the wires which formed the framework of a biplane were of seven-stranded cable. We learnt how to put the covering – sometimes linen, sometimes cotton – on the wings. We had the wing spread out on trestles, and we laid the fabric down and pinned it, and then sewed it together, and then doped it. The dope used to shrink it up so that it became drum-tight.
>
> After we'd received our training on the detailed parts of the aircraft, we were sent out into the flights to work with the men on the actual aircraft themselves. We learnt how to handle them and the special technique of starting up the engines by swinging the prop. Once I'd finished my training, I returned to No. 5 Squadron as a fully fledged rigger, able to take charge of a machine in the flights.

It wasn't just pilots, riggers and fitters who were in need of training. So, too, were the observers – the men who flew with the pilots in two-seater aircraft. Yet in August 1916, when George Taylor was sent out to France, he was completely unprepared:

> I had been posted as an observer to 25 Squadron, but I had been given no training whatever. I'd been on the

aerodrome two hours, getting new clothes, and I was then told I was going up for a trial flight. I went up just before eleven o'clock, and I was flown by Captain Greig. I got into the FE2b, and in my nacelle was an empty petrol tin. I naturally thought it was the seat for the observer, so I sat down. And I stayed sitting. Throughout the flight, I tried to memorize things I saw on the ground, but I was pretty static. I didn't move about, I didn't lean over the side. I just saw certain territory from a distance. When we came down, Sergeant Green, who was showing me round, said that Captain Greig will want a report of where we'd been. I said, 'I don't know much about it!' So he said, 'Don't worry about that. Let's go in the office, get a pen and you can write down what I say.' So I made a good report for that first flight. Captain Greig said it was bloody marvellous!

An observer's other important task was to act as aerial gunner, defending the aircraft from attack. Once he was on the squadron, George Taylor received a little training in this aspect:

There were no textbooks to read, and we never used to meet in rooms to argue about air fighting, or anything. We had just one thing – a model of a German aeroplane made out of canvas, pinned to the ground a few miles from the aerodrome. For our training, the pilots used to dive at this model, and we used to use live ammunition on it. Even then, nobody told us how to use our guns. You wouldn't call it training. The first time I did this, I went up with Lieutenant Davis, and he went into a dive, and I started firing my gun onto the canvas plane. Suddenly, I saw somebody running away from it. It was a Frenchman, who was out for a walk. I hadn't seen him. He was running like hell.

By early 1918, when Howard Andrews was learning to become an observer, new training methods had been adopted:

> For our training, we were given an ordinary machine
> gun with a camera strapped on the front and every
> time you pressed the trigger you took a photograph. We
> were taken up in the air, flown round and every time
> we saw an aeroplane on the ground or in the air, we
> were supposed to take a photograph of it. The first time
> I went up with this gun, I was flown by a Canadian
> pilot – who was a bit of a devil. The aeroplane went
> round and round like a drunk caterpillar. I didn't know
> anything. I didn't know what was ground and what
> was sky. I couldn't see aeroplanes anywhere. The pilot
> swore at me and pointed at the ground – I saw an aero-
> plane on the ground, so I took a photograph of it. Then
> I gave up.
>
> 'Where do you want to go?' the pilot screamed at
> me. 'Hastings,' I said. So we flew to Hastings and he
> went right round the pier. I thought it looked nice so I
> took a photograph of it. I thought to myself, 'I've done
> myself now – I can't get this off.' We came back and
> landed. The squadron leader came racing over to the
> pilot to tick him off as apparently we weren't allowed to
> go anywhere near Hastings. As he came over, I must
> have pressed the trigger again. The next day, they read
> out that somebody got six aeroplanes, somebody got
> five and he said 'Stand up, Cadet Andrews!' I stood
> up and he said, 'You've got one photograph of an aero-
> plane, very nice, one of Hastings Pier and one of the
> squadron leader. And he doesn't like it . . .'

4

And so to War

As the Great War began, and the people of Great Britain united in patriotic fervour, the magazine of the Dover School for Boys – *The Pharos* – indulged in some editorial flag waving:

> The school must be one of the nearest English schools to the seat of war, so near that we are within sound of the guns. This fact alone would enable us to understand how vital is the issue for the future of our country and Empire. For the security of our Empire, as a united England declares, Germany must be conquered resolutely and decisively beaten.

The magazine then went on to record a recent burst of activity at the nearby Swingate Downs Aerodrome:

> A continuous stream of aeroplanes arrived at the hangars. Biplanes, monoplanes – all were there; and the arrival of two dirigibles, the *Silver Queen* and the *Delta*, completed the joy of those enthusiasts who could spend an afternoon sitting on the Promenade, throwing themselves into unearthly positions in their attempts to look at aeroplanes passing immediately over their heads. Unfortunately for these people, both types of aircraft left, presumably for the fighting front.

This 'continuous stream of aeroplanes' was the sixty-three machines of 2, 3, 4 and 5 Squadrons of the Royal Flying Corps, and they were, indeed, heading for the fighting front. In the days leading up to 13 August 1914, an assortment of BE2as, Avro 504s, Farmans and Blériots assembled at Swingate Downs, before flying across the English Channel to Amiens, where they were to regroup before flying onto their final position at Maubeuge, ten miles behind the lines held by the British Expeditionary Force.

These machines constituted almost the entire strength of the Royal Flying Corps. Less than eleven years after the Wright brothers took to the air, aviation was to be put to the test. At the outbreak of war, the largest air force belonged to Germany: 246 aircraft and seven airships. The French had 160 aircraft and fifteen airships, and whilst the official figures recorded that the Royal Flying Corps possessed 189 aircraft, in truth, the majority of these were worn out, broken, or in use at the Central Flying School.

The fact is that the military authorities of none of these countries knew precisely what role their machines would play. Much of the British High Command still refused to believe that they had any role to play at all, short of frightening the horses. As the months passed, however, these machines were to demonstrate their versatility, and in doing so an entirely new concept of warfare came into being; the tactics – and to some degree the strategies – employed came not from past experience or from the upper echelons but from the only men who could develop them: the young flyers themselves. It was up to them to discover what could, and could not be done in the air. If they tried something that worked, they refined it. If it failed, they discarded it. These boys, who wrote letters home describing their water fights, were simultaneously framing the rules of aerial warfare that have played such a crucial part in shaping the modern world.

Before the raggle-taggle Flying Corps had even reached

Swingate Downs, they suffered their first fatalities of the war.
Lieutenant Robert Skene and Air Mechanic R. K. Barlow, of 3
Squadron, crashed shortly after taking off from Netheravon
for Dover. The future air ace James McCudden, at the time
a mechanic in 3 Squadron, started Skene's engine, and
watched as his aircraft flew, tail low, over the squadron's
hangar. He then heard the engine stop, followed by the
sound of a crash, 'which once heard, is never forgotten'. He
ran over half a mile to a small copse of firs, where he found
Skene and Barlow lying dead in the machine's wreckage.
McCudden wrote:

> I shall never forget that morning at about half-past
> six, kneeling by poor Keith Barlow and looking at the
> rising sun and then again at poor Barlow, who had no
> superficial injury, and was killed purely by concussion,
> and wondering if war was going to be like this always.

Kenneth van der Spuy, a cocksure young South African
flying with 2 Squadron, almost suffered a similar fate on
arrival at Dover. In the air, as van der Spuy demonstrates,
overconfidence could amount to incompetence:

> When I arrived at Dover, arrogant young bastard that I
> was, thinking I knew everything about flying, I thought,
> 'I'll show these lads something.' So I came down in a
> steep spiral. I had a big, fat flight sergeant, packed in
> next to me in the observer's seat. As we came down, his
> neck grew redder and redder. I saw where I should land
> between the flags and flattened out. But I didn't flatten
> out where I should have flattened out. Boom, crash! I
> crushed the undercarriage, and there I sat like a bloody
> fool, with three squadrons of the Royal Flying Corps
> marching out to see who this bloody fool was.

If the pilots had such trouble reaching their first assembly
point over land, then the next leg of the journey, across the

Channel to Amiens, was to pose even greater problems. The aircraft flew not in pairs or bunches, but one by one, and any man who ditched at sea would be left to his own fate. Pilots were warned to reach a height of 3000 feet before setting out over the coast, sufficient altitude to be able to glide to France, should an engine failure occur. The first man to arrive at Amiens in his BE2 machine was Major Hubert Harvey-Kelly of 2 Squadron, a man described by Maurice Baring as 'the gayest of all gay pilots'. He arrived at twenty minutes past eight on the morning of 13 August. One after another, throughout the day, the aircraft of 2, 3 and 4 Squadron landed, to be greeted by excited French civilians, relieved to discover that the British were coming. So excited were many that van der Spuy had difficulty touching the ground:

> As I was coming in to land, the whole of the French people in the area – it looked like the whole of France – came surging onto the aerodrome in front of me. Men, women and children. Three times, I had to open up my engine and go up again. In the end, somebody came out with a horse whip, and literally horsewhipped the crowd until they made a path for me to land.

The last squadron to arrive at Amiens was 5 Squadron, including among its pilots a number of special reservists who had joined the Royal Flying Corps directly, without having first been regulars in the British army. One of these reservists, Captain Louis Strange, had a testing time reaching Amiens in an Henri Farman machine, having to contend with fearsome headwinds and a broken longeron (predictable hazards of early flight), and a brutally drunk observer (less predictable). Strange, a name to bear in mind, was the archetype of the spirited, irreverent, free-thinking flyer, and the last pilot to arrive at Amiens.

In the meantime, the Royal Flying Corps Headquarters,

the Aircraft Park, the motor transports, the riggers and fitters and other supporting personnel were making their way to France by road and sea. On the move with 2 Squadron was George Eddington:

I was allocated a lorry of my own and we carried everything required. There were about a dozen vehicles – all lorries except for one tender. The boat which was allocated to take us to France hadn't arrived, so we were let loose in Glasgow until it came. The Flying Corps was getting a wee bit known, and that night, all the cinemas in Glasgow were open free to us. We were back on the docks at night, took our blankets out, and got to sleep as well as we could. After a couple of days, the ship came in and all the lorries were loaded on by cranes. When everything was on, we set sail, we didn't know where for, and the next thing I knew, we landed at Boulogne.

At Boulogne, I was given the job of ferrying the lorries from the various parts of the hold to the cranes. We got them onto the docks and we drove to a rendezvous on the edge of the town, where we joined up with the other squadrons – 3, 4, and 5. From there on, the whole Flying Corps moved as one column, so far every day, and stopped by the roadside where we were. What struck me most was that as we went through the villages, they all turned out. And they called out, 'Aviation Anglais?' 'Oui!' They loaded us up with wine and anything we wanted, and they wouldn't take any money. The French were very friendly indeed. The girls were friendly, too.

James McCudden recalled that the French seemed to be shouting, 'Long live and tear!' With some subsequently acquired knowledge of the French language, he decided that he must have been hearing, 'Vive l'Angleterre!' Edward Bolt, en route with the Aircraft Park, remembers a variety of people having difficulty on the march:

One man was found to be carrying twenty-four tins of bully beef in his haversack and he was placed under arrest. He was caught because he had to drop out. The bully beef was too heavy. Two of the officers with us were Captain Carden, who had one arm, and Captain Moore-Brabazon, who had to walk with a stick because he was partially lame. I don't know what the French thought of this lot.

From Amiens, the Flying Corps (except for the Aircraft Park) made its way to its permanent position at Maubeuge. It was now to play its part in resisting the German army's offensive, whatever that part might be. The strategy of German High Command was to follow the Schlieffen Plan, with modifications made by General von Moltke. The Plan called for an invasion of France, in a large sweeping movement, through neutral Belgium.

No sooner was the Royal Flying Corps in position at Maubeuge than it was put to use in an observational capacity; the development of aerial warfare was underway. The first British reconnaissance flights were undertaken by pilots Philip Joubert de la Ferté of 3 Squadron and Gilbert Mapplebeck of 4 Squadron on the morning of 19 August. Their diaries record the occasion. First, Mapplebeck:

> After dinner, the Major told me I was to make a reconnaissance the next morning at about 9. I was tremendously pleased at this as it meant that I was making the first reconnaissance of the war and was, and am most grateful to the Major for selecting me.
>
> At 8 o'clock on the morning of the 19 August, I and my machine were both ready. At 8.15 Joubert (who was going in a Blériot) and I were sent for by General Henderson, who told us each our particular jobs. Joubert was to go straight to Braine l'Allend via Nivelles, I was to go to Gembloux. He was to be over friendly territory and look out for Belgians, and I was to look

for advanced German cavalry. My special orders were to keep with the Blériot as far as Nivelles then both were to go off to our own districts.

Using large scale maps, followed Blériot. I did not pick up my position on the map, so depended on Blériot's pilot for correct route, including to branch off on arriving at Nivelles. Missed Nivelles, arrived at a large town (I was at 3000 feet and in clouds) but could not place it on map. (On my return I discovered this to have been Brussels.) I flew to the other side of the town, turned round and steered S.S.E.

I then took out a small scale map and picked up my position at Oignies and soon found Gembloux after being in cloud. I made a wide circle round it, being in clouds part of the time, but only saw a small body of cavalry about a mile in length moving faster than a walk in a south easterly direction. At this time I was at 3400 and was just turning a little further when I was enveloped in clouds. I flew on for about 5 miles, and then descended about 3000 feet out of the clouds and saw Namur. I then turned west and passed Charleroi and altered my course a little south. I missed Maubeuge, flew on for about 15 miles after realizing that I had missed it and landed at Wassigny (near Le Cateau) at 11.30 am, and flew back, landing at Maubeuge at 12.

Joubert de la Ferté's diary records a different sort of day:

First reconnaissance with Mapplebeck. Lost myself most thoroughly. Landed at Tournai, where I had lunch with the governor, and again at Courtrai, until rescued by the Irish inhabitants. Finally achieved my task and returned after six and a quarter hours flying.

Aerial reconnaissance reports were initially viewed with scepticism by High Command. Lieutenant Cuthbert Rabagliati remembers the reception he received from the Commander of the British Expeditionary Force:

When you were doing a reconnaissance, you flew at anything up to about 3500 feet so that you could see clearly. The greatest difficulty we had was to persuade the general staff that what we'd seen was true. Their fixed idea was that there were only six or seven brigades coming at us. But nothing would persuade them to believe us.

I took off from Maubeuge and I was told that I should see some advancing German troops. I was very excited as I looked for them. You were very limited in your facilities – you had a map strapped on one knee and a pad with a pencil on the other and it was rather wobbling about. As soon as I got over the area – I didn't see *some* German troops, I saw the whole area covered with hordes of German uniforms. I saw advancing infantry, cavalry, transport and guns. The whole place was alive with Germans. I was completely horrified because it was infinitely more than I'd been told to expect. I made marks on the map, as many notes as I could. I came roaring back and landed whereupon I was put in a motor car by my squadron commander and taken off to GHQ which was in a chateau some miles away. I was ushered into a room with a lot of elderly gentlemen covered in gold lace and all the rest of it. They were all generals and one of them was Sir John French, Commander of the British Expeditionary Force. I'd been brought into his personal conference. Somebody announced me and Sir John said, 'Well! Here's a boy from the Flying Corps! Come here and sit down!'

I was rather terrifiedly put to sit next to him. Then he said, 'Now, where have you been? Have you been flying?' I showed him my map, all marked out. I explained what I had seen and they were enormously interested. But when I began reading the – accurate – figures that I'd estimated, I could sense them losing interest. They seemed to look at each other and shrug their shoulders. Then French turned to me and said, 'Now, my boy, tell me all about an aeroplane, what can you do when you're in these machines, aren't they very dangerous, are they very cold, can you see anything?' I couldn't bring him back to earth because obviously he wasn't interested in what I was trying to tell him. I tried again and he looked at me and said, 'Yes, what you've got here is very interesting, but our information – which of course is correct – proves that you haven't seen as much as you think! You may imagine that you have, but I'm afraid, it's not the case.'

Dispiriting though such a patronizing reception must have been for poor young Rabagliati, in the days that followed, consistent – and accurate – reports of large German troop movements began to demonstrate the reliability of aerial reconnaissance. The German army was pressing on towards Paris, unaware that the small British Expeditionary Force stood squarely in its way, at Mons.

On 22 August, pilots and observers began to bring back reports of the imminent approach of the First German Army under General Von Kluck. Mapplebeck's diary for that day reads:

Many reconnaissances were made. While Wadham's Blériot was near Brussels, he and his observer (Charlton) got into a very big cloud and on coming out of it could not pick up their position. So, thinking that they were in friendly territory, they landed. They were immediately surrounded by peasants, who informed them that they were behind the enemy's first line, and were right in the middle of 11,000 Germans. After obtaining some valuable information, they immediately got back into the Blériot and flew off. Before they had climbed 1500 feet, they surprised a German bivouac. There was immediate activity in the latter, resulting in heavy fire, and the riddling of their machine with bullets. Immediately after this, shrapnel began bursting 100 yards behind their tail, all were short. On their return it was found that Charlton's safety belt was cut by a bullet, the main spar of the right wing pierced by one, and the wings and tail riddled. This was a most miraculous escape.

What Vivian Wadham and Lionel Charlton, of 3 Squadron, had witnessed was the attempt by von Kluck's army, now aware of the British presence, to outflank the BEF. On the same day, Philip Joubert de la Ferté and his observer, Dermot Allen, spotted movement amongst the French forces to the right of the British line. This report was the first that Sir John French and his corps commanders knew of a French retreat.

At the Battle of Mons, which was fought on the following day, a British army of four divisions, made up of 75,000 men, held the German army and on the morning of 24 August, the BEF began its retreat to the River Marne. The value of aerial reconnaissance had been demonstrated, but the men and aircraft of the Royal Flying Corps were immediately forced to withdraw from Maubeuge and they moved south-west alongside the soldiers. The diary of John Bullock, a sergeant with 5 Squadron, gives a flavour of the retreat:

Left *Maubeuge* Monday 23rd August, halted at *Le Cateau*, left at 9 pm. Squadron reached *St Quentin* 9 am Tuesday 24th. Bent front axle on journey, left vehicle on road with Sgt. Bullen to replace it. Had dinner in St Quentin and reached camp at 3.30 pm. Left St Quentin 4.30 pm Wednesday 25th. Raining, reached *La Fère*

8 pm, stopped in farmyard for the night. Started next morning Thursday 26th. Loaded rifles, looking for German cavalry patrol, remained at farmyard all day long. Left at 5.30 am Friday 27th, went to *Compiègne*, arrived 4.30 pm. Albatros flew over Compiègne, dropped two bombs, no damage. Left Compiègne, 10 am Sunday 29th, arrived *Senlis* 10.30 pm. DWF flew over camp about midday, no bombs dropped, fired at her. Left Senlis 2 pm Monday 30th, arrived *Juilly* 6 pm same day.

Left 9 pm Tuesday 31st, arrived *Serris* 3 am Wed 1st Sept. Plenty of fruit, milk etc. Left Serris 10 am Thurs 2nd. Fired on German aeroplane, reached *Pezarches* at 3.30 pm. One of the A.S.C. drivers accidentally shot A.M. Hall, wounded in stomach. Left Pezarches 2.30 pm Saturday 4th, arrived at *Melun* 5.30 pm. Thunder storm during night. Made a bomb rack for incendiary bomb brought by Lt. Finch-Noyes. German aeroplane went over camp, fell in, did not open fire.

These were not the ideal circumstances in which to consolidate its role, but the Royal Flying Corps continued to carry out its reconnaissance flights. Cecil King:

We didn't lose aircraft or lorries on the retreat – we just set fire to the stores which had been amassed at Maubeuge. And the aircraft flew back to a field and we never stopped doing the usual work of keeping the aircraft going and the pilots kept taking reconnaissance views of the advancing Germans and the retreating British.

At Melun, thirty miles south of Paris, the retreat ended. Cuthbert Rabagliati's abiding memory of the withdrawal is of the endurance of the Tommys:

During our retreat, one continually came across units of the army, mostly infantry, coming out of the line, and in many cases, the condition of distress was almost unbelieveable. They were looking like a collection of old men, dragging heavy rifles which were almost too heavy for them to carry.

It was not just the British soldiers who were suffering. George Eddington:

We were in rather more of a hurry on the retreat than on the way to Maubeuge, and we couldn't help seeing the distress of the French villagers who were fleeing and blocking the road. It made us feel rather undignified that they'd hailed us as heroes and now we felt we were letting them down.

But not everybody was suffering quite so badly. On 31 August, Philip Joubert de la Ferté took a break from the retreat. From his diary:

About midday, Grey, Lawrence and I started off for Paris to fetch machines. Arrived there about 3 pm having nearly been shot by an over-zealous sentry. While Grey transacted business at the Embassy, Ikey and I stopped and had our hair cut. Tea at the Ritz, dinner at the Café de la Paix, a most excellent bath and bed at the Ritz, free! Had an amusing talk with a French-American baroness, who was off to London.

At the beginning of September, the Allies assumed that the First German Army, under von Kluck, would continue its march towards Paris. Flying Corps observations, however, began to report that it was changing direction. On 4 September, an aircraft flown by Joubert de la Ferté with Dermot Allen as his observer located the German cavalry corps in a position which confirmed that von Kluck's army was moving south-east towards the French Fifth and Sixth Armies. The Germans had indeed changed direction, and the Allies now had an opportunity to attack them on their right flank. The resulting Battle of the Marne, which lasted for three days, ended with the German army in retreat to the River Aisne, pursued by the Allies. Germany's victorious sweep through Luxembourg, Belgium and France had been halted. At the Aisne, the Germans took a position on high ground. The battle which followed was an inconclusive affair, and both sides began to move northwards in an attempt to outflank each other, digging in as they progressed. Two lines of trenches were created, which were eventually to stretch 400 miles along what came to be known as the Western Front. The war of movement was over. The war of mud, wire, no-man's-land, and attrition had begun. The aeroplane had proved valuable to the Allies' resistance, and in an official dispatch Sir John French was generous in his praise:

> I wish particularly to bring to your Lordship's notice, the admirable work done by the Royal Flying Corps under Sir David Henderson. Their skill, energy and perseverance have been beyond all praise. They have furnished me with the most complete and accurate information which has been of incalculable value in the conduct of operations. Fired at constantly both by friend and foe, and not hesitating to fly in every kind of weather, they have remained undaunted throughout.

Within a few weeks, the laughable birdcages had proved their worth. From September 1914 onwards, however, it was clear that a static front would not call for continued reconnaissance of large-scale troop movements. The aeroplane would have to prove its versatility – and its initial success suggested its adoption in other areas. Most obviously, it could be used to map the lines of trenches, and to look for unusual activity which might indicate a forthcoming attack. It could be used to direct artillery fire, by observing shell bursts from the air and adjusting the aim of the guns. It could destroy enemy installations, with bombs tossed overboard or released from racks. In the meantime, as predicted before the war, the aeroplane would have to fight against those who wished to destroy it. Its conspicuous appearance above the lines made it a visible target for rifles, machine-gun fire, artillery fire and other aircraft. The aeroplane would have to become a fighting machine, and it was up to its pilots and observers to turn it into one.

The first airman to be wounded by enemy activity was Sergeant-Major David Jillings of 2 Squadron. On 22 August, while observing a cavalry detachment approaching Mons, he was struck by a rifle bullet fired from the ground. According to his casualty form, he was the victim of a 'G.S.W. [gunshot wound] in Buttock'. According to Archibald James, he was offering up a generous target:

> David Jillings, a grand looking Guardsman, had an enormous posterior. And when flying as an observer within rifle-fire distance of the ground – that's less than 3000 feet – he was hit in the bottom. And the only known topic on which David Jillings' sense of humour was always lacking was in the fact that he'd been wounded in his enormous posterior.

It was not only the enemy's bullets that airmen had to watch out for. The machines that flew over to France in August had no markings to display their allegiance. Long before foreign correspondents ever spoke of 'friendly fire', infantrymen, unable to distinguish one aeroplane from another, were firing freely at anything that flew overhead. One early British victim of an ally's bullets was Gordon Bell, a pre-war motor car racer and aerial pioneer. Damaged by French rifle fire, his stricken aircraft came down in a tree. Bell was thrown clear, only to be approached by an English staff officer, who asked, 'I say, have you crashed?' 'No!' replied Bell, a stutterer, 'I always b . . . b . . . bloody land like that!'

The solution to the problem of misidentification was clear. Aircraft should be marked with a recognizable symbol. On 27 August, Gilbert Mapplebeck wrote in his diary:

> All German aeroplanes have black crosses painted on the upper surface of their machines, in order to distinguish them from their enemies in case of attack.

In response, the British painted Union flags onto their wings and the sides of their fuselages, but these proved too easily mistaken for the German crosses, so they were replaced by roundels with a red centre, surrounded by white and blue concentric circles. The roundel design was a copy of the tricolor cockades which were being painted onto French aircraft, with the substitution of blue for red, and red for blue, and their use has persisted on British aircraft to the present day.

The first German anti-aircraft fire came from three-inch guns mounted on trucks. Their fire may not have been particularly accurate, but its sheer volume caused problems for pilots. An airman's first encounter with anti-aircraft fire was always disconcerting. Duncan Grinnell-Milne was unprepared for the experience:

> The third jolt, greater than the first two put together, almost unseated me. Like an explosion – it came from beneath my feet, jarring the floor of the nacelle as though some unseen giant had kicked it. And there in front of the machine's nose I saw, unrolling like a ball of soft wool, a puff of yellowish smoke.

Grinnell-Milne's aircraft had not been hit, merely shaken, but constant exposure to anti-aircraft fire came to affect the nerves of many pilots and observers. In a diary entry written only a month after the Flying Corps arrived in France, Lieutenant William Read of 3 Squadron was already wondering 'how long my nerves will stand this almost daily bombardment. I notice several people's nerves are not as strong as they used to be and I am sure "Archie" is responsible for a good deal.' 'Archie' was the name given by the British to German anti-aircraft fire. It originated in September, when Lieutenant Amyas 'Biffy' Borton of 5 Squadron responded to an inaccurate burst by calling out, 'Archibald, certainly not!' This reprimand was lifted from a George Robey music-hall song, where it had been intended for an errant husband:

> A lady named Miss Hewitt got on friendly terms with me.
> She fell in love with me at once and then fell in the sea.
> My wife came on the scene as I threw coat and vest aside,
> As other garments I slipped off to save the girl, she cried:
>
> Archibald, certainly not!
>
> Desist at once disrobing on the spot!
> You may show your pluck and save Miss Hewitt,
> But if you've got to strip to do it,
> Archibald, certainly not!

By 2 November, Harold Wyllie, an observer with 4 Squadron, was confiding to his diary that 'Archibald is getting most accurate in his firing', and two weeks later he records the damage done to a machine by combined Archie and rifle fire:

> Humphries has got about fifty shrapnel hits on his machine, including one longeron, skid, spar, wheels and two wires. He himself has been shot in the jaw (a glancing blow) and in the back of the head. The observer has a bullet through his air helmet, one through his sleeve and another through his coat – he found the bullet inside the lining. From the appearance of the machine, it seems a miracle that they could have got off so lightly. Humphries continued to fly for an hour after he was hit, and, was quite prepared to

fly his tattered machine back to the landing ground at
Poperinghe. Plenty of guts that officer.

The aeroplanes which flew to France in August 1914 did not
carry machine guns, and in the early days many pilots and
observers flew without arms of any kind. Sholto Douglas
(one day to become Commander-in-Chief of RAF Fighter
Command) was an observer with 2 Squadron. When he
first came upon a German aeroplane, he was unarmed,
as was the observer of the German machine. The two men
waved at each other and continued on their way. Such
encounters encouraged the popular conception of the war in
the air as a chivalric contrast to the pitiless war on the
ground. Nevertheless, the realization that machines must be
defended, coupled with the need to prevent enemy aircraft
from carrying out their observations, ensured that British
airmen very soon began arming themselves with whatever
came to hand. Kenneth van der Spuy carried a weapon
more readily associated with bank robbery than with aerial
warfare:

> I took up a sawn-off shotgun, into which I'd rammed
> bullets on strings, so that they might fall and break up
> the enemy's propeller. And I had a revolver. I spotted a
> strange aircraft, which I thought didn't look like any I
> knew, so I sidled up to him and saw that he was a Hun,
> so I got my shotgun out, and I fired it all away. Then
> I got my revolver, and we had a revolver battle up there.
> We were very close to each other, and I could see him
> quite well, and he could see me quite well. I finished
> my six shots and he had finished his. We both waved
> each other goodbye and set off.

Before long, rifles and revolvers were carried as standard, but
they presented little threat in the air. The chances of hitting a
moving machine with a single bullet, fired at an angle from
another moving machine, were very slim. Shots could not be

fired straight ahead in a tractor aircraft, for fear of shooting away a propeller blade, and none of the pilots or observers knew how much lay-off was necessary to counter the effects of movement and wind. S. S. Saunders remembers:

> In the observer's cockpit, you had a rifle, which stood up in a little catch, so you could get it out easily. If you saw an enemy aircraft, you took this rifle out, waited for an opportunity and if he came to within 50 to 100 yards, you let him have it as best you could. Beyond 100 yards, it was a waste of ammunition. Even close up, you seldom got him. You needed a hell of a lot of luck to hit him. If the enemy aircraft was behind you, you undid your belt, stood up and knelt on your seat and watched to see where he was. You had to be very careful not to shoot any of the controls away. If he happened to be below you on the port or starboard side, then you would just lean over the side and if you could get your gun on him, try it that way. If he was directly below you, there was nothing you could do so you had to try to get your pilot to manoeuvre into a position to get your gun to bear on him. After flying with one pilot on several occasions you had a sort of way of communicating with him without actually telling him, and you worked as a team. And then when the ammunition was used up, you said goodbye to him.

Archibald James was an experienced rifle shot, with plenty of faith in his ability to hit a stag on a Scottish hillside. Hitting a German in the sky above France was another matter:

> We met an enemy aircraft at about the same altitude and speed as ourselves so that we couldn't get any closer than 600 yards. I put my sights on the service rifle to 600 yards and fired six deliberate shots – and was miserable that I didn't hit him at all. I've no doubt I was

miles away. Later we learnt with the vibrating platform that effective range rarely exceeded fifty yards.

S. S. Saunders recalls the mistrust that might exist between pilot and observer. Saunders was flying as observer with a new pilot, when an enemy aircraft was spotted at a distance of 400 yards. Saunders refused to open fire. On landing, the pilot could not understand why. He believed that Saunders had frozen in fear. In fact, Saunders knew perfectly well that bullets fired at that range would be wasted, and he bitterly resented the implication that he had been 'funking it'.

Despite the long odds, rifle bullets fired from the air did, occasionally, bring down an enemy machine. Cuthbert Rabagliati remembers his first victory:

> We picked up an Aviatik over the Mormal Forest in August 1914 and we flew round each other for a very long time, the German using a Mauser pistol with a stock set on his shoulder, and I had a .303 army rifle. I fired over a hundred rounds and he did the same with his pistol. At one point, he clipped the lobe of my ear and made it bleed which made me very angry but eventually I made a hole in the sump of his engine and all the oil ran out and his engine seized so that he landed at the edge of the forest and our cavalry picked him and his observer up and made them prisoners. I went back later and got the engine number from his Mercedes engine, which I kept, thinking it would be a prize, but unfortunately somebody relieved me of it and I never saw it again.

Annoying though it must have been, Rabagliati's loss does not begin to compare with that of Gilbert Mapplebeck. His machine was attacked in September by a German two-seater, and he was struck by a bullet in the thigh. Unfortunately, he happened to be carrying loose change in his pocket and the force of the bullet drove a twenty-five franc piece into his groin, slicing away the tip of his penis. In great pain and losing blood, Mapplebeck managed to land safely, only for his wound to become a source of hilarity among the wittier members of 4 Squadron. His casualty form coyly reads: 'Wounded (thighs and abdomen)'. Mapplebeck spent the next three months in bed and only returned to duty in February 1915. He was killed later that year in a flying accident in England.

Even as observers were firing hopeful bullets at each other, one imaginative individual was anticipating the future of aerial combat. Within a week of the Flying Corps' arrival in France, the intrepid Louis Strange had adapted his Farman aircraft to carry a Lewis machine gun, by fitting a makeshift mounting to the top of the observer's nacelle. As the Farman was a pusher machine, the gun could fire directly forward. Strange may not have been the first man to consider using a machine gun in the air, but he was certainly the first British pilot to put the idea into practice in wartime. As with so many good ideas, however, it got off to a bad start. On 22 August, a German Taube machine was flying at 5000 feet over the British aerodrome at Maubeuge. Strange and his observer, Lieutenant Penn Gaskell, ran to their aircraft and took off. The weight of the machine gun proved too great for the poor little Farman, and as Strange, Penn Gaskell and gun struggled into the air, the Taube flew blithely on. By the time Strange had reached 3500 feet, the enemy machine had disappeared. When he reached the ground again, Strange was ordered by Josh Higgins, his squadron commander, to dispense with the gun. 'Machine guns are for use on the ground,' Higgins scolded. He was to be proved spectacularly wrong.

On 5 October 1914, Louis Quénault, a French observer in a Voisin pusher, shot down a German Aviatik aircraft, using a machine gun mounted in the nacelle. Before long, the irrepressible Strange had fitted another Lewis gun onto his latest aircraft, an Avro 504 (the precursor to Robert Smith-Barry's standard trainer), and on 14 November he succeeded in bringing down an Aviatik over Armentières. The Avro was a tractor, so Strange had fitted a crossbar between its central struts, over which he slung a rope, allowing the machine gun to be pulled up into a position from which the observer, seated in front, could fire backwards over Strange's head. The observer of the Aviatik, under attack from Strange's observer, Frederick Small, had fired his pistol and managed to wound Small in the hand. Nevertheless, Small continued to fire and he brought the German machine down behind British lines. Despite the obvious potential of mounted machine guns, it was to be several months before British aircraft routinely carried them. S. S. Saunders did not fit a Lewis gun onto a twin-seater tractor until April 1915. Even then, how best to deploy the new weapon, in such a way that it would not shoot away the propeller, was a matter for discussion among pilots and mechanics:

> We fixed one of these Lewis guns up for the pilot. We decided to attach it to the fuselage on the pilot's left in such a way that it was pointing at an angle so that it just cleared the tip of the propeller as it went round. This meant that the gun was firing at an angle of sixty degrees away from the direction in which the aircraft was facing. When the pilot wanted to change the drum, he could easily do that with his left hand. The spare drums were in racks at the side. The observer had another Lewis gun but at first he had to fire this gun from his shoulder – we fitted a butt to the gun as though it was a rifle. You had to be very careful with this because as soon as you lifted the gun up, the pressure of the air almost blew it out of your hand and you had to hold onto it very tightly. To put this right, we fixed up a rear mounting for the gun behind the observer so that he could swing it about but this limited

the field of fire as we had to be very careful not to shoot away the rudder or the elevator controls. If the enemy was overhead on your tail, diving at you, the fixed mounting meant you had to crouch down in a very small cockpit and trust to luck.

Whilst a machine gun was a distinct improvement on the rifles and revolvers that were in use previously, it was clearly not the ideal method of attack for a pilot to fire at an angle of sixty degrees to the direction in which he was flying. The aircraft would be a far more effective fighting machine if he could fire directly ahead; he could aim his gun simply by pointing the aircraft in the direction of the target. In a pusher machine, this was not a problem, but pusher aircraft were considered inferior to tractors in performance, and were outnumbered throughout the war. Until a reliable method of shooting through a moving propeller could be devised, aerial combat would remain a haphazard affair. Another problem was the large number of machine gun stoppages encountered in the air, far greater than the number experienced on the ground. S. S. Saunders was puzzled:

> We had a lot of problems with the Lewis guns jamming in the air and we couldn't understand why. First of all, we found that they kept getting stuck until the first half-dozen rounds were gone. So we decided to put in fewer rounds which improved the situation but the gun carried on stopping. Then the information went around that if you fired three or four rounds every quarter of an hour, the gun stopped sticking but we couldn't understand why this helped. We found out the problem by accident. One of the riggers happened to send a gun up in an aircraft without oiling it. The gun didn't stick, which started us thinking and we worked out that the oil we were using on the working parts was freezing

up in the air but there was no indication of this by the time we landed. By then it had thawed out.

Such advances in understanding came from the application of a little ingenuity to the trial and error of daily flying. One example of evolution was the development of bombing. Initially aimed at congregations of enemy troops, some of the first missiles dropped by British aircraft were not bombs at all. 'Flechettes' were darts, remembered without affection by Archibald James:

> Flechettes were issued to us in bundles and they were darts about fourteen inches long with a fin to make them fall down the right way. A more useless exercise can hardly be imagined because the chances of a flechette thrown overboard, over the German lines or over a battery site, either hitting the target, or if it did so, penetrating anybody must have been millions to one against. This practice was not persisted in after a fairly short time. I've no idea whose bright idea it was.

James' withering appraisal of flechettes is understandable – and it was not long before their use was confined to squadron dartboards – but it is hard not to admire the spirit that gave rise to them. It was only by experimentation that genuine progress could be made. Another early type of bomb was the hand grenade, tossed over the side of an aircraft. On 25 August, during the retreat, Gilbert Mapplebeck went in chase of a German Taube aircraft. In his diary, he records this very early example of aerial combat and bombing:

> I headed straight at the German who was going in a path across my front. When he crossed the line I was going in, I put my machine almost horizontal and commenced to overhaul him. At this time he was

about a mile and a half or two miles ahead and slightly above. He did a sharp descent and landed, running very fast over what seemed to be extremely bad ground. I prepared my hand grenade. I brought my machine into position to drop my hand grenade. After dropping it, I saw two black marks above the planes of the enemy's machine which looked like the chassis wheels, and I concluded that the machine must have turned over after landing. I did not see my bomb explode though I watched very closely and so returned as my time was limited by orders to half an hour. We heard afterwards from Harvey-Kelly (who landed somewhere near) that the pilot and observer had escaped into an adjoining wood where some cavalry were searching for them.

Cecil King remembers how grenades came to be adapted, so that they would hang from a rack on the side of the fuselage:

The grenades had a plastic cap at the top and when the pilot was ready to throw them down he used to undo the cap, put the detonator on and just take them out of the rack and throw them to the ground. Well, the tail on these bombs was too short. It was about a quarter of an inch iron rod, about six inches long, and it was too short. They wanted to extend it to twelve inches, so they took these bombs without detonators in and they gave them to the smith, who had his little portable forge, and he actually welded a piece of metal on to the live bomb. He was careful to keep it cool all the while with water – but when that job was on we gave him a very wide berth. He would say, 'What are you chaps walking over there for? What's the matter?' And he, merrily, for a day, welded a little piece of metal onto a great pile of these live bombs so that it was better to hang on the side of the machine.

114

Cuthbert Rabagliati, meanwhile, very nearly lost his life when an experiment in dropping shrapnel bombs went wrong in mid-air. Rabagliati's squadron had been provided with a number of different kinds of bombs, and instructed to toss them over the sides of their aircraft. This was a hazardous operation, given the number of wires and struts that jutted from the early machines, so Rabagliati decided to construct a bomb chute that would eliminate the danger. The name of his pilot may be familiar:

We were trying to drop seven-pound shrapnel bombs. They were about four inches wide and eight or ten inches long. I thought I would put a tin tube through the floor of my Avro machine, so that I could push the bomb straight through and it would have no obstruction until it was clear of the aeroplane. I little thought that the wind blowing the bottom of the tube would flatten it, so I gaily pushed a bomb down – and it got stuck in the tube, below the level of the wheels. I tried everything I could think of but I couldn't get it out. I even tried to climb out over the side but I couldn't. I passed a note back to my pilot, Louis Strange, telling him what had happened and I watched him read it and I watched his face. It was a sight. We flew round for a long time, we came back to the squadron, we came very low and I wrote a message, put it in a message bag and dropped it down in front of the hangars, telling everybody what had happened and that when we landed they should keep well away because our machine was going to blow up.

We landed right at the far end of the aerodrome because we were for it, but we didn't want to blow up the whole squadron as well. I suppose Louis Strange was a bit scared. He landed much faster than usual and we skimmed along the ground. The edge of the aerodrome was covered in uncut corn, which was quite high. What happened was that the stalks of corn wrapped themselves round the detonator and wrenched it right out of the bomb. So when we finally touched the ground, there was no detonator, and we got down quite successfully. But if you can imagine the feeling of touching the ground, drawing your knees right up, knowing perfectly well that this was the end . . . and suddenly there was a bounce . . . and another bounce. The lack of incident was quite terrific. I leapt out of the machine while it was still running and Louis Strange must have done the same because when it finally came to a stop, we were lying near each other in silence. I got up to go back to the aircraft and he shouted, 'For God's sake, stay still! You've done enough damage for one day!'

Rabagliati and Strange survived their experiment with a bomb chute. Others did not. James Gascoyne:

We were using ordinary army shells, converting them with a fuse cap which exploded on contact with the ground. These bombs were inserted into aluminium tubes made in the station workshops and a pin was pushed through to hold the bomb in position. When the pilot wished to drop the bomb he leaned over the side, pulled the pin out and away went the bomb.

On this particular day, Lieutenant Cholmondley was in his aircraft, and the mechanic was busy putting the bombs in. The mechanic tried to put the pin through – and one of the bombs came down the tube. He put his knee under it to stop the bomb coming out and the whole thing went up. There were four people killed in that thing including Lieutenant Cholmondley. That's how dangerous bombing used to be – more on the ground than in the air.

The early bombs rarely found their intended targets. There was no means of aiming them, and little understanding of trajectories. Maurice Baring witnessed a lone German aircraft dropping a bomb on Fère aerodrome on 7 October. 'Theoretically,' wrote Baring, 'it was a beautiful shot, practically, it hit a turnip.' Yet bombing raids started to become more ambitious. On 1 November, a raid was carried out near Ypres. Its target was Kaiser Wilhelm II, whom intelligence reports suggested would be inspecting troops at Gheluvelt. The attack was unsuccessful. The most ambitious raids of late 1914, however, were carried out by the Royal Naval Air Service.

The RNAS had not travelled out to France with the Royal Flying Corps. It had been entrusted with the task of defending the east coast of Britain from German air attack and defending shipping in the Channel. To this latter end, a number of cross-Channel steamers were adapted to carry seaplanes. In furtherance of the anti-Zeppelin role, the Eastchurch Squadron, commanded by Charles Rumney Samson, was sent across the Channel to Ostend on 27 August. Shortly afterwards, Ostend was taken by the Germans, and the squadron was ordered back to England, but Samson was a stubborn man, with no desire to give up the fight. On the homeward flight, he landed the squadron at Dunkirk, where he promptly offered its services to a passing French general. Telegrams began to arrive from the Admiralty, confirming the order to return home. According to Samson:

> At last, just as things were getting desperate and I was fully expecting to be marched back to England under arrest, a telegram arrived to say 'Samson's squadron are to operate from Dunkirk carrying out aerial patrols against Zeppelins and aeroplanes and to carry out reconnaissance as required by the French General at Dunkirk'.

Samson encountered no Zeppelins, but, a true innovator in the Louis Strange mould, he began to design and build armoured cars, strengthened with boiler plate from a local shipbuilding firm. He fitted machine guns to these cars and drove out in search of enemy targets. He described the job as 'mopping up' work. Arthur Beeton:

> We called him Sammy, and we would go anywhere with him. He ought to have been an admiral. His first effort was a Mercedes with a Maxim gun strapped to it. He went out chasing Uhlans – the German cavalry. They were patrolling Belgium, and Sammy went out and chased them with his car and his gun. After he came back, our quarters were full of Uhlan lances and helmets.

Samson developed a system whereby the squadron's aircraft would spot for enemy units, which would then be confronted on the ground by armoured cars, led by Samson himself. On 5 September, Samson and his small armoured force entered Lille shortly after the German army had moved out, and he promptly issued a proclamation to declare that he had occupied the town. The proclamation was posted all over Lille and Samson was treated to a hero's reception. He remembers:

> The dense crowds cheered themselves hoarse, and one felt rather as I imagined a Roman general used to feel on being given a triumph.

Having experienced a Roman triumph, he then recreated a Roman legend in the city of Douai. As a large German force was spotted moving towards the city, Samson, a modern-day Horatius, conducted his fleet of cars to the Pont d'Esquerchin, a bridge on the edge of Douai, where he held off the advancing German army, allowing 2500 French soldiers to escape.

In the meantime, in its anti-Zeppelin role, Samson's squadron established a forward base at Antwerp from which

The *Wright Flyer*, photographed in
). 'We were just a couple of kids with a
shop who wanted to get this
raption up in the air.'

Bottom: Samuel Cody (in the white coat) walks
away from the wreckage of his aircraft in October
1908, having made the first powered flight in
Britain.

Archibald James, who joined the Royal Flying Corps in 1915 as an observer, before becoming a pilot and squadron commander. A man of robust opinions, he became an MP in 1931.

erick Winterbotham, pictured in 1942: world traveller, cavalryman, pilot with 29 Squadron
, prisoner of war, secret agent, and Chief of the Air Section of the secret services.

Top: A pupil learns to fly the Boxkite at Grahame White's school at Hendon Aerodrome. 'You were allowed to do hops. You took the machine up on your own and flew about ten or fifteen yards and then put the machine down again.'

Bottom: As a BE2 machine nestles up to a haystack at Hythe near Whitby, in August 1914, its pilot, Hubert Harvey Kelly, smokes a nonchalant cigarette. Kelly would become the first British pilot to land in France in August 1914. He died three days after being shot down in April 1917.

is Strange, a man who hung upside down from his aircraft in 1915, fought against
serschmitt 109s in 1940, and died peacefully in his sleep in 1966.

Top left: Great War aircraft were lightweight, flimsy contraptions, capable of executing difficult landings.

Top right: James McCudden, fighter ace (on the left), began the wa[r] an engine fitter with 3 Squadron. At the time of his death in July 1918, he had 57 kills and a Victoria Cross to his name.

Bottom: The BE2c, the first inherently stable aircraft. Unpopular wi[th] pilots. And pigeons.

orge Eddington was a driver with 2 Squadron in August 1914. In April 1917, he became a
eant pilot with 6 Squadron at Abeele. 'My goodness, I was lonely. Dreadfully lonely.'

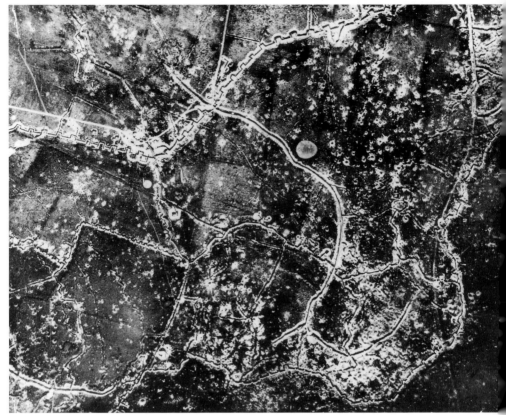

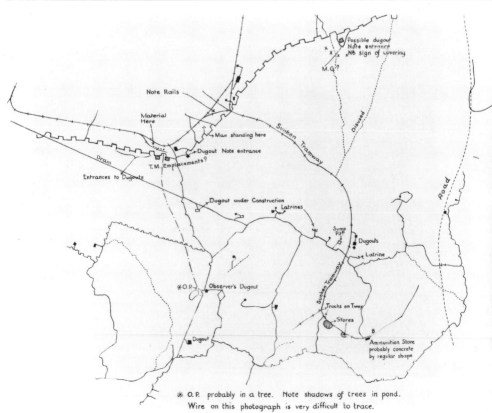

Possible dugout
Note entrance
No sign of covering

M.G.?

Note Rails

Material
Here

Man standing here

Sunken Tramway

Disused

Dugout Note entrance

T.M. Emplacements?

Drain

Entrances to Dugouts

Dugout under Construction

Latrines

Road

Sump
Pit?

Dugouts

Latrine

✳ O.P.   Observer's Dugout

Sunken Tramway

Trucks on T'way

Stores

Dugout

B

Ammunition Store
probably concrete
by regular shape

✳ O. P. probably in a tree. Note shadows of trees in pond.
Wire on this photograph is very difficult to trace.

osite page, top: An aerial photograph of
nbroekmolen, taken in 1916 with the
type camera.

osite page, bottom: The key to the
nbroekmolen aerial photograph. Trained
rpreters were able to identify 'latrines', 'sump
and even 'man standing here'. The area was
prehensively destroyed by the explosion of a
e before the Messines offensive of 1917.

Top: An airman demonstrates the use of the
'C'-type camera.

Bottom left and right: The airmen's view; the
pilot and observer of an RE8 took these
photographs of each other in the middle of
a flight.

Top: An observer demonstrating the use of a Sterling transmitter. Morse messages, tapped on a key to the right of the observer's seat, would be sent to a waiting battery below.

Bottom: The Vickers FB5, or Fighter, or Gunbus. With its Lewis machine gun mounted in the observer's nacelle, the Vickers Fighter represented the birth of the aeroplane as a true fighting machine.

The Fokker Eindecker (or monoplane) onto which Anthony Fokker
d the first synchronized machine gun. The resulting aircraft terrified
ed airmen, who were unable to comprehend how the wicked-
king little scout could spit fire through its spinning propeller.
reatened to clear the skies of British machines.

Bottom: A closer view
of the Eindecker's
synchronized gun.

Right: Oswald Boelcke, one of the first fighting idols, and beloved teacher of Manfred von Richthofen. He was admired by his opponents as well: 'in an enemy sense, he was a gentleman,' according to one British pilot.

Below: The DH2, an agile pusher with a fixed, forward-firing Lewis machine gun, was the first purpose-built British fighter. With help from the FE2b, it overcame the 'Fokker Scourge'.

Above: The Albatros D.III. The Albatros D.I, armed with twin synchronized Spandau machine guns, appeared in September 1916. Responsible for Richthofen's first victory, it won aerial superiority back for the Germans.

Left: Two airmen of 46 Squadron photographed in 1917. It was not uncommon for men of this era to pose arm-in-arm. What *is* unusual is that the man on the left appears to be sending the photographer a cryptic message.

Right: Taking it easy on a summer's day: 'We've had a wonderful, hot summer's afternoon, wearing nothing much but towels, and lazing the hours away by the canal…'.

Below: A BE2e in flames; the petrol tank blazes as the wings and body crumble. In the absence of parachutes, the airman's great fear was a slow burning death. It was the reason why Mick Mannock, amongst others, flew with a revolver alongside him.

Left: Albert Ball, fighter ace, national hero, and Western Front gardener. 'I got my tools and set to work on my garden, for rainy days are just right for setting seeds.'

Below: A stricken aircraft, caught in a reconnaissance photograph, leaves a trail of black smoke.

Above: One RE8 photographs another.

Right: William Robinson Clarke, the first black West Indian to serve as a pilot in the Royal Flying Corps.

to carry out bombing raids on Zeppelin sheds in Germany. The first raid, on Düsseldorf, was carried out in fog, prompting one of the pilots to report that it had been like 'going into a dark room to look for a black cat who wasn't there'. The next raid, carried out a few days later, was more successful. Flight Lieutenant Reginald Marix flew his Sopwith Scout at a height of 600 feet over the Zeppelin shed and scored direct hits with both of his twenty-pound bombs. He watched the roof of the shed cave in as flames shot into the sky. The Zeppelin inside was destroyed. On Christmas Day 1914, the Royal Naval Air Service carried out a daring raid on the Cuxhaven naval base, where the Nordholz Zeppelin station was believed to be located. Nine seaplanes were lowered into the sea off the north German coast, seven of which took off and made for Cuxhaven. The Zeppelin sheds were not located and the majority of bombs fell harmlessly. Nevertheless, all the aircraft survived the raid, and the German navy responded by dispersing its fleet along the Kiel Canal. These raids are important because they represent attacks on strategic objectives. The evolution of aerial bombing was underway.

As the days and months passed, so it became clear that the motley collection of all-purpose aircraft possessed by the Royal Flying Corps would not be adequate to do the range of work necessary. A standard machine was needed for carrying out the squadrons' day-to-day reconnaissance and artillery spotting work, and dedicated attacking machines would have to be developed in order to defend them. The aeroplane chosen as the RFC's standard machine was the Royal Aircraft Factory BE2c – the descendant of the machine taken up by the Royal Flying Corps following the Military Aeroplane Trials of 1912. A tractor machine, powered by a 90-horse-power engine, it was inherently stable, an advantage for reconnaissance work, and for inexperienced pilots, but a disadvantage in the eyes of many. Charles Chabot:

It was recognized that pilots had to be trained quickly and so an aircraft was needed which would be simple to fly, and de Havilland and Busk produced the BE2c. It was the first aircraft to be really inherently stable. The dihedral to the wings and the dihedral between the main planes and the tailplane gave it very strong lateral stability; it wanted to stay on a level keel, right way up, and would correct anything by itself. This had the very great disadvantage that it was very difficult to make it do anything else. You wanted a strong effort to put a steep turn on a BE2c, compared with anything else in circulation at the time.

A pilot under attack from another aircraft had little chance of escape if he could not change direction and altitude quickly. Many pilots were to lose their lives in this first inherently stable aircraft. And it was not just humans that needed to be wary of the BE2c. Robin Rowell:

When I got to Marieux, there was a tame pigeon flying around 'C' Flight hangar. Whenever one of the BE2cs was brought out of the shed to be started up, this bird would fly out and sit on the bottom wing eighteen inches from the body of the machine. When the engine was started up, it would start to fly, slow or fast, according to the speed of the propeller, so that its position always remained abreast of the observer's seat. It was necessary to take a little care when shutting the engine down, so that the bird could land gently on the lower wing again. It followed us when the squadron moved to Bellevue – but unfortunately when an ignorant pilot shut off his engine suddenly, the pigeon overshot its mark and flew into the propeller.

In October, the Royal Flying Corps established its base at St Omer, where it would remain until the end of the war. At first, the four original squadrons collected there, flying from an aerodrome built on a steeplechase course. Maurice Baring lists off his memories of life at St Omer Headquarters:

> A stuffy office, full of clerks and candles and a deafening noise of typewriters. A constant stream of pilots arriving in the evening in Burberries with maps, talking over reconnaissances; a perpetual stream of guests and a crowd of people sleeping on the floor; a weekly struggle, sometimes successful, and sometimes not, to get a bath in the town, where there was always a seething crowd of suppliants, and a charming capable lady in charge, who used to call one 'Mon très cher Monsieur'; hours spent on the aerodrome, which were generally misty; small dinners in the flight messes in the various billets round Longuenesse, almost every day, some inquiry or dispute with regard to a billet; and a tense feeling the whole time that the situation was not satisfactory, but that it would somehow or other come out all right in the end.

Even before the Royal Flying Corps had flown to France, plans had been laid to double the number of squadrons. In November, the Commander of the RFC in the Field, Brigadier General Sir David Henderson, reorganized its structure into distinct wings, each of which would work together with a particular army corps. At first, two wings were formed in France, the first of which was assigned to Major Hugh Trenchard, the man who was soon to replace Henderson. In this way, over time, the squadrons would spread out across the Western Front, each attached to a particular wing.

The first months of the war had proved that aircraft could perform a multitude of roles with considerable success. Development might be a hit-and-miss affair, but the potential of the aeroplane was becoming obvious, even to those who had initially doubted it. Much of the success was due to the originality and irreverence of the men of the flying services, men such as Hubert Harvey-Kelly, who always took a potato and a reel of cotton with him when he flew, on the grounds that if he had to land behind German lines, he was sure to be treated well, carrying such scarce and useful commodities.

Or men such as Robert Loraine, a successful stage actor who wore an entirely redundant monocle, and used to sit for hours in his aircraft with the engine running, imagining himself engaged in successful combat.

Or men such as Louis Strange, whose greatest adventure of all took place in a Martinsyde Scout in May 1915. Attempting to change the ammunition drum of his Lewis gun, 8000 feet above Menin, he found that the drum had stuck. One twisted steel string, a quarter of a millimetre in width, was holding it in position. He stood up in the cockpit, clamped the joystick between his knees and started to pull the drum free. Unfortunately, the port wing of the Martinsyde dropped suddenly, unbalancing Strange, who fell against the joystick, turning the aircraft upside down. He was thrown out of the cockpit and found himself hanging in mid-air, holding onto the drum with both hands, the aircraft above him. A second earlier, he had been attempting to prise the drum free, now he prayed for it to hold. As the aircraft flew on, inverted, Strange used all his strength to pull himself up – only for the aircraft to go into a sudden spin. Dizzy, thrown from side to side, upside down, barely able to hold on, Strange accepted his fate. A moment later, a sudden urge to live gave him the strength to kick upwards, time and time again, until one of his feet hooked inside the cockpit, and then the other foot, and somehow he used his legs to jam the joystick forward. And miraculously, the machine came out of its spin, righted itself, and Strange fell back down into his seat. He brought the aircraft out of its dive just before it hit the ground, and returned to his aerodrome at treetop level.

Louis Strange died quietly in his sleep in 1966, at the age of seventy-five.

5

An Office Job

Tales of the great aces – lone wolves prowling the skies in search of prey – have turned the story of the Great War in the air into a narrative of dogfights and combats to the death. If this were the full story it would make very little sense. Why would either side send men up in expensive machines simply to shoot each other out of the sky? What would be the point? Stanley Walters was a fighter pilot who understood the true nature of his task:

> We didn't do anything for the war, by two fellows fighting in the air, and the loser going down in flames. Nobody could say that Great Britain was winning the war when one German went down in flames. That meant nothing. We fighters were the glamour boys and that was all wrong. What we were doing was protecting the Royal Flying Corps while it did its job.

At the start of the war that job had been to report on the movements of enemy troops during the German advance. Once the Western Front stabilized, the job changed. Observers no longer watched out for large-scale troop movements; they now flew over opposition trenches, looking for more subtle signs of enemy intentions, and, behind the lines, monitoring road and rail activity. They became an insurance against surprise. And they carried out the no-less-important task of directing and ranging artillery fire onto enemy targets. At first, these jobs were carried out by all squadrons. In early 1915, Charles Chabot flew with 4 Squadron:

> My squadron was what you might call a general-purpose squadron. There weren't yet individual squadrons doing individual functions. They got specialized later on, but we were still in the unspecialized state and the general work which we did was reconnaissance, artillery ranging, and if anybody wanted to fight us in the air we were supposed to fight them back.

The daily reconnaissance work was not spectacular. It was thought of as the Flying Services' equivalent of an office job, the aeroplane being substituted for the suburban train. Yet it was essential. The Royal Flying Cops acted as the eyes of the infantry throughout the war, and those eyes belonged, specifically, to the observers, the men who shared the aircraft with the pilots. On arrival at the front, many of these men had little idea of the job in store. George Taylor was one:

> On my second day, Captain Greig came to me and told me that the Commanding Officer wanted to see me. So I went to the reports room to see him. He said, 'Taylor, this is Lieutenant Davis, I want you to take a run round. It's a dud day, there won't be any operations. Just have a look round. Don't go near the line. Keep inland, and you'll be quite safe.' I was introduced to Lieutenant Davis, we got in a plane, and away we went. I thought it would be a real joyride, so I sat down, and made myself comfortable. We'd been up about three-quarters of an hour when Lieutenant Davis nodded that he wanted to speak to me, and he throttled down. He said, 'Where are we?' I nearly fell out of the plane with fright. I had no idea. I hadn't been watching. It wouldn't have made

much difference if I had been watching, because it was only my second time up. He said, 'Bloody well find out!' I looked at the maps on the floor of the nacelle, to see if I could pinpoint some object that might put us on the road to the aerodrome. I couldn't. We came down very, very low. We were practically looking at signposts. Eventually, I pointed out an aerodrome, but I wasn't sure if it was English or German. We landed there, and luckily, it was one of ours. We were taken to the mess, went in and had a drink, and by the time we got out, our squadron had sent a chap in a plane to guide us home. When we finally arrived home, Lieutenant Davis said to me, 'When did you get to this squadron?' 'Yesterday,' I told him. 'Good God! No!' he said. So I asked him when *he* got to the squadron. 'Yesterday,' he said.

Few men could have been less suited to the job of observer than the man who was sent up with Frank Ransley of 48 Squadron:

Starting out on a long reconnaissance with a new observer who had only that day arrived at the squadron, we had no sooner crossed the lines when we met an unusually heavy barrage of anti-aircraft fire which took me all my time to dodge. Black balls of dirty puffs were all around us. As soon as I had a chance, I looked round to the back seat to see how my new observer was taking things. He was on the floor in a faint. I immediately turned back to try and get a seasoned warrior in his place. I had only gone a short distance to the west when I received a tap on the shoulder from my pallid observer signalling me to turn east again. Once more the anti-aircraft fire let us have it. I looked round and the poor man had fainted again. This time I took him right back to the aerodrome, and after some difficulty I managed to get a replacement. He left the squadron the same day, not having unpacked his kit.

A fully conscious observer had a complicated task to perform. He had to become sufficiently aware of military matters to know what to look out for, but not too quick to jump to conclusions. A mistaken observation could have dangerous consequences. On the other hand, an observer with imagination could return from a show with valuable information. Archibald James:

> One made a number of quite chance observations in the early flights. For example, in April 1915 after a dry spell we had some April showers and a warm spell. And the next time I flew over the lines I was able to map exactly how far back the Germans had evacuated the civilian population by seeing the poppies that had sprung up on the chalk and on the clay, and a white flower which had come up on the chalk. It was the first time we knew just how far the civilians had been evacuated, because they had not been able therefore to cultivate their land.

The observer had to learn to interpret what was happening on the ground, and a great deal was visible. Recent digging, for example, could not be effectively concealed. A track which could not be seen by a man walking across it could be clearly made out from the air. Smoke might be evidence of concealed men, while figures on the move were most easily detected by their shadows. Increased railway activity in the evening revealed that troops and guns were moving away from an area, an increase in the morning that they had arrived overnight. Building works, such as new roads, bridges and railway sidings all betrayed an enemy's intentions. The reports gathered were handed on to the army intelligence staff, who assessed and compared reports from many squadrons and formulated a full picture which formed the basis of army strategy. The observers who were compiling these reports understood the importance of their work and this created a bond between them; there was little sense of competition. George Taylor:

> When you went on reconnaissance, you had to watch for new trenches, trains going in every direction, movement of artillery and troops, and when we got back, we used to exchange information. So if I'd seen three trains, but my friend had only seen one train, I used to 'hand' him two trains as well. That meant that everybody had a decent report.

Reconnaissance might have been compared to an office job but the observers had more to fear than repetitive strain injury. As well as attack from enemy machines, they came under fire from anti-aircraft guns. In a diary entry from early February 1915, Harold Wyllie wrote:

> Marsh and myself went on a reconnaissance at dawn and were told to have a look right into Wervicq. We did – and before we could say knife, a battery of guns opened on us from two sides. The shells were bursting under, over and on both sides. There seemed to be no way out of the mess and neither Marsh nor myself thought we should want any breakfast. However, we did get out of it with six hits on the machine from splinters and bullets, and finished the reconnaissance. I never could have believed it possible to be under such fire and survive. The noise was deafening and the air full of smoke.

Two years later, and the air was no safer for a reconnaissance machine. Charles Smart of 16 Squadron, a BE2e pilot, recorded the following in his diary in March 1917:

> Archie was simply fierce. They hammered away at us the whole time we were on the job. There was a terrific

'crump' that seemed to burst about three feet away from my left ear. Several things happened at once, the machine was lifted bodily about twenty feet into the air, a shower of wood splinters flew into my face, streams of petrol squirted all over me up to the waist and a cupboard fixed in the pilot's seat above my feet fell down onto my left foot and practically jammed the rudder. I was frightened to death but managed to turn off both petrol tanks, and switch off the engine. Archie was still bursting all around us. I turned the machine round and pushed the nose down so that we were doing about 110 miles per hour towards our own lines expecting every moment that the whole show would catch on fire, for petrol was pouring out of the back tank and I was having a sort of hip-bath in the stuff.

Fortunately, we were up at a good height so we cleared no-man's-land at about 2000 feet with the Archie 'pops' getting fainter and fainter as we left them behind. Once over the lines, I had a good look round the machine, and saw that the most serious damage was a large hole in the rear petrol tank so I decided to come down low and to try and start the engine up on the front tank. I dropped down to about 1000 feet, turned on the front tank and after some difficulty, got the engine started, all the time trembling in case the machine should catch fire. I managed to get home and felt much relieved when I dropped the machine in the aerodrome.

The Archie which burst the tank went in about two feet in front of my chest and about six inches behind my observer's back. It was the observer's second time in the air and he didn't realize that anything had happened to the machine at all. It seems rather unfair that I should have all this excitement to myself.

When flying over trenches, machines came under heavy rifle and machine gun fire, and sensible pilots like Philip Joubert de la Ferté took precautions:

> I remember very clearly on a day with a strong westerly wind, and I had to fly along a line of trenches into the wind, I decided to try and climb as high as I could. I thought this was a reasonable precaution. When we landed, my observer was absolutely furious. He said, 'I couldn't count the men in the trenches!' 'No,' I said, 'I was up at seven thousand and jolly glad to be there . . .'

The more copious the observer's notes the longer his machine had to remain over dangerous ground. Harold Wyllie, the son of a well-known maritime artist who was to become a respected artist in his own right after the war, sat exposed and vulnerable as he sketched the trench systems below. A diary entry from late January 1915:

> Went out with Leighton in a Blériot to sketch trenches at Messines. Very cold. Got a sketch with difficulty owing to intricacy of the lines of trenches. Two Archies had a game at long bowls with us but didn't make very good shooting though I believe it looked pretty warm to our people who were watching. I suppose they were annoyed at our continual circling round. Came down after two and a half hours. Took a tracing to Brigadier General Lunde. He was delighted with the information contained in the sketch as it showed some saps and a parallel being pushed out by the enemy which they did not know of. I was thanked by the general and he said the information was most important and sent me off at once to report to General Haldane commanding 3rd Division at Scherpenberg. The staff were very interested and General Haldane said he would give orders to have the parallel knocked out at once.

A detailed drawing by a good artist might provide valuable information, but any observer's report, written or sketched, was compromised by the shortcomings of the human eye, and by the difficulty in absorbing information quickly in stressful conditions. The obvious answer was to take photographs from the air, which could then be developed and interpreted on the ground. Indeed, in September 1914, this was already being done; Lieutenant George Pretyman took five photographs of enemy positions on the Aisne. Yet the reaction from one highly placed member of the general staff, on seeing the results, was to remark that he could see 'no future for this sort of thing'. As was so often the case, the impetus for the adoption of a good idea had to come from further down the chain of command.

Frederick Laws was a Royal Flying Corps flight sergeant who had helped to pioneer aerial photography before the war, experimenting with the use of cameras on airships. When he arrived in France in August 1914, with 3 Squadron, he found that nobody had the slightest interest in his area of expertise. He was not even given the opportunity of taking a hand camera into the air, until the squadron's commanding officer, John Salmond, took him up and asked him for a demonstration. In December 1914, Salmond's brother, Geoffrey, was ordered to compile an official report in relation to photography, which led to the formation of an RFC photographic unit. Laws was appointed to the unit, to serve as assistant to its commanding officer, John Moore-Brabazon, the pioneer of flight who had proved, before the war, that pigs *could* fly. Laws remembers:

I was flight sergeant at the time and Moore-Brabazon, who had never handled a camera in his life before, was not frightfully keen to be told what to do by a flight sergeant, so I was offered a commission in the RFC reserve. I rejected it out of hand. I was a regular soldier,

I didn't want any jiggery-pokery. So, instead, I was made a warrant officer, first class. And as a warrant officer you were very powerful. Particularly if you're the top man in your branch. Which I was. As a result, I could get anything. I realized that a camera would have to be designed especially for the work we were to do, and as a result, the 'A'-type camera was produced.

The 'A'-type camera, the first official RFC camera, came into use in early 1915. Weighing ten pounds and encased in mahogany, the observer would grip it and lean over the side of the aircraft to take his photograph. It was discovered that photographs were being distorted by the angle at which the camera was held, so, to the relief of observers, it began to be attached by leather straps to the outside of the machine. It was first used over enemy trenches during the Battle of Neuve Chapelle. A photographic map of the entire German trench system was produced, which was used by the infantry to assist with the identification of objectives. Archibald James remembers using the 'A'-type camera:

> One only took six plates, each of which one had to change by hand. On landing after taking photographs – which I took of things like battery positions and railway junctions – one took them straight to Moore-Brabazon's office where, with his first-class sergeant, Sergeant Laws, they were developed. And one waited there while they were developed because Brab might wish to make comments on the fact that one had been inaccurate in one's pointing of the camera. I always remember one day when the photographs were developed, they were of the right place, but unfortunately Brab had forgotten to change the film in my camera – which he had previously been using himself. And superimposed on all my pictures was a beautiful white horse of somebody who'd come to lunch.

In the summer of 1915 the 'C'-type camera was introduced. It was an improvement on its predecessor, the 'A' type, in that it could take eighteen successive photographs by means of a changing apparatus. The pilot or observer would expose a plate by pulling a piece of cord, and then turn a handle to push the exposed plate into a receiving magazine, before turning the handle back to bring the next plate into position, ready for the next exposure. When, in March 1916, the British Fourth Army took over the Somme front, aerial photographic reconnaissance began on a massive scale; the German trench system was photographed meticulously. Robin Rowell was with 8 Squadron, near Marieux, using the 'C'-type camera:

> The camera was strapped to the right-hand side of the BE2c on the body of the machine. The advantage of fixing the camera to the machine was that the pilot could only take photographs of objects directly below him, and in consequence his pictures were all small maps of the ground, with a correct perspective, and could be pieced together to form a large photo of the enemy's trenches and emplacements.
>
> The pleasures of taking photos were very mixed. As far as results were concerned, the best height to take them was 6000 feet. The anti-aircraft gun 'Archie' became extremely accurate with practice, and as it was almost essential to fly a straight course when photographing, the gunners had plenty of time to make the sky thick with bursting shell. In some parts of the line, it was perfectly amazing to see the amount of stuff they could chuck at you in a minute. The shells would burst far faster than you could count them, and you were compelled to change your direction every fifteen or twenty seconds or you would not last long. But it was well worth taking heavy risks to get good photos. One cannot underestimate the value of good results. In

many cases, when pilots or observers reported any unusual information, such as the concentration of railway rolling stock or large dumps, they were sent straight back over the lines with a camera to take photos of what they had seen. In later days no reconnaissance machine ever crossed the lines without a camera.

Now in a good photo, taken from a reasonable height, 6 to 8000 feet, and enlarged from a quarter-plate to a half-plate, it is wonderful what you can see. You can count railway trucks and engines in sidings; from their positions, you can frequently tell whether they are empty or full. You can distinguish between main lines, temporary light railways, roads, cart tracks and footpaths; and if you march half a dozen men across a field in single file, their tracks can be picked up with a magnifying glass. The gunners spend half their lives trying to hide their guns or camouflage their battery positions and it frequently deceives the casual glance of an observer; but if you once get a photo of the field they are in, you will in all probability see the muzzle of their guns, to say nothing of the limber tracks along the hedges. If they made a trench and enforced it with barbed wire, you will not only be able to see if by the shadows or if it has water in it, but you will be able to see how many rows of barbed-wire entanglement it has in front of it and which way the field was last ploughed.

Cecil Lewis was also taking photographs on the Somme front with the 'C'-type:

My flight commander said, 'You'd better have a go this afternoon. Take Sergeant so and so, and go and have a bang.' So we got on board the BE2c – and the BE2c was totally unsuited to the job, of course. It had the observer in front and the pilot behind, whereas, with any sense, it should have been the pilot in front and the observer behind. But it wasn't. So the observer had four struts very close each side of him, and wires to brace him well in, and a little seat which he could just get into. And he could do nothing at all except keep a look out for enemy aircraft. And when it got at all hot – and you were liable to be attacked from the tail, not from anywhere else – he simply had to get up and kneel on the seat which, you see, was a jolly cold, draughty business at 8000 feet, even in the summer.

So we set out on that afternoon, and the pilot, who was me, had to look after the camera as well. Because with the pilot's seat at least you could look straight down. The camera was one of those real antiques, made by the ancient Greeks, you know. It was absolute mahogany. A good, square mahogany box with the nice, leather concertina pullout, a good, big lens on the bottom, and a little handle that you pulled to change the plates – they were real, good old glass plates. And in addition to that, a bit of wire with a little curtain ring on it, which of course was skittering about in the wind – to pull every time you wanted to take a picture. That was the technique of the thing.

The whole thing was strapped to the outside of the aeroplane and it had a sort of a ball and ring sight at the back. To take the photo you had to lean over the side of the cockpit and look down through this ball-sight, fly the aeroplane with the left hand, move the camera handle, changing the plates with the right; and every time you changed the plate you then pulled the string and waited until you'd flown along a bit more, you had to judge the overlap, and did it again.

So we were going fine. We had to do the second-line trenches, just a few hundred yards behind the German front line, right round the Fricourt salient and up the other side. It was a beautiful afternoon, not a cloud in the sky, and the whole thing looked absolutely peaceful.

One didn't imagine there could be a war. There didn't seem to be anybody firing, the whole thing was asleep. It was really remarkable and just two months before the Somme battle opened. So we got down in position, and started to fly along. Everything went according to plan, and the Sergeant was turned around in his seat, looking over the tail to see if there was anything about. He had a Lewis gun with fifty rounds, waiting until such time as anyone attacked us. We went on for the best part of half an hour, taking these photos, and then we just turned off and came home.

Frederick Laws recalls how the plates were developed in 1916:

The procedure was, when a chap landed, nine o'clock in the morning, the plates were rushed into a darkroom on the squadron, processed and printed. The prints were dried in methylated spirits, so that they could go off straight away. We used to have a huge piece of muslin on a frame, and we'd throw the prints onto this muslin to get air through them after they were methylated. And the first prints went to the local army headquarters, brigades and sometimes down to company commanders. Then the negative would go back to the wing. They would make a distribution to the higher armed formations. The whole thing worked very well.

Early in 1917, the 'L'-type camera was introduced. It was considered a great advance on its predecessors. Its body was made of aluminium, and it was semi-automatic. The pilot or observer made the exposure by pulling a lever, which harnessed the drive of the propeller to change the plate and wind the shutter. The 'L' type contained an adjustable lens, and instead of mounting the camera on the outside of the aircraft it was mounted inside the aircraft, pointing downwards through a hole in the floor. Frederick Laws:

Observers began coming to the section and I gave them lectures on how to handle cameras, what to do in certain circumstances if the camera went wrong in the air, and so on. When the 'L' camera came in, all they had to do was pull the lever. With the old ones, the 'C' and the 'A', they had to really know all about it. They had been very stiff old things to push about.

After the war, a confidential Air Ministry document on aerial photography was prepared. The document was intended 'for use and guidance in any subsequent campaign which may be undertaken during the next few years'. It concluded with an analysis of the scope and success of aerial photography:

Complete maps were produced of the trench works both on the enemy front lines and the reserve lines behind, illustrating the condition of the country in the rear, also the effects of bombing, condition of targets before and after shoots, the flooding of areas for defensive purposes, and the mapping of territory far behind the enemy's lines over which we were likely to advance.

The armies in the field relied solely on photography for the correction and compilation of maps which prior to the war only contained details as to villages, rivers, wells and one or two triangulated survey points. All additional detail to these maps was added from aeroplane photographs which were always taken in a series of overlaps sometimes extending over a distance of twenty or thirty miles.

The rapidity of the Allies' advance was made possible by the information brought back by aeroplanes in form of photographs, illustrating the condition of the roads, railways and rivers, showing in detail every point where bridges had been destroyed over such railways and rivers. They also gave accurate information as to which roads were passable, the junctions of many of which had been blown up by mines. Without such information, the advance would have taken considerably longer than was the case. Also the existence of enemy resistance at points where it could not have been predicted.

While aerial reconnaissance clearly had a crucial role to play in the waging of the Great War, so too did artillery observation. Once the Western Front had begun to stabilize in September 1914, the defences on either side of the lines grew and strengthened. As a result, artillery became the army's most important weapon. When mounting an attack, an artillery barrage would be laid down to destroy opposing defences, and, when defending against attack, opposing enemy guns would have to be destroyed, to prevent them from doing the same. It was crucial to know the precise positions of enemy targets, and, once they were located, to be able to fire accurately onto them. In the past this had been done by using Forward Observation Posts on the ground, from which observers sent information back to the battery. On the Western Front, this was difficult. The landscape was predominantly flat, tall vantage points lay in ruins, a pall of smoke and mist lay over the battle lines and it was difficult to advance forward of the lines unobserved. The obvious solution was to employ airborne Forward Observation Posts – aeroplanes.

Early in the war a variety of methods were used to direct and range artillery fire from the air. One method was the flashing of electric lamps to indicate first the existence of a target, and then the accuracy of the resulting fire. Another method was the discharging of flares. This method was still being used in training in 1915, as Alan Jackson remembers:

We went up in the BE2cs, carrying in the plane a number of different coloured flares. And when we got over the target, and the artillery had fired a shot, we then tried to let them know whether their shot was over the target or short of the target. And by means of dropping different coloured flares – red, say, for over, and a blue one for short – we let them know exactly where the shot had gone. If it was to the right or the left we'd either drop a white one or green one. In that way the artillery got some idea of where their shot had fallen.

Such a system could only offer limited assistance to a battery, and it was soon to be replaced by a relatively new innovation: wireless telegraphy. By sending a message in Morse code an aircraft could give specific directions to a battery, allowing it to range precisely onto its target. The first air-to-ground wireless transmission had taken place in August 1910 in the United States, and within a month of the arrival of the Royal Flying Corps in France the head-quarters wireless telegraphy unit was formed. Two men, both of 4 Squadron, Donald Lewis and Baron James, flew many of the early wireless artillery observations. Both men flew alone, as the size and weight of the early transmitters made it impossible to carry an observer. The Morse instructions that they sent to the batteries read like vivid commentaries. On 24 September 1914, the following was recorded:

4.02 p.m.   A very little short. Fire. Fire.
4.04 p.m.   Fire again. Fire again.
4.12 p.m.   A little short; line O.K.
4.15 p.m.   Short. Over, over and a little left.
4.20 p.m.   You were just between two batteries. Search two hundred yards each side of your last shot. Range O.K.
4.22 p.m.   You have hit them.
4.26 p.m.   Hit. Hit. Hit.

4.32 p.m. About 50 yards short and to the right.
4.37 p.m. Your last shot in the middle of three batteries in action; search all round within 300
yards of your last shot and you have them.
4.42 p.m. I am coming home now.

Both Lewis and James were to be killed while artillery
observing, James in 1915, Lewis a year later.

William Richards was an early Royal Flying Corps
wireless operator who spent his time on the ground with the
artillery batteries, receiving the Morse messages from the aircraft and passing instructions on to the battery commander.
Before the war, Richards had taught himself how to use a
crystal set and a pair of headphones, and this self-education
led him to his unusual role:

I arrived in France in early 1915, posted to 4 Squadron.
And I was immediately sent to Number 6 Siege Battery
at Alainville. I was one of the very first wireless operators to be engaged. There were only half a dozen of us,
for the most part telegraph operators from the post
office. The War Office had decided that wireless for
aircraft artillery observation must be developed. You
must understand that at the start of the war the batteries
were using the same methods that they had used in
the Boer War. Wireless means of communication was
something quite new, and the artillery were not interested to learn because they were so accustomed to their
old systems of communication, like the field telephone
and forward observation with binoculars.

When I came, the wireless set was a very well-
designed little transmitter, designed by a subsidiary
of the Marconi company, but, functionally, it was so
limited; it was only capable of maintaining effective
communication over a distance of about fifteen miles.
And there was no means of avoiding interference when
more than one set was being used in a local area. On

the ground, with the battery, I had a receiver, which was a crystal wireless set with a pair of headphones. It was a heavy thing, about the size of a piano. And I had to put up a thirty-foot steel mast to carry the aerial. When an aeroplane was on reconnaissance, observing local territory, I would wait for it to signal. It would produce signals in Morse code, giving the position of the enemy and the right range to be used. I would inform the battery commander, who would act accordingly. If I wanted to signal to the aircraft, I had to put out cloth strips because there was only one-way wireless communication from air to ground.

Wireless had great possibilities. But it was new and the gunners viewed it with disbelief and regarded it as a nuisance. The artillery, of course, are very proud people, with a background of valuable tradition, whereas the Flying Corps were only public schoolboys out for a joy-ride. What did they know about artillery? And with a strong pair of glasses, or from an aeroplane, the enemy could spot my mast or the cloth strips. It could give away our position – and that was another reason why I was unpopular. So we had to prove that wireless was important, useful, and not just a gimmick.

When I first arrived at the battery, war was all very new to me. I was a new boy completely, and I hadn't been in position more than twenty-four hours when the Germans registered our position and bombarded us with salvoes for the whole of one night. All I can say is I never was so frightened in my life because it was first experience of that sort of thing and I believe I prayed to God, I believe I cried, I believe I piddled in my pants. I was absolutely shattered. Whereas within weeks or months, I got quite hardened to it, and didn't worry if I heard the whizz of a shell coming over. I didn't bother to look round any more.

A great improvement came in 1915, with the introduction of the Sterling transmitter, which weighed only twenty pounds and allowed the aircraft to carry an observer. Frederick Powell remembers his attempts to learn Morse code while training as an observer:

> We sat for a long time with these little electric buzzers learning Morse code. Actually, what we did was to smoke cigarettes and tell smutty stories, until we suddenly found that nobody knew anything about Morse. As a result, instead of going into the hut and just going 'Bip-de-de-bip bip, buzz-buzz', we suddenly thought, 'We won't tell all these stories other than through the buzzer'. And as soon as we got to a four-letter word, we found it very easy to write down the answer. We told all our stories on Morse. Anybody who spoke during the session had to put half a crown into the box. In no time at all we all learnt our Morse – our alphabet was good. We learnt the difficult letters such as Q, L, and F. Q was God Save the Queen – dash dash dot dot. L and F were awkward ones. F was da-da da da, which was 'Get your hair cut'. L was da-da-da-da, 'Get out of it'. Eventually, you don't listen for dots and dashes. You just hear the thing talking to you: 'Get your hair cut; get out of it'. When you got to that stage, you could say, 'I know Morse, and I can pick it up and read it, and hear it.'

The Sterling set was operated by a small key on the right-hand side of the observer's seat on which he tapped in Morse. For the set to work, a trailing aerial, 150 feet in length, had to be unfurled from the aircraft. S. S. Saunders:

> On our aircraft we had an aerial – a piece of copper wire with a weight on it wound round a drum. When we wanted to call the battery, we dropped this down and hung it from the aircraft. Then with the aid of a Morse

signal we were able to contact the battery. If they heard us distinctly they put out a white groundsheet.

Archibald James recalls an aerial-related injury:

A horrid accident happened. Cooper – a very good chap – had a jam when he was letting his aerial out, which you did by turning a handle. He looked over the side, gave a jerk to the handle to try and release the jam, whereupon the drum flew out of its grooves, turned sideways, was caught by the slipstream and hit Cooper on the side of his head making him deaf for life.

A further development in 1915, which allowed an observer to direct a battery's fire more quickly and accurately, was the introduction of the 'clock code'. Devised by Donald Lewis and Baron James, it was a system which simplified the reporting process. K. P. Page, an officer in the Royal Field Artillery:

The normal drill was that the pilot should come up overnight to see the battery and get things worked out. Then, at the pre-arranged time in the morning, he would arrive overhead. He would circle the battery and send down the battery call to tell the battery that he was ready to observe. The battery would put out the ground strip which meant that they were ready to fire. And the pilot, when ready, would signal 'Fire'. And then he would fly in a figure-of-eight pattern, from the battery to the target, and back again. He would know the approximate time of flight of the shell, so he knew that when he sent 'Fire', and then saw the gun go off, he'd think, 'Well, I've got to wait twenty seconds and then I should see the burst.' And when he saw the burst, he reported back to the battery, using the clock code. If you imagine a clock face with the twelve o'clock facing north, and then imagine rings round it at hundred yard intervals – A, B, C, D, E. When the pilot saw the shell burst, he would report down, 'Three o'clock E', and then the battery would know, 'That means 500 yards east.' When the pilot finally saw the hit, he sent, 'Good. OK.'

Leslie Briggs, an RFC wireless operator:

> On average, with a reasonably good battery and a reasonably efficient observer, it might take twenty corrections to find the target. It might even be more than that. A lot depended not just on the weather and the efficiency of the observer but also on the efficiency of the artillery officer in correcting his guns in accordance with the messages. Some battery commanders of the old school were very much against observing by aircraft with wireless. If that was the case, then they were unlikely to make efficient use of the aerial observation and that would affect the time it took to get onto the target.

In 1916 the 'zone call' was introduced. This was a system whereby an aircraft could call down on the artillery to engage sudden targets. Until this time, all targets had been pre-arranged between the aircraft and the battery. Under the new system, the battle area was divided into zones, each of which would be the responsibility of a particular battery. If an observer spotted an active enemy battery or a congregation of troops in a particular zone, he could broadcast the call sign for that zone, and the corresponding battery would open fire. He could then direct it in the usual way.

At the Wireless School, Brooklands, impressive advances had been made in another new technology: wireless telephony. In May 1915, Major C. E. Prince sent the first spoken message from an aircraft to the ground. Leslie Briggs was sent to Brooklands for a course in the use of the 'electronic valve':

About twenty of us had a fortnight's intensive course, and when I first saw the valve, I thought it was just an electronic lamp. When I looked closer, I saw it had three parts and not just an ordinary filament. And it was the means of transmitting speech. Actual speech. It was really the very start of broadcasting as we understand it today. We spoke into what we now call a microphone, and transmitted messages from a station on one side of Brooklands Aerodrome to a station on the other. And we received messages in return.

Despite the excitement it provoked (and continues to provoke with its descendant – the mobile phone), wireless telephony was never applied to artillery observation; spoken transmissions from loud, open cockpits might lead to mis-understandings, and the changeover from the existing system, in terms of equipment and training, would have proved too complicated.

In fact, a changeover from telegraphy to telephony was unnecessary; the existing system worked well, in spite of the difficulties faced by the airmen, who were under near-continual anti-aircraft fire, and subject to persistent attacks from enemy aircraft. They were also subject to inadvertent attacks from the very guns that they were ranging. Cecil Lewis:

> Out of the corner of my eye, when I wasn't really looking, I saw something moving like a lump. I really didn't know what the devil it was. It was mystifying. Then I looked again and focused, and about a hundred yards ahead, there was the business part of a nine-inch howitzer shell right at the top of its trajectory, at about 8000 feet, just where we were. It had come up like a lobbed tennis ball, and it was going quite slowly at the top of its trajectory. It was a pretty hefty bit of metal, and it was turning before it gathered speed again. And

this was such an extraordinary thing to see – because no one imagines they'd ever *see* a shell. However, there it was – and then there were two or three more, and you could follow them right down to burst.

The weather was a problem for the observer; heavy cloud and banks of fog often obscured his vision, and the task of sending accurate Morse messages, over long periods, in bitterly cold conditions, could prove testing. Leslie Briggs:

I had a message once from an observer which said in plain English, which was very much against the rules – 'I am coming in. It's too bloody cold up here.' I reported it to the battery commander who said, 'Would you please tell him that it's bloody cold down here too.' But I couldn't send that message up because we couldn't transmit from ground to air. We only had those American cloth strips.

As the war proceeded and artillery activity increased, there might be so many shells landing that an observer might have difficulty distinguishing which came from his own battery. And some shells were harder to spot than others. Archibald James:

With a high-velocity, flatter-trajectory gun, it was far more difficult to see the shell land and explode, than it was in the case of a howitzer. The bigger the calibre of the gun, the more tremendous the burst; a 9.2 was an enormous gun and that was frightfully easy to see. Shrapnel was extremely difficult to range, bursting as it did in the air. It was awfully hard to judge, from the Very light smoke puff, how far above the ground it was and therefore exactly where the forward impetus would place the little round pieces of shrapnel.

The job of artillery observation effectively gave an airborne junior officer – or even an NCO – greater responsibility over the shoot than the battery commander. When the system of zone calls was introduced, a second lieutenant might call down and summarily take control of a battery. It is perhaps not surprising that many within the artillery found this reversal of the acknowledged order difficult to accept. Just as the aeroplane had stolen the cavalry's long-standing monopoly on reconnaissance, so now it seemed to be robbing the artillery of its independence. Nevertheless, when a battery commander was willing to embrace the new relationship, considerable success could be achieved. Leslie Briggs:

I spent time with No. 82 siege battery which was a twelve-inch howitzer battery. Those twelve-inch howitzers used to be pushed up on a railway by a loco-motive to their firing position, ready for the shoot. They were pulled out of the way again at night. We did several very interesting shoots with that battery. Their commander was very keen on artillery observation from the air. Whilst with them, we did some special shoots in combination with a sixty-pounder battery on our left. The observer was given instructions to fire both batteries at the same target but the idea was that the twelve-inch howitzer shell would arrive slightly before the sixty-pounder shell. First he would give a fire signal to the twelve-inch howitzer; he would allow a little time to elapse and he would then give a fire signal to the sixty-pounder. It was known as 'rabbit shooting' because the high explosive from the howitzer would have such a devastating effect that, whilst the German troops were running for cover, the sixty-pound shrapnel airburst would arrive and catch them. It necessitated very accurate timing because a howitzer shell is much slower than a sixty-pounder fired from a gun. The speed of a howitzer shell is less than the speed of sound – that's why you could hear a howitzer shell coming – but you couldn't hear the sixty-pounder coming as it's quicker than sound. The observer had to work out the time of flight very carefully so that the two batteries *almost* synchronized over the target. That was a very tricky thing to do. It's pretty ghastly to talk about but the idea was to kill as many German gunners as you possibly could – and we did have some marked success.

Pilots and observers engaged in artillery observation were aware of the threat posed by enemy aircraft, anti-aircraft fire and even by the frailties of their own machines. Archibald James recalls an old friend who was killed by none of the above, but by a chain of freakish events that emphasized the precarious existence of Great War pilots, even those merely engaged in an 'office job':

At a later stage of the war we had one of those accidents which is theoretically impossible, but actually took place. A pilot called Newton who'd been an exact contemporary of mine at Eton, flew over the wireless hut and gave the usual tap on his transmitter to check that his set was working, whereupon the aeroplane blew up, and he and his observer were both killed. Exhaustive enquiries were made. The only explanation was that a petrol leak had created a combustible mixture in the fuselage and that the spark from the transmitter set it off. No other explanation was possible. And yet all the expert evidence was that both these things were impossible. Such a combustible mixture could not have been produced. And if it had been produced, it couldn't have been set off by the spark. But the fact is it did happen, and they were both killed, and the machine was blown to pieces.

6

Fighters and the Fokker Scourge

The role of the fighter pilot during the Great War may have been to protect the two-seater areoplanes of the Royal Flying Corps while they were doing their job, but that role quickly gave rise to an entirely new contest. As the fighters went about their business, so they ran into single-seater opponents with the same intentions, and thus were born the gladiatorial battles which have come to epitomize the war in the air.

These gladiatorial battles caught the public imagination, and have continued to do so ever since. In 1930, the epic Howard Hughes movie *Hell's Angels* featured dogfights between SE5as and Fokker DVIIs. Forty-seven years later, the first *Star Wars* film featured engagements between Empire Tie Fighters and Rebel X-wing Fighters. These combats may have taken place in galaxies far, far away from each other, but the nature of the fighting portrayed is not very different. In reality, air fighting changed considerably after 1918. In 1940, during the Battle of Britain, aircraft speeds had increased to the point where pilots were only encountering their opponents for seconds at a time. Prolonged dogfights had become a rarity. Tactical duels in which aircraft chased, harried, circled and strained to get on each other's tail, were essentially a Great War phenomenon. Yet they remain the popular perception of aerial combat to this day. A classic Great War dogfight took place on 23 November 1916, between Manfred von Richthofen and British ace Lanoe Hawker. The fight is described in Richthofen's diary:

> The Englishman tried to catch me up in the rear while I tried to get behind him. So we circled round and round like madmen after one another at an altitude of about 10,000 feet. First we circled twenty times to the left, and then thirty times to the right. Each tried to get behind and above the other.
>
> Soon I discovered that I was not meeting a beginner. He had not the slightest intention to break off the fight. He was travelling in a box which turned beautifully. However, my packing case was better at climbing than his. But I succeeded at last in getting above and beyond my English waltzing partner.
>
> When we had got down to about 6000 feet without having achieved anything particular, my opponent ought to have discovered that it was time for him to take his leave. The wind was favourable to me, for it drove us more and more towards the German position. At last we were above Bapaume, about half a mile behind the German front. The gallant fellow was full of pluck, and when we had got down to about 3000 feet, he merrily waved to me as if he would say, 'Well, how do you do?'
>
> The circles that we made round each other were so narrow that their diameter was probably no more than 250 or 300 feet. I had time to take a good look at my opponent. I looked down into his carriage and could see every movement of his head.
>
> My Englishman was a good sportsman, but by and by the thing became a little too hot for him. He had to decide whether to land on German ground or whether he would fly back to the English lines. Of course he

tried the latter, after endeavouring in vain to escape
me by loopings and such tricks. At that time, his first
bullets were flying around me, for so far, neither of us
had been able to do any shooting.

When he had come down to about 300 feet, he tried
to escape by flying in a zigzag course, which makes it
difficult for an observer on the ground to shoot. That
was my most favourable moment. I followed him at
an altitude of from 250 to 150 feet, firing all the time.
My opponent fell, shot through the head, 150 feet
behind our line.

Such duels stand in sharp contrast to the impersonal nature
of fighting elsewhere during the war years. Infantrymen, who
had traditionally fought opponents at close quarters, were,
after September 1914, largely confined to their trenches,
making only periodic advances and occasional scouting
raids. Naval battles, which had once been conducted with
the aim of boarding an opposing vessel, were now ferocious
artillery exchanges, contested at long range. In the air,
however, pilots and observers were engaged in a human
struggle of skill and tactical acumen. Flying in open cockpits,
at relatively low speeds, dogfights retained a personal aspect.
Airmen could make out the facial expressions of their
opponents, observe their head movements, watch as flames
engulfed their cockpits. The speeds of rival aircraft differed
only slightly; the closing speed of one on another was small.
The contests that resulted have often been described in
chivalric, as well as gladiatorial terms, and it is not surprising
that they created such a lasting impression in the public
consciousness.

In the course of an otherwise faceless war it was to the
airmen that members of the public turned for their heroes.
On the home front, to wear a uniform of the flying services
was to radiate glamour. Alan Bott:

At a tango tea held in the hotel we were pointed out as the intrepid birdmen who had done the deed of the day. Flappers and fluff girls further embarrassed us with interested glances, and one of them asked for autographs.

But undoubtedly, the most glamorous, the most celebrated of the airmen were the fighters; the men who preyed on the enemy. Ira Jones was a young officer with 74 Squadron who flew his first offensive patrol on the morning of 12 April 1918. That evening he wrote in his diary:

The day of days has arrived, and is now almost over. Butler, my cockney batman, called Skeddon and me (we are sharing a hut) at 5.30 am. The sky was cloudy, but the visibility was particularly good. After a cold sponge down and a hot cup of tea and some biscuits, we donned our suits and strolled across to the aerodrome, which is about 200 yards away. Butler came with us to wish us luck. Cairns, Giles, Jones and Begbie were already standing by their machines. As there was ten minutes to go, we were not late. Cairns told us that he was going to cross the line at Merville and work up towards Ypres over the Salient. Everyone was bursting with keenness, each thinking of the Hun he was going to down, and no one of the possibility of death, or worse still – a breakfast of black bread and sausages in the enemy's lines. The CO, Mick and Coverdale were also present to see us off: the former and the latter for obvious reasons, but Mick turned up to ask us not to disturb the Huns in case they were not there when his Flight went on patrol.

We were off the ground punctually at 6 am, and twenty minutes later we were crossing the lines between Forest Nieppe and Merville, which is now the front line of trenches. As we crossed, I looked at my altimeter, and was amazed to find we were only at 6000 feet. This was a ridiculously low height, I thought, as the clouds were quite 10,000 feet. From my observer's experience I knew that the enemy's Archie was fairly good at this height, while there was every prospect of Huns attacking us from above. It was not long before the 'goods' arrived – and it was not wrapped up in brown paper either – it arrived well cooked and on a plate!

Archie bursts soon bounced our machines all over the sky while two miles away and about 2000 feet above, there was approaching a large flight of biplanes led by a Triplane. I watched them for a second or two, and wondered whether they were our machines or Huns. As we were approaching one another rapidly, I dashed up to Cairns, waggled my wings to attract his attention, and then pointed at the approaching aircraft. He signalled back O.K., so I returned to my position at the tail of the Flight, on the right flank. We were flying in the customary 'V' formation with Skeddon and Jones on the immediate left and right of Cairns, then behind them were Begbie and Giles, and behind Giles was myself. This position of honour was given to me owing to my exceptionally good eyesight. It was my duty to warn Cairns of any approaching Huns sneaking up from the rear, or from any other angle. Eyesight plays an important role in air fighting.

When Cairns continued to fly towards and underneath the approaching machines, I naturally assumed they were comrades, but the Triplane puzzled me, and as I couldn't recognise the type of the others, I became more and more anxious. I remembered Mick's advice about fighting Triplanes. Through my mind, flashed the thoughts – Are they Huns? No! Yes! No! Yes! – I couldn't make up my mind, but as we were fast approaching, the black Maltese crosses on their wings soon settled the question. For a moment I was fascinated by those little black crosses. How pretty they looked! And what pretty machines! They were all colours of the rainbow! Black and red, bright blue and dark blue, grey and yellow. It never struck me that they were aeroplanes flown by men – possibly by the crack pilots of the German Air Force. Men whom I knew as Huns. Death-dealing gentlemen, possibly smothered with Iron Crosses and Orders *pour la Merité*. I looked on them for a moment as rather a pretty flock of birds. But I was soon rudely awakened from my reverie.

Cairns, as soon as he had seen the black crosses, turned sharply left to get away and improve his tactical position, as they were diving to the attack. Skeddon and Jones could easily turn tightly with him, and Begbie and Giles, by crossing over positions could turn fairly tightly. But I, being so far behind, was left standing, so to speak. The enemy leader soon took advantage of the gap between me and my Flight, and brought his formation into it, ignoring the remainder of the Flight, and soon he was on my tail, firing sweet bullets of welcome to 74 Squadron. Wisely I kept my head, and immediately put my machine into a vertical bank, held the stick tight into my stomach, kept my throttle wide open, and prayed hard. Following Mick's advice.

It did not take me long to realize that the gentleman who was doing his best to kill me was an old hand at the game. A sure sign of an old hand is that he reserves his ammunition and only fires in short bursts; if he is aiming straight he knows that a burst of twenty is as good as a burst of 200 and much more economical. Having only about 1000 bullets in all, it is foolish for a pilot to use them up when he knows that his aim is not good on the off-chance that the odd bullet may hit his opponent. Once he has used up his ammunition, the then becomes defenceless himself. Mick had warned us that we had to be careful of a Hun who fired in short bursts; on the other hand, if a Hun is firing long bursts at you, he said, you can be sure that he is frightened and probably a beginner. 'Fight him like hell, he should be easy meat.' The Hun on my tail was so close that I could easily discern his features. His machine was painted black with a white band round his fuselage just behind his cockpit, and he was flying it superbly. It seemed to slither round after me. Round and round we waltzed, in what was no doubt, to my opponents, a waltz of death, but this morbid aspect of the situation fortunately never occurred to me. Of course I could see the big idea. The leader was to shoot me down while his eight companions prevented anyone coming to my assistance, or myself from getting back to my lines. Some of them kept above and on the north side (the side that Cairns and his Flight were climbing), and the remainder kept on the west side of me at various heights, so that I would have to run their gauntlet of fire if I chose to quit. As we waltzed around, I kept on repeating to myself, 'Keep cool, he can't hit you. His bullets are going behind.' I could see the track of his bullets as he was using tracers, and this fact encouraged me to keep cool. I had no desire to have a burning bullet roasting my intestines, especially before breakfast. So keep cool.

Occasionally I shouted at the top of my voice at him, telling him to do his damnedest. I also used most indecent language. Of course, he could not hear me, but it gave me satisfaction and temporarily acted as a stimulant to my sorely tested courage. While he flew close to my tail but did not fire, I did not mind very much, but whenever I heard the kak-kak-kak of his Spandau guns, and saw the spurting sheets of flame close behind me, I felt a little anxious of a stray bullet hitting me. Every now and then my attacker would zoom up, and a couple of his comrades would make a dive and zoom attack, hoping that I would get out of my vertical bank – but I wasn't having any as I knew of this old trick. Once they got me out of my vertical bank, the gent on my tail (he may have been Richthofen, Udet or any of the other Hun star-turns as far as I know) would no doubt have soon put paid to my account. After a while I feared, unless I got out of the mess that I was in quickly, the fickle jade Fate might step in and stop my engine, or worse still put a stray tracer bullet through my petrol tank, and send me down to Hunland in a blaze of glory – a glorious death for an airman but not one that I wanted on my first patrol. I wanted to kill a couple of Huns myself first. As we waltzed around one another, sparring for an opening, I kept my eye on the big green mass of trees about five miles away – the Forest of Nieppe. I knew that those trees were in our territory. It was a consoling thought. But I could not make up my mind when to make my dash, the Triplane kept on nagging me with his bullets – so did his companions, and the longer I stayed on as their guests, the more attention they paid me. Occasionally, two or three would have a crack simultaneously. I would sometimes fire for morale effect only.

The seconds passed like years, and the minutes like eternity. The tension grew as the minutes rolled by, until eventually in desperation I decided to make a bid for home as soon as the Triplane did his next zoom. I watched my opponent carefully, as he was then only about 25 yards behind and he seemed to be grinning as I looked at him over my left shoulder; as soon as I saw him commence to zoom up to change his position I obeyed Mick's instructions and 'put on full zoom rudder' and my machine did a turn of a spin. When I came out of it, I found I was facing east instead of west, so another spot of bottom rudder to turn her round westwards was quickly applied, and there in front, a few miles away, was my landmark – the Forest of Nieppe.

Between me and my objective were half a dozen Huns, hungry and angry Huns, just waiting for me to come their way. And their way I went, accepting their challenge, like a mad bull charging a toreador. I knew this was my only chance. It was now or never. So, barging through the middle of them – neither looking to left or right, as I had often done before through a rugger scrum when cornered, I went for home like Hell, kicking my rudder from side to side to make the shooting more difficult for the enemy – and praying hard. It was a grand thrill, that run for the enemy lines – I knew by the incessant angry barking of the enemy's guns that there were hundreds if not thousands of death-dealing bullets chasing my little machine. Occasionally during my mad careering, I looked over my shoulder to see whether I was gaining on my enemies; to my joy I could see I was – but the bullets, I realised, were still faster, and it was not until I knew I was well clear of the enemy – half a mile away, that I knew I was safe. It was a joy to see my little SE5 gaining ground on the Triplane and the Pfalz, and to listen to the fading rattle of the staccato barking of the enemy's guns as my machine gradually outstripped her opponents. I crossed our lines just to the north of the forest, right down close to the ground and fortunately my enemies feared to follow me owing to the approaching of Cairns from a higher altitude. Cairns then chased them miles over their lines.

Throughout his diary, Jones uses the epithet 'Huns' to describe Germans. This term had its roots in a 1900 speech given by Kaiser Wilhelm II to German troops before they sailed to China to suppress the Boxer Rebellion:

Just as a thousand years ago the Huns under King Atilla made a name for themselves, one that even today makes them seem mighty in history and legend, may the name German be affirmed by you in such a way that no Chinese will ever again dare to look cross-eyed at a German.

During the Great War, the Kaiser's words were seized on by British propagandists as evidence of Germanic arrogance and aggression, and 'Hun' soon became a common epithet. Another name consistently referred to by Jones is 'Mick'. This was Edward 'Mick' Mannock – of whom we will hear more – a complex but inspirational leader of men who excelled as a tactician and took great pains to nurture the young airmen in his charge. Jones was one of these men, and he seems to have handled his first show in an alert and sensible fashion. Raymond Brownwell, a young Australian flying with 45 Squadron, was rather less alert during his first patrol in late 1917:

> Off we went and apart from dodging a bit of Archie, we flew along tranquilly enough until at about 12,000 feet, I noticed the leader firing his guns, so I did the same – thinking this was just to warm the gun, and then there was a lot of dodging about and I thought this was a try out for me at keeping with the formation. On several occasions during our patrol, similar manoeuvres took place, and, as instructed, I fired a few bursts at odd intervals to ensure no freezing up took place. However, no matter how hard the leader tried to lose me, I kept my eye glued on him and retained my place at his left in the formation – which I noted had become somewhat disintegrated by this time. Finally we turned for home and landed, and I secretly felt quite pleased with myself for having kept formation – with all the dodging about that I had imagined had been done to test me out. When we got out of our buses and commenced to thaw out, the leader came across to me and said, 'Damn

good show, Brownwell. I saw you shooting at that Hun though I don't think you got him.' I looked at him in amazement and said, 'What Hun? I didn't see any!' The leader said, 'But I saw you close beside me shooting right into one of the enemy buses.' 'I must have been shooting to keep my guns warm,' I said, 'as I never saw any hostile aircraft at all!' I was the joke of the place after that and felt a complete ass.

New boys such as Jones and Brownwell, on patrol for the first time, would have to learn the art of air fighting very quickly if they were to survive.

The birth of the aeroplane as a true fighting machine began in early 1915 with the introduction of dedicated fighters (at the time known as 'scouts') which engaged purely in offensive patrols. The Royal Flying Corps' first fighter – in reality a modified reconnaissance machine – was the Vickers FB5, which arrived in France on 5 February 1915.

The Vickers Fighter was a two-seater pusher, with a forward-facing Lewis machine gun mounted in the observer's nacelle at the front of the aircraft. The pilot sat behind. The Vickers' fighting function led to it becoming known colloquially as the 'Gunbus', a nickname rejected by the prissier members of the Flying Corps; one Flight Commander posted a notice on his door which read, 'There are no buses in this flight. Only aeroplanes', whilst a veteran of 4 Squadron, Charles Chabot, was still reacting angrily to the name in an interview given fifty-eight years after the machine arrived in France:

It would not be the 'Gunbus' because only the dregs refer to 'Gunbus'. We do not talk of 'Gunbus', sir, it is the Vickers Fighter, if you don't mind. It's just as bad as talking of an aircraft as a 'kite'.

Whatever it was called, it had a top speed of seventy miles per hour at 5000 feet, and a ceiling of 7000 feet. It was solidly built, and, for its time, well armed. It initially proved very successful, flying against German machines, many of which were still unarmed. Its engine was a 100-horse-power Gnôme Monosoupape, which could be challenging to fly, as Frederick Powell, a Vickers pilot with 5 Squadron, remembers:

> That engine was an extraordinary thing for a pilot to have to fly, in that it had no throttle at all. It only had one speed – flat out. One used the thumb switch and gave a series of buzzes to taxi, and then one would open up, and let the thing run flat out. But unfortunately as you gathered speed and took off, the fuel/air mixture would change, and you had to keep a hand on the fine adjustment, because the mixture was becoming too rich and the engine would start missing. So you would cut it down until you got a level engine note, but after you had climbed to about 1000 feet, the air would become too rare, and you had to cut down again, always listening to the engine. As you got higher and higher, you cut down again and again. This all had the disadvantage that when you came in to land from some terrific height, like 4000 feet, the mixture would change quickly and many a crash was caused by the engine missing. It certainly paid a pilot to listen because you flew the Vickers entirely by ear.

Powell achieved considerable success, flying his Vickers Fighter on patrol:

> An offensive patrol in the Vickers could only last for a maximum of two hours, because the petrol range was two and a quarter hours' flying. So you had a quarter of an hour to get out to the lines, and back again, and the rest of the two hour patrol was supposed to be flown over the lines, up and down the trenches. As one was flying up and down, always hoping to see a Hun,

sometimes one was lucky and another time one could spend two hours and not see a single thing. But I was fairly lucky, and I was able, thanks to my very expert gunner, to be able to knock one or two of the German aircraft down.

I think the most satisfactory time was when we heard of a new German machine, which we called 'Two Tails'. That was a thing which had two fuselages. We had never imagined a thing of this size. It had a crew of three. The pilot sat in a nacelle, which was positioned between the two fuselages. It was a tractor with two engines, one at the nose of each fuselage, and it had two gunners, one forward, then the pilot, then the rear gunner. To our mind, it must be a very formidable thing.

I was flying one day on one of these patrols, a little bit to the east of Ypres, and I saw a Bosche aircraft called an Aviatik. I was higher than he was, which was quite unusual in those days, so I dived down towards him, shouted to my gunner, and the gunner, being a very good shot, got him. The Aviatik started to swerve down, and as it was going down, I was anxious to see it crash, but at that moment, my dear old Vickers Fighter seemed to want to turn. I was fighting with the Vickers to try and keep my wing out of the way so that I could watch the German, but I could not. In desperation, I swung round on a bank and I saw, just coming up on my tail, this enormous great aeroplane – 'Two Tails'. I shouted to the gunner to stick his gun pointing upwards and to keep his finger on the trigger as I flew underneath 'Two Tails'. To my intense delight, we must have hit the nacelle, or if we missed it, we got one of the engines, because 'Two Tails' went down in a slow spiral, down, and down, and down, and crashed just behind the German lines.

Archibald James remembers a patrol in which he had to deal with two distinct problems:

> I have often been asked what one's sensations were in aerial combat. The answer is it was so exciting that really one's only emotion was excitement. One morning with an observer called Porri I was approaching the lines at the usual height of about 5000 feet. That was the usual height for a Vickers. Just as we were approaching the lines a German biplane crossed in front of us. So we naturally turned and followed it. Its speed was slightly faster than ours and it was obviously doing a very long reconnaissance. In fact it went all the way to St Omer. Directly I saw it was going to turn south to regain its lines I turned inside it and thereby got fairly close. But I could never overtake it.
>
> As we approached the lines again I'd actually pushed the old Vickers up to just on 9000 feet, by far the highest that I've heard of anybody getting a Vickers up to. But of course we were pretty well empty of petrol by that time. Now, Porri was the son of an Italian fish merchant resident in Grimsby, a small swarthy fellow, extremely agreeable, but like a certain number of his compatriots, not a warrior at heart. I had not in the least appreciated how worried he had been at the prospect of his first combat.
>
> However, just as the German was crossing his lines, we exchanged a few shots, perhaps ten or twenty. And I was unaware that the German had in fact hit our heavy two-bladed propeller, about a third of the way up from the boss. And as I was coming down to an aerodrome where I proposed to refuel, the German bullet took effect. About one third of the blade broke off and went with a clatter through my tail boom, which consisted of tubular iron rods which carried the elevator and rudder. It made a devil of a noise.

As the result, with the uneven turning of the two blades, one intact and one with a third gone – the most appalling vibration was set up. So much so that I was afraid that it might jerk my engine off its balance. The only way to reduce the vibration was to come down as flat as possible, near stalling point. It was only then that I realized that the unfortunate Porri had completely collapsed nervously. He was completely panic-stricken, and to my horror he proceeded to put one leg over the side with a view to jumping. So I had the most horrible descent with one hand leaning forward and patting him on the shoulder and saying what a splendid chap he was, and with the other keeping the thing as near stalling point as possible.

On 25 July 1915 the first specialist fighter squadron, No. 11, arrived at St Omer, moving to its base at Vert Galant four days later. Supplied uniformly with Vickers Fighters, 11 Squadron represented a departure from the system of all-purpose squadrons. Robin Hughes Chamberlain, an original squadron member, who describes the Vickers Fighter in four words – 'wonderful view, damned cold' – recalls a less than successful dawn patrol in August 1915:

I was a bit late for going up on patrol so I hurried to Vert Galant, where I put on my stuff, and jumped into the machine. The observer was already in his seat. It was pretty foggy, and I took off, and within an instant I was out of sight of land. After about a thousand feet, I was in blue sky, but the ground was cotton wool. Everywhere. I continued flying up to about 6000 feet, but by this time I was frightened of getting lost, so I made for the lines and counted the minutes until I thought I'd got there. It was about twelve minutes at sixty miles per hour. Then I turned left to go up the front, because I could see balloons sticking out of the fog below. I didn't know whether they were our own or

German, so I couldn't fire at them. After a while, I decided that it would be safer to turn left again, and go back towards our side of the lines, to try and find our aerodrome. But on diving down, I hit the fog again at about 1000 feet, and in case I hit Amiens Cathedral, which would be a spiky place to end up, I pushed her back up into the blue sky. I reached 6000 feet again, when suddenly, all my cylinders stopped firing. That settled it. I had to go down through the fog this time. After fiddling with the controls for a few minutes, the cylinders started up again, but by now, I'd decided that I was going down.

I came out of the fog next to a big wood, which towered up on our left, and nearby I saw a patch of green, and I thought, 'That'll do' and I landed. I didn't have the foggiest idea where I was. It turned out to be a place called Pissy. We got out of the machine, and I told the observer to stay by the Vickers while I went to the nearest telephone. I found one in a café, about half a mile away, and I remembered that I hadn't had any breakfast, but when I put my hand in my pocket, I found that I'd left my wallet behind. After phoning the squadron, I said to the café owners, 'I'm very hungry, I have no money, but I'll see you get paid for it.' They gave me coffee and everything else. They were very nice. Then I thought about my poor wretched observer, who was sitting alone by the machine with nothing to eat, but when I got back to the machine, there was a tremendous crowd all round it. Aeroplanes were very rare in those days. And the crowd was bringing all kinds of things. The observer was eating and drinking, and having a great old time.

Anyway, I'd landed on a strip of clover, and underneath it was some very rough ground. On our right was a cornfield in full sway. So we got into the Vickers and got started, but the bumping over the clover sent my maps up into my face, and I couldn't see anything, and I must have taken my right foot off the rudder, and we veered off into the cornfield. The corn wrapped itself round the Vickers' skids in such a way that the machine turned, very slowly, very gently, and very quietly, onto its back. We fell out.

I went back to the telephone, and said that now I'd gone and put it on its back. This annoyed George Dawes, the squadron commander, very much. He came along in the squadron car, and he could produce a blast of language, I can tell you. I said, 'There's a nice little café here, where they serve rather good drinks. Why don't you come along? And what's more I've got no money so you'll be stuck with the bill.'

The success of the Vickers Fighter led to an aerial arms race over the next three and a half years, in which aerial supremacy swung backwards and forwards between the two sides as they took it in turns to introduce better machines and more effective means of utilizing them. As ever, the impetus for advancement came from the men who flew the aircraft, and who understood what was necessary to overcome the current obstacles; the primary obstacle in early 1915 was the tractor machine's inability to fire directly ahead, through the propeller. Pilots wanted to be able to aim their guns merely by pointing their machine.

A solution of sorts, with impressive short-term results, was introduced by aircraft designer Raymond Saulnier, prompted by a request from French pre-war stunt pilot Roland Garros. Saulnier fitted the propeller of Garros' Morane-Saulnier Type L monoplane, with triangular steel deflector plates, which simply repelled bullets fired forward from a machine gun. It was hardly a foolproof device. Bullets might be deflected onto another part of the propeller or back towards the aircraft. Nevertheless, when Garros took the device into action at the end of March 1915, he shot down five German aircraft in quick succession. Panic spread among German airmen who were unable to understand how an opponent could be spitting fire at them through a spinning propeller. On 19 April, Garros was forced down near Courtrai, behind German lines. He attempted to burn his aircraft on the ground, to remove evidence of his steel-wedged airscrew, but he was prevented from doing so by alert German infantrymen.

Garros' machine was hurried to the factory of Dutch aircraft designer Anthony Fokker, who was handed the new German parabellum machine gun, told to study Garros' steel plates and ordered to produce a copy that could be fitted to German aircraft. Fokker, only twenty-five years old, had designed and built a stable monoplane before the war, which had been rejected by the British, French and Russian military authorities, before it was bought and put into production by the German Signal Corps. Employed by the Germans, he was working very much for himself. He knew that if he could marry his own monoplane with a device for firing through the propeller, he could produce an aircraft which might clear the sky of Allied machines and cement his reputation. He immediately discarded Garros' steel plates, and set to work on a synchronizing gear. This was not a new idea, but it had not yet been made to work practically. Fokker hurriedly built a mechanism whereby the propeller itself fired the gun as it revolved, by striking a cam which was attached to the machine gun's hammer. In this way, a fast-moving bullet was only fired when the slower-moving blades were out of the way, and the machine gun could fire safely through the moving propeller. Before Fokker's solution was made available, he was ordered to prove its capabilities. He was told to fly his own single-seater mono-plane aircraft, fitted with his interrupter gear, over enemy lines, where he was to shoot down an Allied aircraft. He took off, dressed in a German uniform, and spotted a French

Farman machine. As he flew towards it, the Farman took no evasive action. Fokker wrote afterwards:

> This aircraft had no reason to fear me. I was going straight for it, my nose aimed at it, and they couldn't possibly have any reason to fear bullets fired through my propeller.

As Fokker approached the Farman, he made the decision to turn away without firing. He did not have the stomach to destroy an enemy machine, and, as he later wrote, 'no wish to kill Frenchmen'. This act of humanity is somewhat undermined by the fact that he allowed his machine to be taken up by the future German ace Oswald Boelcke, who carried out the necessary kill on his behalf. The following day, another future German ace, Max Immelmann, flew the aircraft, and recorded another victory. Fokker's EI single-seater monoplane (or Eindecker), powered by a 100-horse-power Oberursel engine which gave it a top speed of eighty miles per hour, was to become a feared sight over the Western Front. It was the first true gun platform. Existing aircraft, while often able to match the Fokker in terms of performance, could not match it for firepower.

For several months, the Fokker Eindeckers presented more of a worry than an actual threat to the Royal Flying Corps. They were relatively few in number and dispersed thinly across the Western Front. As 1915 drew on, however, numbers of the later model of the Eindecker, the E.III, increased, and the Flying Corps became compelled to send more fighting machines into the air to protect its working aircraft. In January 1916 an official order was issued, directing that every aircraft engaged in reconnaissance or artillery observation should henceforth be escorted by three fighting machines. This was clearly not a practical long-term proposition, and had it not been for the eventual arrival of a British machine to challenge the Fokkers, and for the fact that many Eindeckers were sent to the battlefields of Verdun in early 1916, it is conceivable that the Royal Flying Corps might have been driven from the skies. The rate of casualties among Flying Corps pilots and observers was certainly driven up, and British newspapers began to report the 'Fokker Scourge'.

The tactics adopted by the Fokker pilots were revolutionary and terrifying to opposing pilots and observers. They took advantage of the Fokker's relatively high ceiling as well as its synchronized gun. The pilot would sit at a high altitude, ideally in the sun and therefore hidden from his victim, before swooping down unobserved to attack from above. Even if he was observed, the speed of his approach would prevent an enemy from mounting any more than token resistance. In order to maintain the attack the Fokker pilot might carry out an 'Immelmann turn', named after its creator. The pilot would dive past his target, before pulling out of the dive into a loop. At the top of the loop, he would perform a half-roll which would leave him in an upright position, with enough height to mount another attack. Another manoeuvre with which Max Immelmann is credited was to pull out of the dive into a climb to the point of stall, and then kick on the rudder, turn sideways and dive once again onto the opponent from the opposite direction. The stable BE2c, the British workhorse, a difficult aircraft to manoeuvre, fell easy prey to such carefully considered and expertly executed tactics. On occasion, however, a Fokker might be outwitted by an inferior aircraft. An entry from Harold Wyllie's diary:

> Cooper of 13 Squadron was on reconnaissance with the usual escort. His observer was hit and both guns jammed. A BE2c which had a cylinder shot away by Archie was just crawling in, but dropping astern all the time, and Cooper saw a Fokker coming up to cut him

off. Without any hesitation, Cooper did a terrific turn and dived straight at the enemy, scaring him so badly that he sheered off, and saving the lives of the pilot and observer in the BE. Cooper, I take my hat off to you! VCs have been got much more easily. For sheer guts this action stands very high amongst brave deeds in this war.

Robin Rowell remembers an even more unlikely encounter:

A boy called Douglas in 8 Squadron arrived home one morning with his face covered with oil from his engine, very much excited and out of breath, to tell us his story of a Fokker who had been chasing him all round the sky. Poor Douglas had practically no means of defence, except a Lewis gun rigged at an angle that it could not be aimed and which jammed directly that he tried to use it. He managed to evade the Hun's fire for some time and finally, in a moment of desperation, he pulled out his Very light signalling pistol and fired it off. The flare happened to be a green one and it went just past the Fokker's wing tip, who instantly turned and made off for home. Never say die.

The rules of aerial tactics were being laid down, and the men primarily responsible for those rules, Immelmann and his fellow Fokker pilot Oswald Boelcke, were to become the air war's first celebrities. Both men were innovators who made the most of their machines and capitalized on the weaknesses of their enemies. As individuals, they were very different: Immelmann was a cold, distant Prussian, with no interest in courting popularity; Boelcke was a pleasantly-natured Saxon, known for bringing gifts to wounded opponents in hospital. Together they were laying the foundations for the future of air fighting. Both would be dead by the winter of 1916.

In August 1915 came an appointment which was to have

great implications for the development of the Royal Flying
Corps at a time when it was coming under increasing strain:
Hugh Trenchard was appointed as its commander in the
field. Trenchard, whose loud, gruff voice inspired his nickname of 'Boom', had served for years as an army officer in
the South Nigeria Regiment, where he had grown stale. He
viewed the formation of the Royal Flying Corps as an opportunity to resurrect his career as well as his enthusiasm,
and despite being thirty-nine years old and too large to fit
comfortably inside a cockpit, he succeeded in learning to fly.
When the Royal Flying Corps moved to France in August
1914, Trenchard had been placed in charge of its adminis-
trative wing in England, which consisted of 'one clerk and
one typewriter, a confidential box with a pair of boots in
it, and a lot of unpaid bills incurred by various officers.'
In November, he was sent to France to command the First
Wing. Trenchard was a man with a reputation for bluntness,
but that may have had more to do with a lack of communication skills than an unpleasant nature. Archibald
James:

> Trenchard was born in the red. When he was an
> impressionable schoolboy, his father fell into dire
> economic and social trouble, and he had nothing
> behind him at all. Everything he achieved was done by
> sheer guts, brains and personality. He was that peculiar
> thing, a totally inarticulate genius. He had no power of
> expression whatsoever either verbally or on paper.

He was therefore fortunate that when he was appointed
commander in the field his ADC was Maurice Baring, a man
who was able to communicate expertly on his behalf. On
Trenchard's appointment, their first meeting was typically
short and to the point. Baring wrote:

> General Trenchard sent for me, and told me he was
> willing to keep me for a month. He would see by that

time whether I should be of any use to him, and if I was of no use I should have to go.

Baring would prove to be of great use to him, and Trenchard, for his part, would come to demonstrate genuine concern for the officers and men under him, as well as for the finer points of Flying Corps business. Trenchard's attention to detail is evident from the first notes that Baring made for him on 22 August, during a visit to the First Wing:

> I have down in my notebook for that day that the General wants some Oxford marmalade for breakfast, that the road near No.3 Squadron is too dusty and steps must be taken to remedy this, that the first Wing are not to press at present to send home observers to learn to fly, that Christie wants some more double clips for his elevator control.

Baring came to understand Trenchard implicitly, and was able to smooth over his prickly dealings with others. One man with whom Trenchard had a good understanding was Sir Douglas Haig, Commander of the First Army. In March 1915, during the build-up to the Battle of Neuve Chapelle, the two men had met and Trenchard had impressed Haig with his realistic assessment of the contribution that the Royal Flying Corps could make to the forthcoming attack. In return, Haig had told Trenchard that he would probably cancel the offensive if bad weather prevented aircraft from materially assisting with reconnaissance and artillery observation. The battle achieved only minor gains for the British force, but it confirmed that genuine faith was being placed in the abilities of the air services.

One effect of this increased faith was that aeroplanes were encouraged to carry out new duties. During the Battle of Neuve Chapelle, attempts had been made to carry out 'contact patrols'. These involved the use of low-flying aircraft to observe the positions of advanced troops during an attack, and to report these positions back to headquarters. In this way, the extent of the advance might, in theory, be closely monitored. Quite apart from the dangers posed to airmen by flying low over heavily defended enemy positions, contact patrols presented other problems, as Archibald James discovered in May:

> I was sent to observe the progress of the Battle of Festubert. It had been arranged that in order to let the air see how far they'd got, the most advanced troops would from time to time put out white strips of cloth about eight feet long and a foot wide. To my astonishment when I arrived with almost the first light, the whole of the battle front was covered with white strips. What in fact had happened was that the methodical Germans had lined their trenches with wooden boards. And our bombardment when it hit a trench blew out a number of planks, which scattered round and were quite indistinguishable from the white strips the troops were supposed to have put out.

Another new duty allocated to aircraft was the dropping of spies in enemy territory. The first spy drop was carried out in September, and is described in a contemporary Royal Flying Corps memorandum:

> In the early hours of the 13th September, Captain T. W. M. Morgan left No. 6 Squadron aerodrome with an agent, Van de Leene of Courtrai, and pigeons, to land near the village of Oyeghem (near Courtrai). It was necessary to land near a wood and the field selected was very enclosed. In landing at 4.45 am, the pilot struck a tree and tore a wing off. Both were injured in the crash and taken prisoner. The agent's life was only saved by the large pigeon baskets he carried in front of him. He had both legs broken and suffered slight internal injuries.

Five days later, news was received from an agent giving information of the crash and stating that it was an hour before the Germans arrived and in the meantime all papers which they had with them were saved by the help of friendly civilians. These civilians saved, as well, the two pigeons which were still alive and were placed in hiding. The wounded aviators were placed in hospital at Courtrai.

The pilot, Tom Mulcahy-Morgan, who had broken his jaw in the crash, was later to escape from captivity, arriving back in England in 1917.

A subsequent spy drop was carried out by Sergeant Sidney Attwater, an air mechanic turned pilot. Attwater received orders to drop an agent by night on a German aerodrome. He remembers:

On the next moonlit night, we went. The agent's name was Monsieur Victor, and he was in French uniform, with a No. 13 on his cap. I didn't fancy that number much. But at 1.15 am, a large basket which contained pigeons, ammo, money and other things, was fastened on the starboard wing and Monsieur Victor arrived with an old fashioned string bag full of dainties and presents for his wife and family. I asked him how he was going to get away when I had landed him – we had to land as there were no parachutes in those days.

When we arrived at the target, he wished to be taxied to a wood at the end of the aerodrome, which I did. He had his bag and the basket off in a jiffy. He told me to turn round, ready for the take-off, and wait for another agent to get in and fly back with me. I was getting a bit windy by the time this other agent came and got in. Well, he let off a few rounds at the hangar and I took off and got back OK.

There were quite a few bullet holes in the plane on examination, so someone had a bash at us. I asked the new agent how they got away after landing, but he wouldn't tell me. He just said it was impossible for them to be caught. I'm sure they are the most courageous men in the world. He said they had to dress in uniform to avoid both of us being shot as spies, if we were caught. I was given that job quite a few times, not always at the same place, of course. And I've never worried about number 13 being unlucky since.

It has subsequently been suggested that the two agents dropped by Attwater were, in fact, identical twins, posing as an individual behind enemy lines.

In late September 1915, the British mounted an attack on Loos, to support an assault by the French on Vimy Ridge. The Flying Corps was engaged in the usual artillery cooperation, as well as the bombing of railway lines and further contact patrols. No strategic gains were achieved during the battle itself, although it is remembered for two reasons: the first British use of poison gas and the subsequent removal of Sir John French as commander-in-chief of the British Expeditionary Force, to be replaced by Sir Douglas Haig, a man who supported – and had the support of – Trenchard. As the year drew to a close, and the Western Front remained as deadlocked as ever, this relationship gave rise to a new way of thinking within the Royal Flying Corps.

The army's intended strategy in 1916, as shaped by Haig and the French commander-in-chief, General Joffre, was an aggressive one: to grind down enemy resistance until the opportunity arose later in the year to deal a decisive blow to the German army. This was to be mirrored in Trenchard's aerial strategy. The Royal Flying Corps must achieve air superiority and it must do so by seeking out and destroying German scouts and two-seaters at every opportunity, particularly over their own lines. Such aggressive flying would force German machines back and away from British territory, and so prevent them from carrying out bombing, artillery observation, and reconnaissance work. At the same time, the British two-seaters would still have to carry out their own work fully and effectively, even if this now meant taking greater responsibility for their own safety.

Trenchard understood that his offensive strategy would result in a sharp increase in aircraft losses and casualties, but such an increase, he believed, was a reasonable price to pay for a contribution to a British victory. One immediate result of the new strategy was a renewed determination to eradicate the Fokker Scourge, and the problem promptly (and fortunately) met its solution with the arrival on the Western Front of the DH2 scout, the first purpose-built British fighter. The DH2, a Geoffrey de Havilland-designed machine, may have been a pusher, but it was an agile single-seater with a Lewis machine gun fixed straight ahead, a top speed of eighty-five miles per hour at 7000 feet, and a ceiling of 14,000 feet. It was fitted with the same Monosoupape engine as the Vickers Fighter, but its performance was a great deal better, and it proved to be more than a match for the Fokker monoplane. One clear advantage was that its Lewis gun had an unrestricted rate of fire, whereas the Fokker's rate of fire was compromised by its synchronizing gear. At first, DH2s were distributed piecemeal around the squadrons, and it was considered an honour to be chosen to fly one. Frederick Powell:

> The DH2 was faster and more manoeuvrable than other aircraft and it was the prize for any pilot in the squadron to call himself the Scout pilot. At the time, an aeroplane and its pilot were indivisible. No pilot went and flew another pilot's aircraft. They were guarded as jealously as one's girlfriend. You can imagine the excitement of young fellows in their teens all wanting to be the squadron scout pilot. That happily came to me after I had had some success with the old Vickers Fighter.

On 7 February 1916, 24 Squadron arrived in France. Equipped only with DH2s, and commanded by Lanoe Hawker, its purpose was to lead the charge against the Fokker scourge. John Andrew, a flight commander with the squadron, remembers flying against the Eindeckers:

We could take on the Fokker singly in the DH2, because we had better manoeuvrability and better diving power. We usually patrolled five to ten miles. Quite a long way over, in time, not in distance. I could always get a good height, being lighter than some others. And that, of course, was the whole secret – to be above the other bloke. Because you could always translate height into speed if you were coming down. The fact that he was faster than you on the level didn't really matter, as long as you shove your nose down, which you could with the old DH2.

In the early days, up to the Somme, the Fokkers were coloured a sort of battleship grey. The Fokker's technique, when it attacked, was to get above you and come down on your tail. If he tried to dive on my tail, I could do a climbing turn, and then come down onto *him*, because the DH2 was solid in the air – it was strong. And then he would always put his nose down to the deck and dive away. But he couldn't do that against a DH2 because the one thing a DH2 could do was dive like a brick. It fell out of the sky! So when he started diving and he looked back, there was my DH2 sitting on his tail.

I used to fly in silk gloves with ordinary gloves over them otherwise my fingers got thoroughly frozen. I had enormous sheepskin boots with a rubber sole, the sheepskin on the inside, that came up to my thighs like salmon waders. I always wore silk underwear, then woollies on top. Never a collar and tie because I always wanted to be looking around and a collar would chafe my neck. And then a scarf and a leather coat on top of that. I was sat on the floor, in a wicker basket with some very thin runners which bolted straight down onto the floor.

Gwilym Lewis flew with 32 Squadron, the second DH2 squadron to arrive on the front, in May 1916:

The Fokkers tried to keep away from us because they knew we could outmanoeuvre them. We put them out of business. The excitement of a dogfight was very considerable. The odds were that you would be killed, or you would kill the other chap, and those are pretty big odds to play with, but as a rule, the Germans would try to disappear. Coming down again, after a dogfight, after that type of excitement, I would find that I was kind of exhausted. I would frequently get onto my camp bed and fall fast asleep for a couple of hours.

As the DH2 won control of the air back from the Fokker Eindecker, it was assisted by the bulky FE2b, a two-seater pusher machine, which for a time carried out a multi-purpose role; fighter, bomber, reconnaissance aircraft. George Taylor describes the FE2b's firepower:

There was a pilot and an observer. The observer was in the front nacelle, and the pilot was behind him, in front of the engine. In the observer's cockpit, you had one gun that could be fired in three positions. There were three clips for the gun to be mounted on: one firing down, one firing to the right and one firing to the left. When you fired, you had to put your knee against the mounting, or else the gun would blow out with the recoil. In the rear, you had one Lewis gun firing over the top plane. That was on moveable mounting, a plunger arrangement, where you pressed the plunger underneath and the gun used to go as high as possible to fire over the back plane.

In his diary, Harold Wyllie recorded a frustrating patrol during which his FE2b flew into the middle of a fight between DH2s and German LVG two-seaters. Wyllie's diary records that his observer could not take advantage of the opportunities which presented themselves:

> Went on patrol. Ordered by CO to take up Corporal Porter. Could not send him with Studd, the new pilot, so had to take him myself. At 7.55, we got into a hot action with five LVGs over Arras. They had been engaged and thrown into utter confusion by three de Havilland Scouts. I never saw such a mix up in the air. They came down for a couple of thousand feet with the little scouts after them like angry bees. We got into the middle of them at 9000 feet. Unfortunately, Corporal Porter completely lost his head. Magnificent shots, one dead nose on, and the other 200 feet under – but I could not get him to fire. He sat like a sick monkey doing nothing. The air was full of lead, and at last I banged him on the head and yelled, 'Fire, you bloody fool!' he woke up then and got off a drum at a machine overhead. My God, I was mad. We ought to have got two machines. As it was it is a great wonder we were not shot down. A damned silly way of getting killed too. I saw one Hun do a vertical nose dive for a couple of hundred feet, but I was too busy to follow his movements. Hope he was down and out. I think the action of the three scouts was the finest thing I have ever seen.

Archibald James remembers a disconcerting encounter with an FE2b pilot:

> One morning while we were having breakfast in the squadron, in walked an Irishman called Callaghan, a tall fellow, who had been a pupil at Norwich in my time, and whom we had all regarded as being something of a boastful character. He had spent some time

in Canada and claimed to have done a lot of cowboy and blah-blah, what have you. We all rather wrote him off. However, into breakfast walks Callaghan. And I said, 'Good morning, nice to see you.' And he said, 'I'm bloody hungry. Can I have some breakfast?' I said, 'Of course.' So I called the mess waiter to bring him some bacon and eggs. And he sat down and started eating.

And I then said to him, 'What are you doing here by yourself like this?' He had his full flying coat on. 'Oh,' he said, 'I got a lift here. It's the nearest aerodrome and I got a lift here.' So I said, 'You got a lift, what do you mean by that?' He said, 'I had an accident.' So I said, 'Well, what sort of an accident?' 'Well,' he said, 'you see, I was flying my FE2b and I bumped into three Fokkers. And we had a bit of a mix-up – and then my engine got hit and lost most of its power. So all I could do was to run for our lines. And I had an awfully nice man as my observer who'd done jolly well. And what the Fokkers did was to fall in turn behind me and shoot. But of course as they were only hitting the engine which protected me entirely it didn't make very much difference. I had plenty of gliding room. But unfortunately, in a pause in the attacks, my observer was stupid enough to look behind. And to do that he leant out sideways, whereupon a Fokker blew his head off.'

He carried on, 'I landed five or six hundred yards behind our lines, luckily close to a trench and I popped into it. And from there I was given a lift in a car to breakfast here. Thank you very much.' Which just shows one should never judge too quickly.

The arrival of the DH2, with support from the FE2b overcame the Fokker Scourge. The Royal Flying Corps took control of the skies, but the balance of air power had not shifted for the last time. Many different aircraft would come and go – as would so many of the young men who would fly them. The gladiatorial contests might evolve, as larger scale formation combats became common, but their essential nature would remain unchanged. Norman Macmillan, a pilot who joined 45 Squadron in 1917:

> There was, undoubtedly, a sense of chivalry in the air. We did not feel that we were shooting at men. We did not want to kill men. We were really trying to shoot down the machine. Our enemies were not the men in the machines. Our enemies were the machines themselves. It was a case of our machine is better than yours. And to try and down theirs was almost like a game of nine pins, a game of skill, a game in which we pitted ourselves against them and they pitted themselves against us, each to prove the other the better man. It was a difficult game, a game in which, in combat, we were swilling round without regard for horizon or for any other aspect of flight. We had been trained to fly with our noses on the horizon so as to keep our aircraft level, so we could turn right or left, roll the machines in accordance with the horizon which we could see. But in flight, in combat, there was no horizon, there was only a sphere. We flew like goldfish in a bowl, in all directions, swimming around the sky, sometimes standing on our tails, sometimes with our heads right down, sometimes over on our backs, sometimes at right angles to the ground; at any attitude. The only attitude which mattered was the one that enabled the nose of the aircraft to point where you wanted it to point – in the direction of the enemy, so that the guns could register hits. It was a fantastic type of flying and our machines could turn in such tiny circles that we simply swerved round in an amazingly small space of air, missing each other sometimes by inches as we swerved, missing enemy aircraft, missing our own aircraft, dodging in and out amongst the others in the sky, weaving the most fantastic patterns

and aiming all the time to place our noses where they ought to be.

In the first chapter of this book, we read Duncan Grinnell-Milne's impressions of flying over the Western Front; of the godlike and judicial sensations that overwhelmed him, and separated him from the world below. This sense of otherness was transformed into something darker by the individual nature of combat. Macmillan:

> Flying in the war bred a new type of man. A man whose attitude to living and fighting was distinct from that of any other men in the war. We had tremendous isolation that drove us in upon ourselves. Spiritually and emotionally we were shut in.

Such isolation set the airmen apart from the infantrymen who lived, fought, and died together. When courage was needed, the ground troops could look to each other for support. In the air, every man was reliant on his own efforts; he could not rely on another for inspiration at the crucial moment. Courage had to be drawn from within. Tryggve Gran was a Norwegian who flew with the Royal Flying Corps:

> Many times I have tried to define what is meant by courage. During my attachment to 70 Squadron I had the opportunity of seeing so many examples of daunt-lessness and bravery that I came to a conclusion. In my opinion, courage is the consequence of a strong will. Many a time I have seen a man make his way to his aircraft pale and dejected. The same man I have seen returning in a cold sweat and shattered, but with results which threw a lustre far beyond the Squadron's boundaries. A strong imagination makes the individual anxious and it is only by willpower and a sense of duty that he is carried through to the field of battle, where death stands ever at the door.

But what is willpower? How did one exercise it? Could a man simply climb into an aircraft, stiffen his sinews, conjure up the blood, and cry 'God for Harry, England and Saint George'? Some had little problem doing so. Tryggve Gran:

> I knew individuals who were naturally fearless. They lived for the moment and what they did not feel, they didn't see and what *could* happen, did not bother them. They lived and died unworried.

Most, however, had to overcome their fears, and it was in the many and various methods of coping with these fears that willpower was exercised. In the pages that follow, we will examine the lives of airmen on the Western Front, and their efforts to survive in a solitary, unfamiliar and often terrifying world.

7

Life and Death

Over a short period of time in early summer 1916, Albert Ball, fighter ace, wrote a number of letters to his parents:

> Will you do me the great favour of sending me one packet of marrow seeds, one of carrots, and a good big packet of mustard and cress? Also I would like a few flower seeds, one packet of sweet peas, and also a few packets of any other flowers that will grow quickly.

> I have only just missed being done in today. I was on the 7 o'clock patrol and I saw over the lines a lot of transports in a wood. I went over the lines in order to have a good look, so that I could report the place, but the old Huns did not like it. They surrounded us with shells from their Archie guns, and at last we were hit. One of my cylinders was smashed off, also the machine got a few through it. Only just missed my leg.

> I got up at 6 am. It was raining, so I could not fly. However I got my tools and set to work on my garden, for rainy days are just right for setting seeds. In three hours I just managed to dig a piece of ground 12 feet by 6 feet. In this I planted green peas. I hope to get in a few rows of beans tomorrow, if I have time to dig up another piece of ground.

L. P. Hartley's *The Go-Between* opens with the words 'The past is a foreign country: they do things differently there.' It would be easy to dismiss Albert Ball's letters as quaint reflections of a different era, but that would be to miss the point. The best way to understand the feelings of the Great War airmen is to examine their conduct in their spare time. It was then that they reflected on their fears and faced them in a multitude of different ways. Some, like Ball, with his peas and mustard and cress, sought refuge in normality. Some imposed themselves on their surroundings with acts of defiance. Some drank themselves into a stupor. And some, like Stanley Walters, could not face their fears at all:

> It would start by nightmares. Going down in flames.
> The flames all around me. I would wake up screaming
> and shouting. After a time, it affected everything.

We may live in a world of more freely expressed emotions, but such emotions did not begin with us. And nor did the attitudes that people adopt to being alive. Some people are, broadly speaking, optimists, who believe that life is light, interspersed with brief periods of darkness. Others are pessimists. Some live for a purpose, others do not. Some think the world a funny place, many find little to laugh about. Some engage with the world, some rebel against it and some merely endure it. For many, the key to survival is simply the ability to strap on a pair of blinkers and face the day.

And now consider the young British airmen in France, almost a hundred years ago. These men were stepping out of their accustomed lives into a quite unfamiliar world, where each day brought closer a likely fate. They feared death, they feared injury, they feared the loss of their friends, and they feared their own fears, which might betray them as cowards, or drive them mad over weeks and months of torment. Ira Jones, of 74 Squadron, describes the sensation that overcame him at the end of the patrol described in the last chapter:

> The feeling of safety produced an amazing reaction of fear, the intensity of which was terrific. Suddenly I experienced a physical and moral depression which produced cowardice. I suddenly felt that I was totally unsuited for air fighting and that I would never be persuaded to fly over the lines again. For quite five minutes I shivered and shook while my aeroplane careered about the sky almost uncontrolled. I had completely lost control of myself and my moral resistance was at its lowest ebb.

Men such as Jones might be forgiven for viewing this new world as an unhappy place that must be endured. Did they have the imagination or the luxury to search for light in their situation? Or humour? How might they rebel against a military machine, mount a challenge in such bleak circumstances? Were these men not having to strap on their blinkers every morning, along with their leather helmets and silk scarves, in order to be able to face the day?

Not necessarily. We have already seen that many of the airmen were (non-ideologically speaking) free thinkers and individualists, innovators and risk-takers. The risks that they took were not confined to the air, and, set down in a world of military conformity, these men appeared both rebellious and confrontational. When Archibald James came back from leave, he brought with him eight breaches of discipline:

> Before returning to France I had bought from the local pack of harriers in Sussex, four pairs of hounds. These I took out with me to France. And when I arrived, they were greeted with a minimum of enthusiasm by my ardent soldier commanding officer, but with great applause by my brigadier. A considerably strained relationship ensued but the hounds were great fun. I

hunted hares of which there were quite a number in Bayeux-Armentières sector, with a most distinguished field, beautifully mounted on their first chargers. There were only two or three little thorn hedges in the whole of our area, which extended nearly up to the gun lines. And these we periodically jumped as often as possible to keep up the illusion that we were a hunting club.

Given his propensity for novelty, and his relatively comfortable, stable living conditions, it is only an airman among Great War combatants who could feasibly have attempted to mimic the life of a country gentleman while actively engaged in a struggle as bloody as the hare's. It is a measure of the airman's reputation as a breed apart that he was allowed to get away with it. And what was Archibald James doing if he was not laughing at his situation?

When Frederick Powell was placed in command of 41 Squadron, in August 1917, he devised a novel means of passing the time:

> As the squadron commander, my most important duty was to keep up the morale of the squadron, all the pilots. That meant that one had to keep them occupied during the non-flying periods. I was fortunate enough to have a spare hangar on the aerodrome, and I thought what a marvellous thing I could do, if I got a lot of cement, which was then very hard to come by, and make myself a rink where the officers could roller skate.
>
> In order to get our skates, it was an order that anybody who went on leave had to come back with two pairs of roller skates, and it seemed in no time at all, we had quite a nice rink. But then unfortunately the supply of cement ran out. The way we got round that was that my sergeant major knew the sergeant major up the lines, and with a bottle of whisky offered here and there, I received so many bags of cement. Unfortunately

I couldn't get enough cement for one last corner of the rink.

Just at that time, our squadron was visited by General Higgins, and as he was walking past this hangar, he could hear my officers inside, making the dickens of a noise. I tried to steer him away, but to my horror he walked straight up to the hangar and looked through. He turned to me and said, 'That's a very excellent idea!' and snapping that remark up quickly, I said, 'Well, I'm sorry sir, but I can't finish the thing, I'm short of two bags of cement to finish the far corner.' He said, 'Well, if you put in a requisition in a way in which I can supply it, I'll see that you get two bags.' So I said, 'Thank you very much', and I wrote in and asked if I could have two bags of cement for the floor of my erecting shop. No one knew what an erecting shop was; neither did I, but sure enough I got my two bags of cement and finished the rink.

We used to play badminton on roller skates in there. We even played rugger on roller skates, but as it was a cement floor, I had to flood it with half an inch of water so that when you fell, you at least had the chance of sliding rather than grazing yourself. I think we must have been the only unit in France with its own roller skating rink.

On this occasion, as befits a squadron commander, Powell was acting in the collective interest – although collectivity seems not to have stretched quite as far as the rank and file. All the same, Powell's initiative certainly brought the officers together, united in the preposterous and therefore healthy pursuit of roller badminton.

A particularly fine example of ingenuity took place in early 1917. It came from the enterprising mind of well-known actor and commanding officer of 41 Squadron, Robert Loraine. Loraine built a theatre on his aerodrome at

Léalvillers, and began mounting productions, the parts being taken by officers and men of the squadron. Quite how the 'actors' managed to combine their evening performances with combat flying is a matter for conjecture, but one wonders how many suffered stage fright after a day spent under attack over enemy lines. In February 1917, this makeshift repertory company performed two anti-war plays by George Bernard Shaw – *O'Flaherty VC* (performed by the officers) and *The Inca of Perusalem* (performed by the men). The wondrous circus of good intentions had come to town, and Frederick Powell was there to enjoy it:

> Robert Loraine, our CO in 41 Squadron, had seen a Red Cross hut which nobody seemed to own. So all the officers went off in cars, and we dismantled the hut and brought it back to our aerodrome and rebuilt it. It made a wonderful theatre, once we'd put in a stage. It held about 250 people and we started doing plays. We had decided to stage two unpublished plays of Bernard Shaw's, when, one day, I saw an article in *John Bull* written by Bernard Shaw, urging young men not to enlist. I saw this and I said to Loraine, 'You know, there is a job for a public assassin, a fellow trained by the Government to kill people like this.' And then, one week afterwards, who should arrive to stay with us – but Bernard Shaw himself.
>
> Loraine introduced me. 'Oh, Shaw,' he said, 'this is Powell. This is the boy who wants to shoot you.' 'How do you do?' said Shaw, 'I am very pleased to meet you. And you know, you might have chosen somebody worse.'
>
> At dinner, Loraine excused himself, and said, 'I've got to go down. We are doing a dress rehearsal for the men, *The Inca of Perusalem*, one of your plays, Shaw. Powell, will you bring Shaw down as soon as he's finished his meal?' So I took Bernard Shaw down to the theatre and I sat on a seat just behind him, and I was

worried to see that all the way through this play he roared with laughter. He roared so much that he actually cried and brought out a handkerchief to wipe his eyes. In those days, Shaw had a ginger beard, and I sat behind him, watching it wobbling up and down.

It struck me at the time that it was extremely bad form for a playwright to laugh at his own comedy until he cried, and I leant forward to him, when it was finished, and I said, 'I am so glad, sir, that you appreciate our poor efforts at your play.' He turned round, still wiping his eyes, and he said, 'Do you know, if I had thought it was going to be anything like that I wouldn't have written it . . .'

The majority of airmen did not chase hares, wear skates or slap on the greasepaint, but many defied the war on a more modest scale. Some became genuinely fascinated by their new surroundings. One of these accidental tourists was Harold Wyllie, who recorded the following in his diary in late 1914, while an observer with 6 Squadron:

Went into the town and looked at three churches. All were built of yellow brick, two apparently built 1300–1400. The detail was not good but one of them contained some magnificent Renaissance wood carving which had more go in it than anything of the kind I have ever seen. It seems funny to be studying Flemish church architecture with the guns booming away outside.

It may seem funny to Wyllie, but to act normally in the midst of war is a true act of defiance. As is the ability to maintain a sense of the ridiculous. The following entries from Wyllie's diary were written in early 1915:

Chinnery and Barton were loafing round one of the French towns when they saw 'Femme Sage' on a brass plate, and jumping to the conclusion that 'Femme Sage' meant a fortune teller, they knocked at the door and asked to see Madame. An old hag answered the knock, shook her head and placed her hands before her stomach with a gesture indicating great size. 'Non! Ici pour le bébé', she said, to the great joy of the crowd that had collected to see what on earth two British officers might want with the local midwife.

Russell was wandering round a church and stopped in an absent-minded way near the altar when a Frenchman came up and crossed himself whereupon Russell acknowledged the salute. The first time a British officer had taken a salute for the Almighty, I suppose.

Arthur Rhys Davids, of 56 Squadron, had been a King's Scholar at Eton College, and was waiting to take up his place at Balliol College, Oxford, once the war was over. He was an intelligent, contemplative young man, who once told Maurice Baring that he carried a small volume of Blake's poetry in his pocket just in case he should come down behind German lines. According to Baring:

> He was passionately fond of books and poetry, and his mixture of scholarship, enthusiasm, fun, courage, skill and airmanship made one feel that if these were the sort of pilots we had, whatever else might happen, we should never be beaten in the air.

In a letter to a friend, Rhys Davids wrote:

> My present existence here [56 Squadron at Estrée Blanche] is a delightful mixture of fact, which is the tiresome though somewhat amusing war, and imagination, which is the time I spend reading books and letters. I have discovered a Belgian worth considering – one Maurice Maeterlinck whose poems have been translated into very good English by one Miall. It is very obscure à la Blake, but quite thrilling.

If we consider these men, perhaps the common denominator is that none of them remained passive. Whether driven by amusement, defiance or curiosity, whether engaged in grand schemes, absurd hobbies or the pursuit of normality, they shared a determination to retain control over those parts of their lives which could be controlled. For many airmen, however, free time was more likely to be spent engaged in a less active pastime: drinking. In today's newspapers we are bombarded with tales of the 'binge drinking' habits of the young. We are supposed to be shocked by the recent decline in public morals. It is enlightening therefore to discover that not only did Great War airmen consume large amounts of alcohol, but they too described their activities as 'binges'. In a letter posted after Christmas 1916, Horace Heales, a sergeant in 24 Squadron (and a teetotaller) wrote to his sisters, describing the squadron's seasonal binge, conducted just behind the lines to a backdrop of continuous gunfire:

Now for the 'Christmas Tales' (not by Charles Dickens). On Xmas Day, the corporals and men had their dinner at 4.45 pm and the mess orderlies were, for a change, the Warrant Officers and Sergeants. The dinner consisted of roast pork and turkey, brussel sprouts, potatoes, Xmas pudding and custard. Nearly every man had two helpings. This was washed down with copious draughts of BEER and lemonade. The tables were laid with white muslin cloth, two clean plates per man, no licking of the plates for the pudding and plenty of glasses. The Major and Captains came in and wished the men a Merry Xmas and a speedy and successful end to the War. The men replied with 'He's a jolly good fellow', three cheers, and 'God save the King'.

After dinner a concert was held in the Mess room, all officers and several trench officers were present. A stage had been rigged up, with footlights, scenery, etc and a good entertainment was enjoyed, songs and con-juring by officers and men being given. During this, there was a plentiful supply of fruit – apples, oranges, dates in the small oval boxes (which you both fancy), figs, grapes, fruits of all kinds. And, whisper it not near a Band of Hope meeting, BEER, WHISKY, CHAM-PAGNE etc. As was to be expected, there were some comical and pitiable sights to be seen, but taken as a whole, things went very smoothly. The concert finished about 10.30 pm, but not for the Sergeants' Mess. We were soon joined in there by several of the officers (I forgot to say that they were also in our mess until 3.30 in the morning on Xmas Eve) and between the lively spirits there was a lively time.

On Boxing Day, it was our turn for a feed and social evening. We had a similar dinner to that the men had on Xmas Day. With the addition of a few fancy pastries made by our cook. This was at 5.30 pm. In the evening, our concert was again invaded by the officers (who seem to prefer our evenings to those in their own mess). They turned the place upside down, broke plates and glasses, also the door off the hinges, fell through the floor, bulged the walls, went outside and came back covered in mud, having fallen in rain water pits. Some of the officers and two of the sergeants got hopelessly drunk. One officer got his eye kicked by a sergeant whilst dancing, you can guess that it was not a gentle waltz.

One sergeant kept on crying hysterically for a pilot who had been lost the same day, and couldn't be pacified. Another was drinking neat whisky and Benedictine liqueur like water and soon became lively. By the aid of grease paints, they gave this man a gorilla-like appearance, which caused immense fun. He tried to kiss and cuddle the officers, who thoroughly enjoyed it, and accepted the embraces gracefully.

Three sergeants tried to get to bed early, but were sorry afterwards. The whole of the remainder, officers as well, went to their bunks and dragged them out of bed, giving them no opportunity to dress and took them back to finish the evening in their pants.

You would hardly imagine a scene like this just behind the lines, with guns booming all the time, and if anyone enjoyed themselves better than this squadron, they were lucky. You may wonder, after all this tale, if I was merry with wine, but they know in the Mess that they cannot force me to do anything that I don't want to do. In fact the Sergeant Major describes me as the jolliest teetotaller that he has ever met.

As one side was getting drunk, so was the other. Hans Schröder, a German leutnant flying on the Eastern Front experienced a night of wildness similar to Horace Heales' but with a touch of added aggression. At the beginning of his evening, late in 1916, punch was added to the usual champagne, and the fun started when a guest had a glass of champagne tipped over his head. The guest protested but was informed, with Teutonic directness, that if he didn't like it, he could leave. Suddenly, another man was seized by four airmen, dragged outside and tossed into the dirt. Returning with handfuls of mud, he began to hurl it around the room, whereupon somebody turned out the lights and an orgy of destruction began. Plates, bottles, glasses were smashed, tables overturned, chairs hurled through the air, until the man who had been dragged outside left the room. A group went to find him, but could not, and in their understandable disappointment they broke his windows and fired their pistols into his door. On his eventual return, he was appointed 'master of the revels' and the evening continued. One unsuspecting guest was subjected to the 'funnel trick'. A funnel was slid under his belt, a coin placed on his forehead and he was told that he had to deposit the coin into the funnel without using his hands. He arched backwards, with the coin on his forehead, but as he was about to attempt the feat a group of airmen rushed forward and poured wine and beer into the funnel, flooding his crotch. As they did so, 'the spectators indulged in Indian war whoops'. The party continued until the early hours of the morning, and the following day, according to Schröder, the walls and ceiling required 'a thorough whitewashing'.

Such binges may have seemed hilarious and high-spirited, but in a sense they were anything but. The men who drank so heavily were not engaging with the world, they were anaesthetizing themselves against it. They were accepting the unhappiness of their situation. Frederick Powell:

> The centre of every Royal Flying Corps squadron seemed to be the bar. That may offend a lot of people, but it is perfectly true. When you think of these boys, with the tensions they lived through, they would come in, in the evening, and ask about their best friend, 'Where is he? Where's George?' 'Oh, he bought it this afternoon.' The gloom would come, the morale would die and the reaction was immediate: 'Well, come on chaps, what're you going to have?' That was the sort of spirit that kept us going, and though people are against alcohol, it played a magnificent part in keeping up morale. It was to avoid the crying.

Winged Victory is an extraordinary novel, published in 1934, which relates the experiences of a Sopwith Camel pilot, Tom Cundall, during the last year of the war. Although a novel, the book is very carefully crafted from the genuine experiences of its author, Victor Yeates, who flew Camels with 46 and 80 Squadrons in 1918. While the aerial combats are vividly described, it is the internal life of the central character that grips the reader, in particular his struggle to control his fears, a struggle which closely mirrored the author's own. This may be fiction, and the conversations may be imagined, but the sentiments were once deeply felt. In one passage, Cundall contemplates the nature of his fears. He decides that he is weak-nerved, as he cannot reason his fears out of existence. That being so, he wonders whether his nerves stem from a fear of death or from a love of life. It is the latter, he feels certain. 'So long as there was warmth in the belly, so life was worth living; the delicious glow of base animal life in the cunning belly.' The animal within him, Tom decides, is responsible for his fears, and the best way to appease the animal is to indulge it, feed it alcohol, offer it girls, while threatening it with the knowledge that, if it cries, it will be shamed. It cannot be reasoned with – only menaced and cajoled, and Tom spends much time cajoling it. When the reader experiences the world through Tom's drunken eyes, we feel his relief, as the memory of a dead friend is consumed in the alcoholic swell:

> Tom sat drinking himself dead to the world. There was a crowd. What was it all about? He ... he ... didn't know. Didn't want to know ... Someone killed ... Bill. No, there was Bill. Someone dead ... didn't know ... He tried to get up. Hands helped him. He was clinging to Bill. Bill was clinging to him. They were outside. A lot of people were laughing. Damn funny. He laughed. He was on the ground. He swore. He couldn't walk. His feet got tangled. Bill was as bad. They were rolling in a ditch. Hell. The world was spinning. Couldn't get out. Sleep there. Then he was in bed, alone. The pillow was sinking, sinking down endlessly.

But drunken relief only lasted so long:

> Whenever Tom woke up depression returned like a load in the pit of his stomach; he felt sick with it. In the morning, breakfast filled him with nausea.

E. F. Van der Riet, a South African pilot with 55 Squadron, recalls the end of an alcoholic evening within the squadron in late 1917:

> I noticed the feelings between Collett and Jones to be running pretty high, so I tactfully suggested bed. We turned in and Collett, to my surprise, locked the door. It was a wise precaution for almost immediately the door was tried and Jones demanded admittance. We took no notice and he repeated his demand and threatened to blow the door open, and true to his word fired his revolver through the keyhole. Lead sprayed into the room, missing us but puncturing Collett's immaculate cavalry boots which he had just taken off. With considerable intrepidity, he grabbed open the door and wrested the gun from Jones. It was all rather ridiculous for Jones then went quietly off to bed without another word.

Orlando Lennox Beater, an officer in the same squadron, wrote in his diary at the same period:

> For the past three or four nights there has been a rum issue which by the way, has had a most demoralizing effect on some of the younger squadron members. They say the army has been the making of a good many youngsters, I should be surprised if it has not ruined a great many more.

Of course alcohol was not always knocked back with desperate abandon. Reginald Fulljames, a pilot with 53 Squadron, points out that 'life was always dangerous, and a wise man was not drunk too often.' Most airmen drank only to the extent that they could relax and enjoy each other's company. Cecil Lewis recalls a typical evening's entertainment:

> There was an old upright piano in the mess with keys so yellow, they looked as if the keyboard had been

smoking for about fifty years. And we had one chap who played the piano, and he'd sit down in the evenings, and there were three notes missing and it was out of tune. It was a terrible piano. But it didn't matter. He'd play the tunes of the time, the reviews on in town, the things we knew by heart and used to sing in chorus. Occasionally a bit of Chopin on the nights when we felt that sort of thing was appropriate. All very easy and go as you please.

The tunes that the flyers sung were often airmen's adaptations of popular songs. A song called 'The Only Way', from a musical comedy, *Tonight's the Night*, was turned into this, which can be heard sung by Simon Ward in the 1976 film *Aces High*:

> If by some delightful chance,
> When you're flying out in France,
> Some old Boche machine you meet,
> Very slow and obsolete,
> Don't turn around to watch your tail,
> Tricks like that are getting stale;
> Just put down your beastly nose,
> And murmur, 'Chaps, here goes!'
>
> *It's the only, only way,*
> *It's the only trick to play;*
> *He's the only Hun, you're the only Pup,*
> *And he's only getting the wind right up,*
> *So go on, and do not stop*
> *Till his tail's damn near your prop.*
> *If he only crashes this side in flames,*
> *Well, you'll only know they'll believe your claims –*
> *So keep him right*
> *In the Aldis sight –*
> *It's the o-o-only way!*

Some of the most popular entertainment available to everybody on the front, not just the airmen, was provided by the concert parties. Tommy Keele had served in the 11th Middlesex Regiment, before joining the Ace of Spades Concert Party in 1917. In an all-male acting troupe, Keele played the female roles, making him one of the British Army's most unusual – and if we believe his protests, one of its most misunderstood – corporals:

> People didn't always know I was a man dressed up as a woman. At Arras, some officers from one of the regiments came to see our show and they teased their colonel that one of the girls in the show was a real girl and the other one was a female impersonator and they bet him 50 francs that he couldn't pick out the real girl. Dolly Clair, the other 'girl' appeared first. He was much fatter than me. I didn't come on stage until the end of the show. I walked on in a very low cut evening dress. Halfway down my chest I used to put a dark red line and then shade the line off so the side was a little pink. It looked like a cleavage and when he saw me the colonel said, 'That one is the female.' So I had to go along to his barracks to prove I was a little lance corporal in the Middlesex Regiment. He was disgusted.
>
> We were playing in the evening, and in the afternoon the theatre would show films. In these films, girls would be slightly naked and when a girl had her leg up in the air, the cinema operator would stop the machine so we could all have a jolly good look. Well, the 'girls' from the other concert parties would come to watch the films and we would sit there and listen to them talking to each other. They made pansy bloody noises to each other and I just hated them. They were nearly all poofs. All those sissy sounds coming from them, I thought, 'Am I going to be lumped in as a sissy because I'm playing girls?' Ooh, how I hated playing 'girl'.

Airmen were not tied down to the official army entertainments, however. They could – commanding officer permitting – jump on a tender in the evening, travel into a nearby town, and take advantage of whatever pleasures they could find. For Robin Rowell, this meant a favourite restaurant in Amiens:

Leading out of one of the main streets, there is a tiny by-way down which one would not venture without good reason, for even its name 'Rue de Corps Nu Sans Tête' seems to tell of a horrible crime. Three or four doors down on the left, you will find 'Aux Huîtres', a fish and oyster shop, measuring some 15 by 24 feet in all. At the far end, you will see a spiralling staircase leading up to the room above known as 'The Restaurant', which has a long table down one side directly over the counter in the shop below and another table across the window, leaving room for two or three people to stand up at once on the remaining unoccupied space. Its total seating is probably eighteen and you must keep your appointed time, or you don't eat. The habitués are mostly Frenchmen, with the addition of the few Englishmen who got to know of it. As you enter for your meal, you must do so in the correct manner, saluting as you open the door, and saying to everyone, 'Bonjour, messieurs!' – 'et mon Capitaine!' if you happened to spot any French soldier of high rank. By this time, you will have lost your hat, stick, and coat, and some guilty person will rise from his seat looking as if he had no business in the place at that hour, and with a word of profound apology, he will offer you his seat. Once seated, you must get on with the job, for everything there is done in double-quick time by Jeanne, who talks nineteen to the dozen at the age of forty. How she gets through the work, I don't know. The cooking is excellent. You can get anything to eat that you can think of, if only you can find its right name; and if you don't mind my giving you a tip, order a rum omelette to finish up with. But do it properly – order it first, then wait till Jeanne is halfway down the room, turn round in your chair, and shout, 'Eh! Jeanne! Dites donc! N'oubliez pas le rhum!' You will then hear Jeanne talking all the way down the stairs, mumbling about the scarcity of rum in the land of the Lily.

There were other reasons for going into town. Frederick Powell:

On the bad days, that is when it's pouring with rain with a low cloud ceiling, there was no flying. We then used to get into the cars and go off to the various towns, places like Amiens. And St Omer, that was good, and that was where most of these boys learnt a little more about life than they would ever have done in normal civil life, because we used to go to the various estaminets, and then every town of any size at all had its house of entertainment, which I believe is called a brothel, and so people gathered, although they were young in years, it wasn't long before they were quite worldly-wise men.

These houses of entertainment, which Powell believes are called brothels, became very important to young men, barely out of childhood, brought up on Victorian notions of virtue. Away from home, unlikely to survive the war, these boys were at least discovering something of the world before they left it:

On dud nights, we'd go into Toul or Nancy, have a good feed and then go round to see the girls. They were always pleased to welcome 'Les Anglais Aviateurs, plenty money'. The meeting room, as we called it, reeked of cheap scent and the floor was bare for dancing and over in the corner was an antiquated piano, minus a few ivory keys. On the walls was a display of nude females and underneath, scrappy quotations. Madame would see us all with a drink, clap her hands, and in would stream the mademoiselles with a piece of tulle draped diagonally across and shoes and stockings. The piano stool was placed in the centre of the room and each female mounted in turn and posed as Venus, one of us revolving the stool, to allow the audience to pass comment, favourable or otherwise. There was Marguerite, the little tubby one who looked lovely. Fifi, the tall, dark one was also a favourite. There was one with a very flat nose like a boxer, who we nicknamed 'Pug' and a very big girl with fat legs that we called 'Tiny'. Fun ran high and we spent a lot of money on cheap champagne, which was all that mattered to the girls.

Some of the young men discovered a little too much of the world. Venereal diseases were not uncommon amongst the men of the flying services. The fictional airman Biggles may have fallen in love with a French girl who turned out to be an enemy spy, but his creator, W. E. Johns, received a surprise of his own from the opposite sex: according to his casualty form, Johns, a pilot with 55 Squadron IAF, was admitted to hospital in 1918 suffering from both syphilis and gonorrhea. Biggles reacted to his experience by keeping women at a safe distance for the rest of his flying career. Perhaps *Affaire de Coeur*, the story in which he meets his femme fatale, ought to be read as a morality tale. But there were many happy affairs, flirtations and friendships formed between English airmen and French and Belgian girls. Archibald James:

Merville, a little Flanders country town, was quite an agreeable place and earned a certain measure of renown

from the fact that in the Estaminet de la Gare, a little
inn on our side of the town, there was a ravishingly
pretty girl called Marie Louise, who became the subject
of 'Marie Louise of Merville' – a song sung in the
London music halls. I got to know Marie Louise very
well, and after the war, when I went back to do a tour of
the old battlefields, I enquired about Marie Louise, and
I was told that she'd married a man in Boulogne, and I
got her address. I called on her, but she wasn't there.
I'd have loved to have seen her again.

For all the stresses brought about by wartime flying, and
the various means of relieving them, the fact remains that,
in physical terms, life on the squadrons was a great deal
more comfortable than life in the trenches. It even compared favourably with life back at home. George Taylor, an
observer with 25 Squadron, was aware of this:

> I'd been home on leave to find that everybody was
> hungry. In the trenches, you were lucky to get a hot
> meal. But in the Flying Corps, we had nice mess
> rooms, nice billets, we had good food, no shortage. We
> had breakfast, dinner and high tea. For tea, we'd have
> cold meat and vegetables. For lunch, we'd have a hot
> meal, a roast, steak and kidney puddings. Eggs and
> bacon for breakfast. I don't know anybody in England
> who was getting that. I don't even know where it came
> from.

The officers and men of 56 Squadron, commanded by Major
Richard Blomfield, led a life that would have been the envy
of those in the trenches, had they known of it. The squadron
had its own band, made up of professional musicians,
as well as an extremely well stocked shop. Hubert Charles,
an officer who served as an engineer in 56 Squadron,
remembers:

When we arrived, you couldn't get anything at Vert Galant, so Major Blomfield opened a shop. The two men he provided for the purpose were grey-haired men who had been shopkeepers in peacetime. And Blomfield was clever – all the stock came from the 'back stairs'. The shop belonged to the men's mess, and all the money that it made was men's mess only – the officer's mess never got a penny. Well, it was such a fantastic success that it made money like water. When the men wanted to buy an expensive ice cream machine to add to the mess, the profits from the shop bought it. On a hot day, it would be nothing unusual for the shop to sell 400 bottles of soft drinks. Every squadron was sending somebody along to buy half a dozen. You could get razor blades, chocolate, postcards, anything you wanted.

The lives of airmen differed from those of the men in the trenches in many ways. When 74 Squadron was visited by General Plumer, Commander of the Second Army, in May 1918, the general was somewhat taken aback by the casual appearance of the flyers he met. It was most unmilitary. Ira Jones recorded the visit:

He [the general] flattered us with his praises of our fighting efforts but I have suspicions that he did not approve of either the cleanliness or the mode of our dress. Naturally, when off duty, we are not particular about our dress as we believe in being comfortable to-day, as tomorrow we may be dead.

The desire for comfort extended to the airmen's surroundings, which could be almost palatial. Frederick Powell:

The mess I was in was a chateau, a beautiful chateau with wonderful inlaid doors and chandeliers. It really was a magnificent place, and it belonged to a gentleman who was supposed to be French, but whose name

203

was Schatzmann. And Schatzmann tried to discipline us and he put notices all round the hall saying, 'Officers will put their hats in the cloakroom and not leave them in the hall' – things like that. My commanding officer was Robert Loraine, the actor, and he spoke the most marvellous French, and he and Schatzmann did not see eye to eye. Schatzmann was so interested in his chateau, he had no thought of us fighting his confounded war for him. Our aerodrome was on his land, and on one occasion one of our boys overshot and ran into a cornfield, where he crashed. I was up in the office that morning, and Schatzmann came across and he said, 'Excuse me, major, I understand you have had an accident. One of your planes has landed in the cornfield.' I thought he was being rather decent, so I said, 'Oh, thank you, Mr Schatzmann, for your enquiry, but the boy wasn't hurt at all.' And he said, 'I was not thinking of your boy, but about my corn.' This was why Schatzmann was not very popular with us. And I am afraid we damaged his chateau terribly, disgracefully.

Of course, the standard of the billets could vary. No. 32 Squadron had spent the summer of 1916 living comfortably at Vert Galant, but on moving to Léalvillers in October the standard of accommodation fell sharply, as Gwilym Lewis moaned in a letter to his parents:

> We have really come to a most 'delightful' place, and if anyone wanted to become thoroughly miserable for any length of time they have only to come here . . . We live in tents and most of us have tent boards, so of course we ought not to grumble. It is a mere detail that everything is covered in a thick film of moisture; after all, I have a perfectly good wick lamp to dry my socks by, and although one's servant does deposit a nice layer of slime on the floor every time he enters, there is nothing to beat a hearty indoor slide, is there? . . . The 'Mess'

consists of a large hangar, inside which is a perfectly good table. This is surrounded by a rather superior type of mud, the rain being cleansed before it falls on it by filtering through the canvas. This is where one sits during the better part of the day and either gambles or waits for the next meal.

Despite Lewis' sarcasm, the fact of the matter was that, while infantrymen were forever being shunted between the front line and the rear, airmen could settle into stable surroundings and relax in between shows. Arthur Gould Lee, in a letter to his future wife:

> We've had a wonderful, hot summer's afternoon, wearing nothing much but towels, and lazing the hours away by the canal, swimming, reading, writing (especially me!), but now it's close on 6 o'clock, and I must get ready for patrol.

Probably the greatest single influence on morale within a squadron was its commander, often a young man in his early twenties. When 85 Squadron was commanded by distant Canadian ace, William 'Billy' Bishop, between April and July 1918, it was an anarchic squadron, but when it was taken over by Edward 'Mick' Mannock it became a more comfortable, assured unit. Raised in poverty, abandoned by his father, a prisoner of the Turks early in the war, aged almost thirty when he arrived in France, a committed socialist, a supporter of Irish Home Rule, a future Victoria Cross winner, a man with a hatred of Germans, 'society' women, and the British class system, Mannock might not seem the average British airman, but he represents a definite type within the Flying Corps: the social outsider who finds a home in an edgy, extemporal world. Mannock was a greatly admired pilot, possibly the finest British tactician of the war, and generous in his nurturing of young pilots. As well as giving them advice and encouragement, he would on occasion share an undoubted personal victory with other members of his patrol, in an effort to unite those around him.

Despite his active role as leader, Mannock was careful not to distance himself from the men under him. According to Ira Jones, his favourite prank, which every newcomer to the squadron would have to experience, was to enter the new boy's room in the early hours of the morning, accompanied by another airman. Pretending to be helplessly drunk, Mannock would make retching noises as though he was about to be sick, at which point the accomplice would splash some water from a jug onto the floor. The new boy would jump up in horror, and receive the rest of the water over his legs. Yet for all Mannock's efforts at uniting the squadron and allaying its collective worries, he was himself engaged, as will be seen, in a bitter ongoing struggle with fears of his own.

No. 85 Squadron may have had a good commanding officer, but other squadrons were less fortunate. In his diary, Harold Wyllie recorded the damage that could be done by an ineffectual leader:

The commanding officer asked me the reason for the state of nerves of so many of the officers and I could not give him the only answer: 'A fish rots at the head first.' The squadron has got demoralized and jumpy, simply because officers, in addition to the great strain of the work in the air, have been so hunted and insulted by the commanding officer on the ground that they don't know where they are at all. And yet the commanding officer would never realize what he is doing or think otherwise than that he was a most efficient squadron commander – and not a subject for ridicule and contempt throughout the whole corps. Another squadron commander remarked to me the other day, 'Oh, that fellow – he didn't say 'fellow' – is so incompetent that he is certain to be made a wing commander soon.' Ever since he took command of this squadron, I have been obliged to use the utmost tact to keep on speaking terms with the other flight commanders and their officers. The same thing has occurred with regards the senior NCOs who have been daggers drawn. Truly a pretty kettle of fish.

By concentrating on the wellbeing of others, a squadron commander could significantly improve his own state of mind. In June 1918, Mick Mannock had been at home on leave, and without his flying or his men to occupy his mind, his underlying fears erupted into obsessional thoughts of death. In this state, he visited his old friend and father figure, Jim Eyles. Eyles remembers:

On one occasion, we were sitting in the front talking quietly when his eyes fell to the floor, and he started to tremble violently. This grew into a convulsive straining. He cried uncontrollably, muttering something that I could not make out. His face, when he lifted it, was a terrible sight. Saliva and tears were running down his face; he couldn't stop it. His collar and shirt front were soaked through. He smiled weakly at me when he saw me watching and tried to make light of it; he would not talk about it at all. I felt helpless not being able to do anything. He was ashamed to let me see him in this condition but could not help it, however hard he tried.

At the end of his leave Mannock returned to France, where he was promoted and given command of 85 Squadron. The foisting of a new responsibility onto Mannock's shoulders focused his attention outward. He wasted no time in imposing himself on the squadron, encouraging the pilots and passing on his knowledge. His new men were inspired and Mannock himself was revitalized. The terrible dreams that were plaguing him abated, his preoccupation with death faded and he discovered new energy and enthusiasm – if only briefly. But it was not long before the death of a friend renewed his miseries.

It is all very well to speak of defiance, humour and an engagement with life as key elements of an airman's mental survival, but the modern reader may feel that these attitudes are mere sticking plasters to be placed over the essential problem; a fundamental unwillingness to admit to, and deal with, the fears themselves. It is certainly true that such issues were rarely acknowledged or discussed, but to criticize this approach is pointless as it fails to consider the attitudes of the time. Men were conditioned to display self-control and repress fear. Mannock's shame when he breaks down in the presence of Jim Eyles is an example of this; the fact that his fears have been seen does not, in any constructive manner, ease them.

The world of the squadrons, with its horseplay and emotional reserve, was the world of the English public school, transported to France. When the newly formed 74 Squadron suffered its first casualty, its young officers were shocked when that evening's dinner and games went ahead as usual. Mourning, it was made clear, would take place only in private. The world of the public school, and the attitudes it engendered, were discussed by E. M. Forster in his 1920 essay, *Notes on an English Character*. According to Forster:

> With its boarding-houses, its compulsory games, its system of prefects and fagging, its insistence on good form and *esprit de corps*, it [the English public school] produces a type whose weight is out of all proportion to its numbers. They go forth into the world with well-developed bodies, fairly developed minds, and un-developed hearts. And it is this undeveloped heart that is largely responsible for the difficulties of Englishmen abroad. An undeveloped heart – *not a cold one*. For it is not that the Englishman can't feel – it is that he is afraid to feel. He has been taught at his public school that

feeling is bad form. He must not express great joy or sorrow, or even open his mouth too wide when he talks – his pipe might fall out if he did. He must bottle up his emotions, or let them out only on a very special occasion.

And if he is scared to feel in the ordinary run of things, how much more must a Great War airman be afraid to feel, when he is terrified that if he does, he will not be able to stop, and will end up by breaking down. These men had to fly day after day, for nobody knew how long. It is not at all surprising that they behaved as they did, and sought means of controlling their fears, other than by expressing them. We should not judge these men by modern standards.

Notwithstanding their resistance to visible emotion, it was important for airmen to be surrounded by others who had the same feelings, whether they were articulated or not. From *Winged Victory*:

> It was a balance of fears that kept him [Tom Cundall] going, fear of his friends balancing fear of the enemy, and reasoning was only the accompanying shadow play. And practically everyone was a coward: very few seemed to lack fear, and they were dolts without imagination or decent feelings; heroes. Cowards were the salt of the earth if they could fight their cowardice and poise themselves on.

There existed a silent understanding: it was accepted by all but a few that everybody was afraid. This amounted to an unvoiced empathy, which was appropriate to a situation in which too much expression might be dangerous. W. H. R. Rivers, psychiatrist at Craiglockhart War Hospital and the Central Hospital for Flying Officers, drew the conclusion that the individuals least prone to what he described as 'anxiety neuroses' were those who could acknowledge that fearlessness was an impossible ideal. At first glance, such an acknowledgment seems to stand at odds with the attitudes in the *Winged Victory* squadron. After all, these men would not admit to their fears if challenged. Yet, it was a necessary condition of their silent understanding to accept that each of them was flawed. They shared a secret, and one that brought them closer to each other. Norman MacMillan:

> On the ground we had the comradeship of the men around us, we had the intimate society of being thrown together. One knew that they were there, they would back one up and one would back them up. We had a feeling of community, a feeling that we were all together in the same thing, each helping the other, each one the intimate companion of all the men about him. Almost like a pyramid of strength.

The friendships forged between these men might serve as a haven against extremes of fear and stress, so it is little wonder that activities which brought men together, whether roller skating or singing round a piano, were so important. And neither is it surprising that the death of a friend could have a shattering effect. In July 1918, Mick Mannock heard of the death of his great friend and fellow ace James McCudden. According to Ira Jones:

> His death was deeply felt by Mannock because they had spent much of their time together during his last leave; Mannock felt the void left by McCudden's death as he meditated on his passing, and he gave the impression that he felt more than ever that the Shadow of Death was drawing nearer to himself.

For the members of 6 Squadron, based at Abeele, the death of a friend might be borne more easily – perhaps even denied – if the lost friend could maintain a presence within the squadron. T. E. Rogers joined 6 Squadron in November 1917:

After a pilot or an observer had been there for a day or two he was sent down to the photographic office. He went inside and the photographers took a silhouette of his head, and they'd cut it out in black paper, and it went onto a white frieze in the mess. One looked up at the frieze, and some fellows were still with the squadron, some had gone home for a rest, and some had gone for an eternal rest. And the thing that struck me as very strange – they'd refer to fellows whose silhouette was on the wall, refer to him by name, and tell you all his faults, all his goodness, and exactly what sort of pilot he was, as though he still lived. They'd tell you all about the fellow, in a very friendly way, and in a way that they missed him intensely. Silhouettes of pilots and observers, dead and alive.

Horrifying as it must have been to lose a friend, there were those who did not have friends to lose. Fewer in number, sergeant pilots might find themselves isolated from the officers, the only men who could understand their situation. George Eddington:

I was an NCO pilot in 6 Squadron and I couldn't make friends. I didn't have access to the officers' mess and I never knew what they were thinking. But in the sergeants' mess, they were all riggers and fitters and I wasn't in their world any more than they were in mine. My goodness, I was lonely. Dreadfully lonely.

Arriving at a new squadron could be another lonely experience. When Arthur Gould Lee arrived at 46 Squadron in May 1917 he received a cool reception from established squadron members. In his diary, he wrote:

I was speaking to Stephen in the mess last evening, a jolly nice chap who thought he'd met me somewhere, though he hadn't. It was just a way to open up talking. He and another fellow called Dimmock were the ones I spoke to most, apart from my hut mates. The original members of the squadron are a little inclined to be stand-offish. Some of them have been in it since it formed in England a year ago with two-seater Nieuports and I fancy they look on us newcomers almost as interlopers.

Such a cold welcome was perhaps not surprising at a point in the war when the life expectancy of a new pilot might be little more than a fortnight. The new boy might be replacing an old, trusted friend and he probably wouldn't be around for very long anyway. He was hardly worth welcoming. When, in April 1917, Mick Mannock first arrived in France as a newly trained pilot with 40 Squadron, he found acceptance difficult to gain. Lionel Blaxland remembers Mannock's early days in France:

His manner, speech and familiarity were not liked. He seemed too cocky for his experience, which was nil. His arrival at the unit was not the best way to start. New men took their time and listened to the more experienced hands; Mannock was the complete opposite. He offered ideas about everything: how the war was going, how it should be fought, the role of scout pilots, what was wrong or right with our machines. Most men in his position, by that I mean a man from his background and with his lack of fighting experience, would have shut up and earned their place in the mess.

To make matters worse, Mannock was already suffering from nerves which he found difficult to disguise, and the more experienced airmen felt that he was avoiding combat whenever he could. In fact, as an older, perhaps wiser man, he was flying conservatively in an attempt to gain an understanding of aerial warfare. He believed, quite sensibly, that mindless risk-taking ought to be replaced by more considered tactics. When he was asked by a fellow squadron member whether he was scared, he did the unthinkable and admitted that for a while, he had been terrified every time he went up on patrol. He qualified this admission by alleging that he had since overcome his fears – which was certainly not true. By the mere fact of his continued survival, however, Mannock began to gain acceptance and friendship. But though his reputation as air fighter and tactician grew, his fears did not diminish.

It was the fear of death, of course, that was ultimately responsible for all the diversions, strategies and mind games played out in the squadrons. And death was all around. Young men, once accustomed to the funerals of elderly relatives, were now attending those of their friends. Arthur Gould Lee:

> After coming back from St Omer this morning, I went to Stephen's funeral. He was buried next to Gunnery. It was a gloomy party, nobody saying a thing. As we stood beside the grave, I heard the padre's voice, but didn't take in a word of what he said. On the way home, riding in the back of the Crossley, with the other pallbearers, in complete silence, my mind drifted to the funerals at Filton, and how we marched behind the local band (I believe it was the Salvation Army), and how they always played the same slow march, the only one they knew for certain, Chopin's Marche Funèbre. Then I caught others staring at me oddly, and I realised I was quietly whistling it.

The same young men were having to write letters informing families of a change in circumstances. Frederick Powell:

> My most difficult duty was having to write to the next of kin to advise them of the death of their sons. That

was a horrifying thing for a boy of twenty-one to have to do.

Some deaths hit home particularly hard. The Reverend R. W. Dugdale, chaplain to 13th Wing RFC, in a letter to his mother:

> Young Swann was shot down in no-man's-land and killed. It has knocked us all very badly: he was a perfectly sweet and adorable little boy, and extraordinarily loved by his whole squadron. His major and I went up to the line to see about bringing the body back and we buried him near his squadron. I could hardly read the service for the first time since being out here. His flight sergeant said to me on Sunday evening 'His death has almost broken my heart' and it's just the same with all the men in his flight – he was a dear boy and looked about 15 years old. He was a brilliant pilot and put up an awfully good show before he was killed. One of the men in the squadron said to me, 'You felt like kissing him rather than shaking hands with him.' It's a contrary world.

When a man knew that he *ought* to be dead, there was very little to be said:

> When I landed, I noticed everybody looking at me strangely. I stopped, wondering what was up. Then I realized. Both the elevator and rudder controls were shot away. The wires trailed behind in the grass, just lying on the ground. For a moment, I couldn't believe it. How could I possibly have got back? I saw bullet holes in the fin, in the rudder, the tailplane and up the fuselage. None as far forward as my seat – obviously some Hun had got a terrific burst into the tail, cutting the control wires. Yet I was still alive. How? Corporal Ellins, my rigger, was there with McFall, my fitter. 'How could I have got back, Ellins, with these wires gone?

How could the controls still have been working?' For a moment, he said nothing; just looked at me with steady eyes. Then he spoke. 'Well, sir. You came back the other day with some bullet holes in the tailplane. I thought, maybe, one day, they'd get your control wires. So I spliced up some new wires and duplicated the controls.' He just stood there in his brown overalls. No drama. No great emotional scene. What could I say that could be any kind of answer to the thoughtfulness that had saved my life? In the end, I said, 'Thank you, Ellins.'

What of the men who could not take the strain? For these men, whose minds could not tolerate life as an airman on the Western Front, what lay ahead? For some, an existence racked with self-loathing. The diary of an anonymous airman in training:

> I was down for flying for 11.30 but I got one of those spasms of wind-up and dodged it. I do not think I shall ever make an airman. I am on tenter-hooks all the time I am up, and dare not for the life of me climb to 3000 feet, getting most terrible wind-up as soon as I reach 1200. And I shall be in France next month, so God help me. I am hoping that I shall suddenly acquire a liking for flying, as I sometimes hit on things when almost in despair. Whilst flying, I often think of going to the adjutant and asking him to have me transferred as an Observer (because I am not nervous so long as I have not control); and then, when flying is over for the day, I think about Mother, Father, Rene and Jack and think what a damn coward I am.

Some lost the ability to think and act normally. Tryggve Gran's diary entry for 15 October 1917, whilst with 101 Squadron:

A sad incident occurred tonight. When I returned from a sortie, I learned that Lt. Gladstone had crashed at the airfield and had been seriously injured. I ran down to the place where some red flares indicated that one of our machines was in difficulty and was met by a sad sight. A silent train of men marched slowly through the trees of a wood which was lit by the flares. Shoulder high, on a stretcher, they bore the young officer. Blood gushed from his wounds. Poor lad. Early that afternoon he had asked me to give him a good observer, for he did not feel too sure of himself at the moment. I did not take much notice of this but ordered the best observer we had to accompany him. When in the evening I was ready to take off, I noticed that his aircraft was far from being ready. I shouted to him and gave him a good talking to. Then I took off. Half an hour later, Gladstone was ready for take-off, and they said his face was quite pale. His plane was seen to roll down the runway and disappeared into the darkness. Suddenly a loud noise was heard and the people ran up, only to find Gladstone under the turned-up machine. The observer jumped out and escaped uninjured from the wreck. He related that they had just got into the air when the machine started to sink and the next moment it hit the earth and overturned. There was no doubt. The young man who had previously shown the greatest courage and sense of duty had suddenly lost control of his nerves. Instead of letting the aircraft gain flying speed, Gladstone, out of pure nervousness, had tried to get the heavily laden machine off the ground too soon. I am afraid his injuries will be mortal, though of course, a wound looks worse before treatment.

Gran's diary, a day later:

This afternoon some of us drove over to the hospital where Lt. Gladstone was a patient. When we arrived, he had just died.

George Jones, a pilot in 2 Squadron, Australian Flying Corps, managed to stiffen his resolve before he suffered a similar fate:

I ran out of petrol when I was engaged in a fight, and my opponent got his sights on me and shot away the wing bracing wires on one side. I could do nothing but glide. The engine on my Camel had stopped. He chased me for a few miles, and I had no way of retaliating. There was nothing I could do, but then, for some unknown reason, he turned and left me. I couldn't do anything! But he turned and left me! I was six miles over the enemy side and at 6000 feet, and I had to glide towards our own side of the lines, but I wasn't quite sure where that was.

I pushed the rudder bar to try and make her go faster and finished up by crossing what turned out to be the front line at 100 feet. I glided down a gully, landed in a shell hole, and turned over. I got out my Very pistol and was about to set the aeroplane on fire, because I didn't know whether I was on the wrong side of the lines, but fortunately, some soldiers appeared, and their uniform was khaki and not field grey. So I was taken down to the trenches, and they gave me a very stiff drink, and I slept all day, and that night, my people came and collected me.

But my nerves were badly shaken up, and after they returned my Camel, I took it up and brought it into land at what they said was 120 mph, whereas I should have brought it in at 65. It shot right across the aerodrome, turned over again, turned upside down in the mud, and I stood there on my head until they lifted the fuselage off me. My nerves were terribly shaken up by now. It took a lot of hard thinking to get myself into a condition of stability to keep myself flying. Every time I thought of it all, I couldn't hold a knife and fork when I was having a meal. They would fall out of my hands. But I did manage to overcome it and I kept on flying.

For those who could not overcome it, and were not killed in the attempt, a breakdown lay ahead. The medical case sheets, on which hospital patients were diagnosed with either 'Shell shock' or 'Neurasthenia' make sad reading. Usually handwritten in a doctor's scrawl, some begin with the cause of the complaint, and continue with the patient's symptoms, which are updated, often in different handwriting, until a decision is made on his future. Others are less complete. It is immediately clear from the tone of many of the comments, and from the references to 'illness', that these men were treated sympathetically, and not as malingerers, weaklings or cowards. There is no sense that they should be punished for failing to carry out their duties, rather they are being treated for a genuine inability to do so; although perhaps 'treated' is rather an optimistic description of the rest cure that these men received. Even after so many years, the physical and psychological torment of airmen who have tried and failed to suppress their fears is very affecting:

2 Lieut F. P. Blencome 22 years, RFC
Maghull Military Hospital
Neurasthenia

12/2/18 – On admission, this officer was in an intensely nervous condition, tremors, twitchings of facial muscles. He suffered from insomnia and dreams of aeroplane crashes. He had had sleeping draughts for 9 months every night before coming here.

6/4/18 – This officer has rapidly improved in every respect. He is sleeping well and had got over his night-mares and is putting on weight. Having regard to this long illness, he is being invalided out of the service.

Neurasthenia: 2 Lt James Baxter, 33rd Kite Balloon Section, RFC
40 year old man with 21 years service behind him.
Was a balloon observer. Broke his upper denture and became unable to masticate his food at the Front. Suffered much in consequence and finally suffered a nervous breakdown after his balloon was brought down and he had to witness the violent death of his friend. He has suffered from insomnia and distressing dreams, dizziness and headaches.

Neurasthenia S. Beaumont
Joined RFC in August 1917. His first and only crash in November 1918. He was not in charge of the machine. He was not physically injured by the crash. About a week later, he developed fear symptoms and became fatigued. The nervous symptoms became aggravated with depression, memory defects and lack of power of mental application. Irritability of temper was marked, war dreams, insomnia developed together with head-aches and nausea. He spent three months in hospital but did not improve. His legs became so shaky that he had to use two sticks. He harbours mistrust and sus-picions of everybody around him and is easily upset. There are no physical signs of organic disease.

2 Lieut Baird, aged 22
Craiglockhart, 12/9/17
Disease – Neurasthenia

Very healthy before the War. Was a commercial traveller. Was in the Artillery in this country till Dec 16.

Then joined RFC. To France June 1917. On 28 June, he had a crash, his engine giving in, aircraft pancaked and fell with a nose dive. Was not physically damaged, and only felt a little dazed. Two days later, began to feel nervous and chary. Went up again five days later, and was all right while up in the air, but fainted on alighting. He then went off his sleep, developed headaches, deafness and amnesia.

15/8/17 Sent to England. Admitted to 4th London General Hospital. Was badly upset for two days by an air raid in London.

12/9/17 Transferred to Craiglockhart.

23/10/17 Feels much better but any sudden bang makes him jump and he feels sick after it.

27/10/17 Much improved and has been sent to light duty.

2 Lieut C. R. Alston
Shell shock

Arrived in France in April 1917. Flew every day in Arras offensive. Flew every day in Messines offensive. Got on all right till June 19, when he had to make forced landing in a thunderstorm and crashed and caught fire in telegraph wires. He was thrown out of the aeroplane. His bombs exploded. He was dazed and stunned. On admission, restless, irritable, tremors.

July 8: has improved greatly but is still restless and irritable and in my opinion requires a further rest before starting to fly again.

August 13 – Discharged

2 Lieut L W Brisks RFC,
Mrs. Mulliner's RFC Hospital, Clifton Court, near Rugby

Since this officer arrived here two months ago, the wound in the left thigh has healed, and the injured right knee has got well. The condition of his nervous system is unsatisfactory and he has not made much progress – he suffers from very disturbed sleep with haunting dreams of his crash, and nervous irritability with defective power of mental concentration. The reflexes are increased, there is much loss of weight and a feeling of general debility. This place does not seem to agree with him and a change to a convalescent hospital in lighter air is recommended.

2 Lieut Bertram Brown, 11 Squadron
Admitted 10/11/17 from France, labelled 'mental'

Physically normal. Mentally depressed, very restless, self deprecatory, unhappy. He stated that while shaving he was suddenly seized with a strong impulse to cut his throat and fearing that he might not be able to resist this, he reported to the M.O. but failed to report the full facts. Afterwards, afraid to re-enter his room as he had a loaded revolver in his kit. He slept poorly except with Veronal. Restless all day and wants to be doing something, asks foolish questions and quickly forgets what is said to him. He has not felt well for some months and had greatly felt the loss of friends, over which he brooded until the suicidal impulse struck him. He impulsively said, 'You know what is the matter with me, there is no doubt I have funked it. I will never fight again, it's all up with me.' Stated he did not know what he was doing. He took no interest in anything, yet ceaseless activity seemed obsessive. His room mates complain of his silly questions.

And finally we present the curious case of Lieutenant Boxer and the lost winter weekend:

2 Lieut Edward Maurice Boxer, Dec 6 1917
Lapse of memory, brought here by police, found wandering.

I have examined this patient today. He complains of headache and seems a little dazed. His hands are slightly tremulous. Pupils not unduly contracted or dilated. Both react well to lights. Knee jerks a little brisk.

So far as his present condition is concerned, there are no definite signs of nervous disorder beyond those of general fatigue which would be expected from the history of the case. I can find no signs of memory for any events from the time of his arrival at Marylebone Station, when he says he remembers giving his luggage to a porter, to the time when he found himself wandering in the street and was helped here by a policeman. He has recently suffered from headaches since an accident six months ago after which he was put on light duties for a time.

Dec 7 – Family history from father. Eldest brother in an asylum for two years. Now all right again. No other history of mental trouble. Patient was always bright and healthy, but never very vigorous. His father notices a great change in him mentally.

Dec 8 – This officer impresses me favourably as to the truth of his story. I think it is a genuine case of loss of the highest consciousness, not uncommonly observed in specific cases.

Dec 11 – Headaches much better.

Dec 18 – Memory returns. This officer now remembers that he met Lt. Head at Marylebone Station and that he had a whiskey and soda with him. He then went to Bayswater and called upon a girlfriend who was out. He then went to Waterloo Bridge where he took off his belt and tunic and threw them over the bridge into the river. He then sat on the bridge and a policeman flashed his light upon him several times. He then spent the greater part of the next day (without his tunic!) in a small street on the south side of the Bridge. A police-man then took him on the top of an omnibus to King George's Hospital and from there, brought him here. All this story requires an investigation.

13 Feb 1918 – Found unfit for duty for one month following an examination by RFC Standing Medical Board.

[Subsequent records show that in June 1918, Edward Boxer was passed fit and returned to active duty. A diagnosis of temporary amnesia was presumably accepted. He survived the war and remained in the Royal Air Force until 1919.]

One wonders what happened to these men as the years passed, whether they ever fully recovered, whether they could bring themselves to speak of their wartime experiences. For many, the post-war years can have offered little comfort. Writing in 1934, Ira Jones:

Those who have survived the war must have had to fight an even greater battle in the effort to return to normal. How many have failed! Peace had stripped these veterans of their last resources of emotional reserves. We meet them daily, men who faced death and untold horrors in the war, beaten and cowed by the remorseless struggle for existence, unable to harness their shattered emotions to the stresses and strains of civilian routine, and fleeing defenceless into the gutters of the world's highways. In a 'get on at any price' world, these men have little chance to recoup their emotional reserves, and to our lasting shame we cannot yet adjust our social order to give the war veteran who has been unable to get to grips with life a chance to live the remainder of his days a little more easily than those who escaped the deluge.

One man who never had to face the post-war world was Mick Mannock. The great ace, and Victoria Cross winner, who had broken down so utterly in Jim Eyles' front room, continued to suffer anguish. Terror of burning alive inside his aircraft drove him to carry a revolver with him, in a canvas pocket at the side of the cockpit, so that he might put a bullet through his head rather than burn. His behaviour towards the enemy turned increasingly cruel. On 30 April 1918, he dived half a dozen times at a downed German machine, spraying the still-living pilot and observer with fatal bullets. 'The swines are better dead – no prisoners for me!' he crowed on landing.

He had long since turned to black humour to assuage the fears. Whenever he brought an enemy pilot down in flames, he would laugh feverishly and joke of 'flamers' and 'sizzlers'. Ira Jones, who witnessed his mania, wrote:

> Having finished in a frenzy of fiendish glee, he will turn to one of us and say, laughing: 'That's what will happen to you on the next patrol, my lad.' And we all roar with laughter.

Mannock's worst fear was realised on 26 July 1918 when his SE5a was hit by tracer from a German machine gun and burst into flames. According to an eyewitness on the ground, as the machine's cockpit caught fire Mannock was still wrestling with its controls. It is not known whether he lifted the revolver out of its pocket, raised it to his head and pulled the trigger, or whether he was consumed in the blaze. Either way, the 'King of the Air Fighters' died only sixteen months, give or take a few days, after his arrival in France as a fighting novice. Such was the intensity of the airman's life on the Western Front.

Bearing this in mind, it is worth reading again the excerpts from the letters of Albert Ball that begin this chapter. A request for flowers to be sent from home is one thing; a request for flowers that will grow quickly is another altogether.

8

Over the Top

Bernard Rice was an officer with 8 Squadron who wrote a series of vivid letters home to his father in 1916 and 1917. In one undated letter (which was never finished and never sent) he decided to offer his father a share of the observer's seat during an artillery observation:

> If you like to squash yourself very small, and hop in alongside o' me when nobody's looking, and have a decent box of gaspers behind you when you get out, you can come out with us, and do an artillery show. The machine you are getting into is exactly the same as those they are building at the old works. You get into the forward seat, and just mind where you're putting that foot, you clumsy old beggar! We don't want a hole through the fabric just yet, they will come on their own later on!
>
> 'Switch off, petrol on, suck in!' That is 'Wind Up', our pilot. Not a bad lad, but he's a nasty lust for Hun scrapping. Don't believe in looking for trouble myself.
>
> 'Contact, please, sir,' – 'Contact' – Whirrrr – Pleasant here isn't it? Just keep under the cowl, and you won't get your teeth blown out. Bit bumpy getting off, eh? Now we're off the ground. Feel your insides trickling out of your boots? It will take us twenty minutes to get our height, and more if you hang out like that! Keep under

the cowl 'till we're up, man! Plenty of time to admire the country then.

'Hulloah!' – that is my speaking tube to the pilot. 'Have you let out the aerial yet?' 'Thank you.' Now look out for the acknowledging letter in white cloth strip on the aerodrome. No! No! Not out there! Underneath, look! On that patch of green, the size of a penny. Got it? Our wireless is working now and we can turn off to the lines.

Rather quaint to see the clouds underneath, isn't it? Sun is nice and bright though, isn't it? Cold outside the cowl. Those patches of molten lead? Oh, they're lakes. If you look again, you'll see that most of them are complete with chateaux, gardens, drive, and trees. Of course you can't see people, unless they are in bunches. It all looks exactly like that *Daily Mail* map, don't you think? The roads twisting about, the villages and towns. It isn't hard to find where you are, is it, by noting the road 'shapes' on the map?

Yes. That is the line. I thought you would know it when you saw it. Everyone does. The trenches show up well – all white and black lines – don't they? Good Lord, no! Those aren't *all* ours. You will notice there is a narrow strip of brown unbroken earth winding down nearly the centre of all that conglomeration of trenches. That is the 'no-man's-land'. You see it is almost a continuous front line, those bits going back are communication, support, and second line trenches. All that muddled looking lot of trenches behind are the foundations which carry that thin front line. You will notice the Hun trenches are just the same.

You mustn't miss the 'crump' holes. See all those myriad of 'stars', that show white just like the trenches, <u>they</u> are shell holes. Things are pretty quiet this morning. Pity. See! There! Those white puffs! There, another, see it burst? A speck of red flame there! Now it is only a puff of white smoke. That is Hun shrapnel. I bet that came from our 'job'. Let's have a look at the map. Yes, that artillery that we are going to knock out, is over there alongside that long thin wood. I thought so! Did you see them fire? Four little red spurts? I will just wave to the pilot to take us back to the ground station, and see if they have put any signals out. I've been calling them up with this little 'tapping key' here at my right hand. There it is! Now for a shot. Do you mind sticking your right hand out your side and old 'Wind Up' will turn us round and head over the lines. Thanks. Now watch the top end of that wood. There. I've fired them. It will take about twenty seconds for the shot to get there. Watch carefully. Splendid! See it? That cloud of black smoke and dust that shot up? Right on the target, twenty yards short. I'll send them that correction and we'll have another shot.

I say, do you notice how flat all the country looks. All the hills and downs seem to have flattened out. The earth looks like a great saucer, doesn't it, sort of coming up to meet the sky on the horizon all around? And do you see how ground <u>detail</u> tails off into a greeny blue <u>form</u> towards the horizon? By jove! Over there! See that strip of pale misty blue between the sky and earth, with a thin broken white line along the top of it? That is the Channel, and the white line is the cliffs of Dover.

Now for the wood again. I am ready to fire. What is 'Wind Up' pointing to? I don't know. Never mind him, let's watch our target. Good! That was an 'OK' on one gun. Hi! Look out! Get the gun out. Hun!! Hun!!! Quick – onto the side mounting! Now! There go fifty rounds. Some must have hit him. See, he's trying to get under our tail. Now hold tight, we're going to dive at him. Whoa! Up!! He's got a dose! After him! Keep firing. He's going down – had enough – I wonder if he's hit? See the signal lights he's dropped? Now look

out for Archie. Here they come! Crump! Wallop! Hang
on tight, we'll have to do some dodging to get out of
this . . .

And so the letter ends with the Rice family stranded in
mid-air over the German lines. As well as giving a vivid
description of a flight over the lines, the letter demonstrates
how static the war on the ground had become. As machine
flew against machine over the Western Front, and the
balance of air power shifted backwards and forwards, the
ground armies sat facing each other, for the most part
attritional and stagnant. The war in the air was having no
obvious effect on the stalemate. Which begs a number
of questions. Was aerial superiority of any consequence in
terms of the war as a whole? Could an overall aerial victory
have won the war? And if not, could the sacrifice of men and
machines be justified?

To answer the first question, air superiority was clearly
of consequence. Aerial reconnaissance, artillery observation
and bomb dropping were crucial to both sides, as contact
patrols and ground attacks were to become. Air superiority
allowed the aircraft with the upper hand to carry out more
of this work as well as preventing the other side from doing
so. 'It is important for the winning of the war that we should
not only secure air predominance, but secure it on a very
large scale' concluded the Smuts Report on aerial operations
in August 1917. In propaganda terms, air superiority offered
a morale boost to the public at home, and immediate and
visible encouragement to the men in the trenches. Alexander
Stewart, an officer with the 3rd Scottish Rifles:

> Our peace and comfort in the trenches very largely
> depended on the superiority of our fighting men in the
> air, and when Boche came hurling or flopping down
> to earth, cheers went up to heaven all along our line.
> Judging from personal experience, it seemed obvious

that the success of the army in the field primarily depended on the initiative in the air being obtained and maintained. Nearly every time an enemy aeroplane was permitted to fly over or behind our outpost line, and to return to its own lines in safety, both our infantry and artillery shortly afterwards suffered from severe and accurate shell fire.

Nevertheless, it is difficult to imagine how an aerial victory for either side, such as seemed possible at the height of the Fokker Scourge, could have won the war. To win freedom of the air would certainly offer great advantages; the dominant side could attack on the ground with near-total surprise while it could defend with knowledge of the enemy's intentions. This might encourage a more offensive strategy, but attacks did not guarantee success; battles still had to be actively won by the myriad men who faced each other across that narrow strip of brown, unbroken earth, and that, as we shall shortly see, was no foregone conclusion. Throughout the war, aeroplanes would remain ancillary to ground forces. As for the final question, whether the sacrifice of men and machines could be justified, perhaps that can be left to the reader to consider. For the time being, it is enough to say that neither side could back out of the aerial arms race once it had begun. Technology was advancing, potential was being explored and results were being achieved. It is a measure of the respect earned by the flying machines and their pilots that as the DH2 was overcoming the Fokker Scourge, mastery of the air was considered a prize worth winning.

In the summer of 1916, the aggressive strategies of Generals Haig and Joffre came to a head in an attempt to make the great Allied breakthrough that would end both the stalemate and the war. The Battle of the Somme was to be launched on 1 July by the British Fourth Army and a single corps of the Third Army, together with eight divisions of the French army over an eighteen-mile front between Maricourt and Gommecourt. Trenchard, keen as ever to place the Royal Flying Corps at the disposal of the army, had overseen the creation of a new brigade, made up of two wings, one of which was to carry out artillery observation and aerial reconnaissance over the Somme, the other to be placed under the direct control of the Fourth Army. The artillery bombardment in advance of the battle began on 24 June and lasted for a week. The barrage was intended to destroy the enemy's defences, so that the infantry would face little resistance as it walked across no-man's-land, over the destroyed barbed wire and through what remained of the German front line. Cecil Lewis carried out reconnaissance flights with 3 Squadron in the middle of the most ferocious barrage ever seen:

> These jobs were among the most terrifying I did in the whole war. Because we were flying down to about 1000 feet. And when you had to go right over the lines you were midway between our guns firing and where the shells were falling, and during that period the intensity of the bombardment was such that it was really like a sort of great, broad swathe of dirty looking cotton wool laid over the ground. So close were the shell bursts, and so continuous, that it wasn't just a puff here and a puff there, it was a continuous band. And when you looked the other side, particularly when the light was failing, the whole of the ground was just like a veil of sequins that were flashing and flashing and flashing. And each sequin was a gun.
>
> The artillery had orders – we were told – not to fire when an aeroplane was in their sights. They cut it pretty fine. Because one used to fly along the front on those patrols, and your aeroplane was flung up by a shell which had just gone underneath and missed you by two or three feet. Or flung down by a shell that had

gone over the top. And this was continuous, so the machine was continually buffeted and jumping as if it was in a gale. But in fact it was shells. You didn't see them, they were going much too fast. But this was really terrifying.

I remember two days before the attack opened, when we *had* to get some photographs because they were terribly badly needed, we were down to about 1000 feet in murky weather, with a cloud bank overhead, and this grey swathe on one side, and this flashing, these continual flashings – one had the feeling, they're firing at us! It's us they want to get! This was ridiculous, of course, but it was quite terrifying at the time. And then at last, having finished the photos, and having got out of the buffeting, you thought, 'Heaven's alive! I've come through that!' because so many of the boys, my best observer, many of my friends, were hit by this barrage and destroyed.

Shortly before the infantry advanced, Lewis was in the air. At this point, the bombardment was at its heaviest and the chaotic scene that was playing out beneath him was to become even more hellish with the detonation of huge mines under La Boiselle:

On the morning of 1 July, when the zero hour was to come, I was on the first patrol, on the northern part of the salient, from Pozières down to Fricourt. And at Pozières they'd put down two enormous mines. Hoping to clear the whole of the front line with this enormous burst. This was what we were looking for. We had our watches synchronized. We were up at about 8000 feet, and really it was a fantastic sight because, when the hurricane bombardment started, every gun we had – and there were thousands of them – were all let loose at once, and the thing was wild. You could hear the noise of the guns above the roar of the aircraft almost like rain on a pane. Extraordinary, this roll of thousands of guns at the same time.

And then it came at last, eight o'clock, and we were looking at La Boiselle Salient, and suddenly the whole earth heaved, and up from the ground came what looked like two enormous cypress trees. It was the silhouettes of great, dark cone shaped lifts of earth, up to 3, 4, 5000 feet. And we watched this, and then a moment later we struck the repercussion wave of the blast and it flung us right the way backwards, over on one side.

Despite the undoubted ferocity of the bombardment that Lewis had witnessed, the sheer length of the front had weakened its effect, and it failed to destroy the many heavily reinforced dugouts and shelters that had been constructed along the line. The majority of German troops survived the onslaught and when the barrage lifted they had time to regroup before mowing down the advancing British infantrymen with machine gun and rifle fire. The result, as is all too well known, was carnage. By the end of the day, 19,240 British soldiers had been killed and 35,494 wounded. Above this carnage flew airmen on contact patrols, attempting to locate infantrymen who had made it past the German front line. The system of contact patrols had changed since the white strips of cloth that had confused Archibald James at Festubert the year before. Cecil Lewis:

We went right down to 3000 feet to see what was happening. Of course, we had this very well worked out technique which was that we had a klaxon horn on the undercarriage and I had the button and I used to press out a letter, and that letter was to tell the infantry that we wanted to know where they were. And when they heard us hawking at them from above, they had red Bengal flares in their pockets, just like the little things one lights on the fifth of November. And the idea was that as soon as they heard us make our noises above they would put a match to their flares, and all along the lines, wherever there was a chap, there'd be a flare. And we'd note these flares down on the maps and Bob's your uncle. But, of course, it was one thing to practise it, another thing to really do it when they were under fire. Particularly when things began to go a bit badly. Then of course they jolly well wouldn't light anything, and small blame to them, because it drew the fire of the enemy onto them at once. So we went down on that particular morning, looking for flares all around La Boiselle, and down to Fricourt, and I think we got two flares on the whole front. And of course we were bitterly disappointed, because this was our part to help the infantry – and we weren't able to do it. And in fact it did never work, until two months later, when the attack had gone further forward.

The first of July 1916 may have turned into an unprecedented human disaster on the ground, but in the air British superiority had not been challenged. As numerous British aircraft patrolled the skies over the battlefield, very few German machines dared to challenge them in combat. And yet, although the first day of the battle was fought at a time when the Allies had air superiority, and despite the fact that the Royal Flying Corps was led by a man who was doing all that he could to offer support to the army, the airmen had been able to do little to influence events on the ground. The Battle of the Somme lasted until November 1916, by which time the opposing armies were even more deeply entrenched, and aircraft were so indispensable to the military authorities that a request was made by senior generals to have the corps squadrons placed under the aegis of the Royal Artillery. But at no point could air power alone have dictated the outcome of the Great War, even though it would not be very long before it was capable – one thinks of the Battle of Britain – of changing the course of history.

During the Battle of the Somme the development of the aircraft coincided with the first use of another invention. Cecil Lewis practised contact patrols with this top secret contraption:

> One afternoon the commanding officer said he wanted me to go off on a special job, and he gave me a designation on the map, and I and my observer, went off. And when we arrived, we saw these curious sort of heavy looking iron vehicles, and they were lumbering over the ground at about two miles an hour, with a whole lot of chaps standing round, and a kerfuffle going on. And these vehicles were, of course, tanks. And so, from that moment on, we started doing mock attacks with them. In order to get them to light their flares, note where they were, and take back records to the brigade headquarters.

Gwilym Lewis of 32 Squadron, flew overhead as the tanks rumbled slowly to war:

> Our big day was 15 September. That was the day the tanks went into battle for the first time. They were a complete surprise to the Germans, and we boys in 32 Squadron were quite determined that no German air force would interfere with them. The tanks were moved up into their position covered – they never showed themselves until the 15th, and on that day we were up as much as we could, only leaving enough time to fill up our tanks. I'm pretty sure that the tanks were not interfered with by the German air force, and the battle was a success up to a point – we made a breakthrough – but after that it failed.

During the spring of 1916, British air superiority had been reinforced by the arrival of new aircraft over the Western Front. One of these was the Nieuport 17, a single-seater French scout, powered by a 110-horse-power Le Rhône engine, with a Lewis machine gun placed above the top wing to fire over the propeller. Another was the Sopwith 1½ Strutter, the first British aircraft equipped with a synchronized machine gun. The Strutter, a two-seater, was intended for use as both a fighter and a reconnaissance machine. Its Ross system of synchronization worked on the 'interrupter' principle which employed a mechanism to prevent the Vickers machine gun from firing when a propeller blade was in its path; this allowed 300 rounds to be fired per minute, but on the early Strutters the Vickers' ground trigger remained in place as an alternative to the synchronized trigger. This meant that the pilot could risk a shattered propeller by firing the gun normally and doubling his rate of fire. The Strutter also carried a backward-facing Lewis gun in the observer's cockpit, and it soon became a well-regarded if not very generously distributed machine.

The first Strutters to arrive in the Royal Flying Corps were borrowed from the Admiralty, and their very existence bore out the pre-war naval decision to rely on private enterprise to design and construct its aircraft. In mid-1916, in the midst of a struggle for aerial superiority, the greater the choice of aircraft the better, and the impact of subsequent Tommy Sopwith machines would demonstrate the short-sightedness of the army in its belief that it could rely solely on Royal Aircraft Factory-designed aircraft. At the same time, a shortage of aero engines was making itself felt. A large proportion of them were still being imported from France, and competition had developed between the RFC and the RNAS to get hold of the limited number available. Such a conflict between organizations that ought to have been working together was clearly not in the Allies' best interests.

As new machines arrived at the front, so more thought came to be devoted to the theory of air fighting. A 1916 lecture delivered to pilots in training by Captain J. H. Simpson gave a lesson in combat tactics:

> First of all a scout pilot must have absolute control of his machine, i.e. he must be able to put it into any possible position and get it out again without in any way inconveniencing himself.
>
> It is absolutely essential of all things, to keep a good look-out, because there is not a machine made that has not a blind side and if you fly with that side blind for any length of time, it gives an enemy machine an opportunity to approach you unseen, and gives the enemy the chance of surprise, which of course is the great factor in air fighting.
>
> Never fly straight for any length of time. That of course works with keeping a good look-out because if you are keeping a good look-out in every direction you cannot be flying in a straight line – you must swing.
>
> The scout is essentially an offensive machine and the only thing they have to do is attack. It is your whole job, and when you see a hostile machine, go for it. In attack, your main object is to get to close quarters. Don't open fire more than 200 yards away. Under present conditions it is practically impossible to do any effective firing from more than that distance. It is only a waste of ammunition and you are simply warning the enemy of your approach. Always reserve your main burst of fire until you are quite close – say 50 yards – and if possible, closer still. Always make your attack vigorous. Don't hesitate. Go right in and don't give him any rest. If the first attack fails, get your gun ready again and get at him, without giving him a chance of recovery.

Additional notes to this lecture were added by a greatly respected pilot who had achieved success during the Battle of the Somme flying a Nieuport 17; this man was renowned for his daring single-handed attacks on large formations of enemy aircraft, and his notes reflect the fact:

> If a scout attacks a large formation of hostile aircraft, I think it is best to attack from above and dive in among them, getting under the nearest machine. Pull gun down and fire up into hostile aircraft. If you get it, a number of hostile aircraft will put their noses down and make off. Don't run after them, but wait for the hostile aircraft that don't run, and again take the nearest machine. If they all run, wait for a bit and look for a straggler. One is nearly always left behind. Go for that and give it a drum, at the same time keeping your eyes as much as possible on the other machines, as they may get together and get round you.

This respected pilot was Albert Ball, the young man whose letters to his parents appeared in previous chapters. Just as Ball preferred solitary pursuits on the ground, so in the air he preferred to fly alone, and he was usually granted the freedom of a roving commission. One of Ball's favourite tactics was to fly at an opponent head-on, confident in the belief that his adversary would be the first to break away to avoid a collision. As the opponent turned, he would leave himself vulnerable for a split second, and in that second, Ball would fire and claim another victim.

Such nerveless behaviour might seem at odds with the childlike nature of his letters, but perhaps it is what one might expect from a boy who has arrived from a public school where duty is valued above other qualities and he has been taught to 'play the game' for all that he is worth. Ball was known for taking risks that bordered on reckless-ness. He would often return to his aerodrome, his machine riddled with bullets. His most famous exploit occurred after he engaged two enemy aircraft in combat, both of which slunk away and headed home. Angered by their cowardly behaviour, Ball flew over their aerodrome and dropped a note, challenging them both to a contest at the same time on the following day. Sure enough, a day later, he arrived over the aerodrome to find two enemy machines waiting for him. He immediately launched into his favoured manoeuvre, flying his Nieuport head on at one of them. Suddenly, he became aware of three other enemy machines close by; he had been lured into a trap. He pulled out of his attack and steeled himself to fight all five enemy machines, but each time he drew close to one, he was set upon by others. Eventually, he ran out of ammunition, and, as all five opponents circled around him, taking it in turns to fire, he put his Nieuport into a dive. Believing that he had been hit, the enemy machines followed him down. Ball made a rough landing in a field, and slumped forward over his controls as if unconscious. Two of the enemy machines landed nearby, and their pilots hopped out and ran towards him. All of a sudden, Ball sat up, opened his throttle and took off, leaving his opponents stranded in his wake. The other three enemy machines had returned to their aerodrome, giving Ball a clear run home.

It is little wonder that with stories such as these circulating (and it has on occasion been suggested that this particular exploit was little more than a story) Ball was fêted by the public back in Britain. He was a dashing young hero in the midst of a faceless, mechanized war. Archibald James remembers:

> The first of the stars was Ball. He was the first of the great fighter pilots. But he was bound to be killed, because he had absolutely no regard for his own safety whatever. Whatever the odds he went bald-headed into the attack.

By October 1916, Ball had been awarded the Military Cross and two Distinguished Service Orders. He was the first true British ace of the war, but his greatest challenges – and his Victoria Cross – were yet to come.

Although Trenchard disapproved of public recognition for individual fighter pilots – on the basis that it belittled the work of less 'glamorous' airmen engaged in reconnaissance duties – he cannot have failed to notice that Albert Ball's approach to air fighting mirrored his own aggressive strategy of taking the fight to the enemy. This strategy was easy enough to bear when the British possessed superior machines, but it would be harder to accept were the balance of air power to swing back in the enemy's favour. And that is precisely what began to happen in the autumn of 1916.

In August, the first German Jagdstaffel (Jasta) was formed. This 'hunting squadron' was a fighter unit made up of fourteen aircraft, and it was put under the command of Oswald Boelcke, who immediately set about finding the right men to join him. One of those he chose was an arrogant young Prussian with a fondness for hunting who had been flying observation aircraft on the Eastern Front. His name was Manfred von Richthofen. Boelcke spent weeks instructing his protégés in shooting, formation flying, aircraft recognition and fighter tactics. Throughout this training period, Boelcke was the only member of the Jasta who flew in combat. Each morning he would fly off alone before returning to tutor his pupils. If, on his return, his chin was blackened with powder from his machine gun, then his 'cubs' knew that he had seen action.

On 16 September, Boelcke's Jasta took possession of the latest German fighter, the Albatros DI, with its cigar-shaped fuselage, 160-horse-power Mercedes engine and twin synchronized Spandau machine guns. It had a top speed of 109 miles per hour, and a ceiling of 17,000 feet. Each member of the Jasta received one of these impressive machines and was told by Boelcke that it was the best fighting aircraft in the world. One of the cubs could not wait; whilst on a familiarization flight that evening, he came across, and shot down, a British pilot. The next morning, Boelcke allowed five of his pupils to fly their Albatri (as the British pluralized them) in combat for the first time. Led by Boelcke, the Albatri encountered a formation of FE2bs near Cambrai, where their outstanding speed, climb and rate of fire overpowered the pushers. An FE2b, piloted by Lionel Morris, with Thomas Rees as his observer, was forced down after its engine was knocked out by a stream of bullets. In a letter written from a German prison camp two months later, Captain D. S. Grey, the leader of the FE2b formation, wrote to Morris' father, describing what he had seen of the crash landing:

> We were attacked by hostile aircraft. I was ahead with two other machines and one of them which I believe was your son turned back to assist those in the rear. I was then attacked myself and know no more of the fight till I reached the ground. About a minute after landing, I saw one of our machines come down and disappear behind some trees and houses about 500 yards from us. We subsequently passed this machine when we were driven in a car under escort. It was crashed beside the road, near an embankment, with a crowd of people round. Our car drew up, and I gathered from the German officer that the observer was killed and the pilot injured and had already been removed in an ambulance.

The Albatros pilot responsible had followed Morris' machine down and found the two British airmen slumped and unconscious in their cockpits. They were dragged clear of their aircraft. Rees died within minutes, Morris was hanging on to his life. Captain Grey's letter continues:

The next afternoon, we were told Morris had died that morning. He had been wounded in the air and injured by the crash. We were told he was conscious most of the time and when admitted into hospital was able to give his name etc. He was very quiet and I think suffered little pain. I would have liked to have seen him but he was already dead before we knew very much about it and we were somewhat dazed and put out by our experiences ourselves. I should like you to feel assured that your son met with a most gallant end, going as I believe to the assistance of his comrades and that his sufferings were not great. He was one of the most reliable and brave pilots I have met and I say this without exaggeration and not merely through desire to gratify. I am certain he gave a good account of himself. No officer in the Flying Corps could wish to meet with a better end.

However gallant Morris' end, it was certainly significant. The pilot who had shot him down and followed him to the ground was Manfred von Richthofen; Morris and Rees were the Red Baron's first confirmed victims. In a letter to his mother, written after the engagement, Richthofen admitted that he had nearly yelled with joy when he saw the FE2b's propeller fail. British air superiority was coming to an end, and the career of the most notorious ace of the war had begun. He quickly began to notch up victories. Two months and one week after his first, he achieved his eleventh: his victim was Lanoe Hawker, and we have already read Richthofen's account of the classic fight.

As one career began, so another ended. On 28 October 1916, Oswald Boelcke was sent plummeting to his death by a mid-air collision with a member of his own formation. Richthofen, like many others, had come to idolize Boelcke, and in his diary, he wrote:

It is a strange thing that everybody who met Boelcke imagined that he alone was his true friend. I have made the acquaintance of about forty men, each of whom imagined that he alone was Boelcke's intimate. Each imagined that he had the monopoly of Boelcke's affections. Men whose names were unknown to Boelcke believed that he was particularly fond of them. This is a curious phenomenon that I have never noticed in anyone else.

On hearing of Boelcke's death, British squadrons dropped wreaths over the German lines to be placed on his grave. Even in late 1916, opposing airmen still shared a bond unknown to those engaged in the anonymous conflict below. Gwilym Lewis, of 32 Squadron, no conspicuous lover of the enemy, made an exception for Boelcke:

> I didn't like the Germans as a whole, but I had respect for certain of them. The great commander Boelcke. I respected him tremendously. He was a splendid chap, and in an enemy sense, he was a gentleman.

In October, an improved Albatros – the DII – was introduced, with a sharper rate of climb and a lower top wing. Its two synchronized Spandau guns became as feared as the Fokker E1's single Parabellum had been in early 1916. The twin guns were to interfere with the sleep of Herbert Thompson, a pilot with 8 Squadron RNAS:

> The whole flight was on patrol and my flight commander decided to dive on two German aircraft. I obediently followed, quite excited because they appeared to be dead ducks. I didn't realize that they were a decoy for the aircraft up above. There were eleven of them, in all. I was busily engaged in shooting down one of the decoys when there was suddenly a frightful uproar behind me. Two Spandau machine

guns going flat out. I panicked and dived away, which I shouldn't have done because I couldn't outdive an Albatros in my Sopwith Triplane. Immediately, the noise stopped so I pulled out of the dive and turned round to see if I'd been damaged. The main spar of my top plane had been shattered – there was wood flying off in all directions. The only thing I could do was go straight home. As I landed, the Triplane just flopped down because the balance wire had been severed. Although I'd managed to land back at my own aerodrome, it was a technical shoot down. When my flight commander landed, he said, 'I didn't think you'd get home!' He had come behind me and shot the Albatros off my tail. He had saved my life. That night, I woke up to find myself outside on the cold, wet grass. I'd crawled out of my tent and I was sleep walking. I did this for a whole week. More than once, I was collected and brought back by the sentry.

By the start of 1917, the Royal Flying Corps had increased in size and now consisted of five brigades, but of its thirty-eight squadrons only eight were single-seater fighter squadrons. Trenchard was aware that an increase in fighter strength was crucial, and early in the year, two new Sopwith aircraft arrived at the front: the Pup and the Triplane (as flown by Thompson above). The Pup, a scaled-down, single-seater version of the Strutter, was considered a delight to fly. It had a maximum speed of 110 miles per hour at ground level, a ceiling of 18,000 feet, and a synchronized machine gun. Russell Smith, of 54 Squadron, was flying a Pup when he confronted a German formation in early 1917:

I started to regain altitude keeping a sharp lookout all around – especially above me – but there was no one close. I soon spotted three aircraft in 'V' formation, below and behind, coming up from the east to attack. I carried on, watching them, and looking for any others. When they got closer, before they started to fire, I turned quickly and dived on the middle plane on a collision course, firing continuously. The two outside planes fanned outward in climbing turns and the leader pushed his nose down and passed under me. Then my engine misfired and I knew I had run out of fuel. Without the engine there was only one defence. I closed the throttle and put the machine into a tight, vertical spin, intending to come out of it at low altitude and land. There was no indication that my attackers were following me down and I didn't see them again. It may be they thought they had finished me.

Smith pulled out of his spin and crash-landed near the front lines, unaware of which side he was on. He jumped into a shell hole, still warm from the explosion which had created it. He blacked out and the next thing he remembers is kneeling in the bottom of the shell hole, swaying slowly from side to side:

I felt hot and removed my leather flying helmet and found it soaked with blood where it had covered my right ear. I jammed the helmet back in place and pressed the fur lining against the wound. Then I began to black out again.

When he came round for a second time, Smith noticed a chunk of damp clay next to him with a metal shell splinter protruding from it. It was the result of a nearby shell burst and the reason for Smith's loss of consciousness. Now that he was fully awake, Smith had to decide whether to make a dash for safety in broad daylight or to wait until dark, by which time he might be weak from loss of blood. He decided on the former:

I crawled up the side of the shell hole and out on top; nothing happened, so I started to run with my head and shoulders as low as possible. Glancing back to the right toward the place I had left the plane, I saw wreckage only; to the left I saw a body in German uniform lying on the parapet of a communication trench; and looking straight ahead I saw a tin hat slowly rising above a parapet in front of me. The tin hat stopped moving, leaving only enough space below the brim for the wearer to see me. Then two more hats came up, one of either side, and stopped. That was a wonderful sight, for they were NOT German helmets. I raised my hands above my head and struggled forward. When I reached the parapet, they were still there, and they reached forward and pulled me into the trench.

The Sopwith Triplane was another aircraft that was loved by those who flew it. It could not compete with the Albatros for firepower, but its three banks of wings gave it a phenomenal rate of climb. At first, it was only in service with the Royal Naval Air Service in the area around Dunkirk, although in April it would come south to fight over Arras. Herbert Thompson adored it:

It was at once my favourite aeroplane. She was an absolute beauty. She was really a glider with an engine, and she had no bad manners. Of course, you realised you mustn't play any tricks with her because there was only one set of flying wires, and I noticed that when I was diving very hard, I could see the strain on the centre section; there would almost be a curve on it. But she was so delightful that I remember one shocking occasion, when it was very hot, and I was coming home from a very high patrol, and believe it or not I went to sleep. Only momentarily. Really the culprit was her manners. She was so beautiful.

omfortable sleeping arrangements at Mons-en-Chausée.
e Flying Corps, we had nice mess rooms, nice billets, we
ood food.'

Bottom: Men and animals of
42 Squadron at Bailleul.

Opposite page, top: A chair occupied at breakfast might be empty at dinner, but the surviving officers would always dine well.

Opposite page, bottom: A rather uncomfortable encounter, as the Royal Flying Corps Kite and Balloon Section prepares to perform Cinderella at Bapaume.

Above: A wounded British airman is half-dragged to a dressing station by German soldiers. The airman is holding tightly onto his thigh-length flying boots, but he is unlikely to need them in captivity.

Left: Mick Mannock, winner of the nation's highest award for gallantry, a spontaneous man in an extemporal world.

Top: An officer buried with full military honours. 'As we stood beside the grave, I heard the padre's voice, but didn't take in a word of what he said.'

Bottom: Two British airmen buried where they crashed. aircraft stands guard.

he SE5 may have seemed a disappointment to Albert Ball
ιe pilots of 56 Squadron, but its speed, solid build, and
mance – once a number of modifications had been made
ed it into 'the honey machine of the war.'

Bottom: British airmen ready
to face the cold.

Top: William Bond, pilot with 40 Squadron, and author of a parody of Lewis Carroll.

Bottom: A Sopwith Camel. A sensitive and unpredictable machine, with a violent right turn that made it 'a terror to Huns'.

Opposite page: A Camel performing a loop you do is pull back the joystick, right bac your stomach, and the machine goes up, and then drops. As it drops, you switch o engine and come smoothly out into a gli

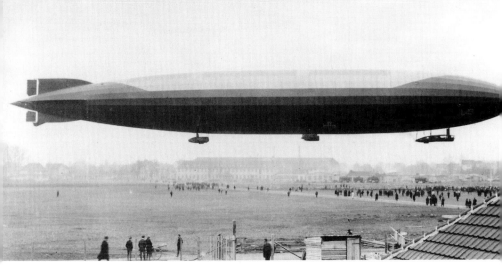

Above: German naval airship L43.

Right: Zeppelin bomb damage to the London and South-Western Bank on the corner of Aldgate High Street.

ipe, having the date of June 1916

7660 A   LIEUT. WILLIAM LEEFE ROBINSON, V.C.   ROTARY PHOTO, E.C.

"HE ATTACKED AN ENEMY AIRSHIP UNDER CIRCUMSTANCES OF GREAT DIFFICULTY
AND DANGER, AND SENT IT CRASHING TO THE GROUND AS A FLAMING WRECK."

*her engines — since then
airships have ventures into Essex*

ge from the diary of Essex schoolgirl Nell Tyrell, containing a picture of her hero –
am Leefe Robinson. Robinson's transformation from pilot to paladin was sudden.
es, flowers and hats have been named after me, also poems and prose have been
ated to me. Oh, it's too much!'

Right: German airship SL11 plummets to the ground in flames. Shot down by William Leefe Robinson, flying a BE2c, SL11 was the first German airship to be brought down over English soil. 'As I watched the huge mass gradually turn on end, and – as it seemed to me – slowly sink, one glowing, blazing mass – I gradually realised what I had done and grew wild with excitement.'

Below: The Bristol Fighter, the two-seater fighter-reconnaissance machine in which Robinson was shot down over Douai on 5 April 1917. Once the Bristol Fighter began to be flown in the manner of a single-seater, it proved a great success, remaining in service with the RAF until 1930, and with the Royal New Zealand Air Force until 1938.

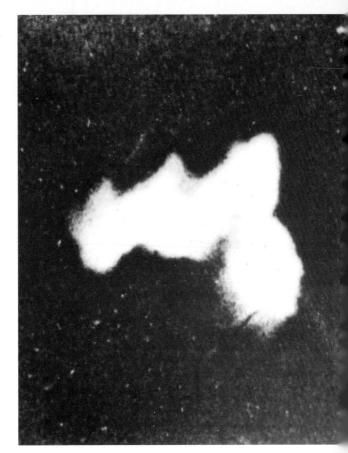

A Handley Page bomber being handled into position for take-off. Handley Page machines were the first h heavy bombers, and could handle oloads in excess of 1800 pounds.

Bottom: Werner Voss, a German pilot of great skill and aggression, who achieved 48 victories in just over ten months. He was killed whilst flying alone in combat against seven SE5as of 56 Squadron. The bullets which finally brought him down were fired by Arthur Rhys Davids.

Top: Werner Voss' silvery blue Fokker Triplane, with its moustachioed face.

Bottom: Manfred von Richthofen (in the centre) surrounded by fellow German pilots. His brother Lothar stands to his left. Richthofen achieve his first victory in September 1916, and his last in April 1918. He commanded the first Jagdgeschwader (mobile fighter wing) which cam be known as the Flying Circus by the British. His 80 victories made hin highest scoring pilot of the war.

hofen's room 'decorated' with serial numbers cut from British aircraft he had shot down, chandelier made from a rotary engine. Richthofen considered himself a hunter; these were phies.

Top: The foreshadow of death: the frontal view of Manfred von Richthofen's red Triplane.

Bottom: Richthofen's Fokker Triplane after it wa down on 21 April 1918. It resembles a carcass p clean by animals.

he funeral of Manfred von Richthofen at
ɪgles. Four officers are placing wreaths from
ι squadrons on the grave. It is worth noting the
ɪ the far right of the photograph. It belongs to
ɪber of the Chinese Labour Corps, transported
ɔhina to the Western Front.

Bottom: King George V inspects cadets of
the recently formed Royal Air Force in
August 1918. The initials of the new
service are made up of cadets standing on
the hillside in coloured shirts and shorts.

Arthur Rhys Davids. Born – 26 September 1897. Died – 27 October 1917.

Another new aircraft was the RE8, the two-seater replacement for the ageing BE2c. At first, the RE8 gained a reputation as a dangerous aircraft, prone to spinning. George Eddington was forced to do the unthinkable and put his RE8 into a deliberate spin:

We were going on a shoot, a routine daily job, to silence the guns. I had with me Lieutenant Dormer as observer, who hadn't been with the squadron very long. He'd been twice with me before. I took off and we reached the target, and it was quite a clear day. I think we were about 6000 feet, and we started the shoot. He did all the sending of the position, using the clock code. My job was to get as near over the target as possible. When we were fairly well over – having had some experience I said, 'You'll have to keep your eyes skinned' because there was no one about at all, which was sometimes a bad sign. 'Alright,' he said. And after a while he said, 'Can you go further over, I can't see the target properly.' 'Well,' I said, 'you've got to be careful. There's a bunch of Huns over there on the right.' He said, 'They're not Huns. They're British Nieuports.' I said, 'Well I'd watch them anyway if I were you.' And then he got on me again, and I thought, 'I suppose he thinks I've got cold feet', so I said, 'Alright, we'll go further over.' And I made up my mind to keep an eye on them myself.

I could see where the shots were falling and I was getting quite anxious to see them creep into the centre. And all of a sudden, without any warning, I heard a burst of gunfire. What had happened – these 'Nieuports' turned out to be eight Albatros. I could count them in the distance. They'd crept up on us – they saw easy prey. The usual method of attack, especially when there was only one to deal with, was to dive down from the back and pop off the gun. They let off a burst, and that startled me. I looked round, and there was Mr Dormer on the floor, flat out. I thought, 'That's it. They got him in the first burst.' Well, there I was, with eight of them round me. I was over the line but not very far, at 6 or 7000 feet. I was alright, I hadn't been touched. I had to depend on my own initiative. I decided to try and avoid them by making a wide flat circle, which deprived the enemy of being able to make a straight line dive on me. If you fly straight or if you dive he's got a straight line sight on you. If you're crawling around it's like a slow moving vehicle in a stream of traffic: he can't do much about it. All the time losing height. But I knew, in the end, they'd get me. And this went on for a while. I glanced round and I saw one of the aircraft diving on me as though he'd realized I had no gunner and was out to make a job of it. So I had to do something pretty quickly.

One always has to bear in mind that one has strict instructions never to do any stunting in an RE8 because it would break up on you if you did. But here was this man coming down at me, holding his fire, so I was left with no option. I decided to stand her up on her tail, pull the stick right back, kick the left rudder just as she comes on stalling point, and she will drop and start spinning. And of course spinning is the quickest way to get down. As long as you can get out of the spin. No one ever did it but it was the only way out, because there was another one behind him and if he didn't get me the next one would. So I stood on her tail, pulled the stick back, kicked the left rudder – I won't say shut my eyes, because it was too exciting. You'd be surprised but I was quite cool. Even at that stage somehow one doesn't think of death.

And down she went. Of course, the firing stopped. There was nothing to fire at for the moment. And I suspect that what happened was that the Huns could see me spinning down and thought, we won't get trapped on the wrong side, we'll just wait to see the shower of sparks. But I knew the supposed way of getting out of a spin was to centralize everything – rudder, joystick and the lot – and it will come out and do a straight dive. That's what the theorists told us so that's what I did and just as I was coming out of the dive, into the straight, I heard two sharp bangs. I didn't have to look round to know what had happened – both the wing extensions had broken off short, up against the struts. They carried the top ailerons right away. So I was left with no lateral control at all.

So there it was. I was going down straight, fast, and there was nothing at all I could do about it. I shouted at Dormer – 'We're going to crash!' But he was out. The only thing I could think of was to wait until I got within thirty feet of the ground, and then I thought I could break the back of it without diving straight into the ground. I put both hands onto the stick as hard as I could, far back into my stomach, and that pulled her back a bit, but then she dived into the ground with one colossal bang. I nearly never used the safety belt because it restricted my movement, but by a fluke I had it done up this time. There was an almighty crash, and I remember no more until an artillery officer came up to me and dragged me out. They'd already got Dormer out, and I remember him saying, 'Oh, you're alright!'. Well, obviously I wasn't alright but there was nothing broken. 'You made a jolly good show. I was watching you,' he said.

They bundled me into an ambulance, the old model T Ford, and they took me off to the casualty clearing station. I was there three or four days. Turned out to be nothing more than bad bruises and quite a lot of shock. I had a week's rest there and then I went back to the squadron. But the commanding officer, Major James, said, 'I'm going to send you back. You're not fit for any more operational work.' I was due for it anyway, I think. My nerves. Post-accident reaction, you might call it.

These aircraft, the Pup, the Triplane and the RE8, were really provisional measures, which would soon be superseded by a new wave of machines. For the time being, the Albatros held superiority of the skies. As a result, the Germans became bolder in their flying. Large formations of Albatri began to sweep the lines in search of two-seater machines, and once again British fighters were forced into an escort role which limited the patrols that strategy demanded. At the same, it was becoming accepted that British fighter aircraft should patrol in formation, directed by a leader; a formation offered greater protection when flying against a superior aircraft, it gave an ambushed opponent fewer escape options and it reduced the likelihood of being outnumbered. Cecil Lewis recalls a typical formation patrol:

> We used to take off on these big, squadron-offensive patrols, usually in the afternoon. Kitted up, of course, in our long sheepskin thigh boots and leather coats, and little motorcycle helmets and goggles. And by the time you got all that into a cockpit there wasn't much room. We were wedged into our cockpits, ran our engines up for two or three minutes; water-cooled engines, took time to get them warm. And then you took off severally, and at about 500 feet would begin to get into formation and head slowly out towards the lines. We were about 20 miles or so behind the lines, so we had to climb up on our way over. Our business was offensive, that is to say we used to climb up to get height on this side of the lines and then, when we'd got our height, go over and look for trouble. And we usually got up to about 15 or 16,000 feet before we crossed the lines into enemy territory. This was a good

height and, of course, very cold. And our eyes were, of course, continually focusing, looking, craning our heads around, moving all the time, looking for those black specks which would mean enemy aircraft at a great distance away. And we'd be, perhaps, between clouds, and not be able to see the ground, or only parts of the ground which would slide into view like a magic lantern screen or something, far, far beneath. Clinging close together, about 20 or 30 yards between each machine, swaying, looking at our neighbours, keeping our throttles, setting ourselves just right so that we were all in position.

Then, sooner or later, we would spot the enemy. If lucky, they would be below us. But in those days we were always under the enemy. That is to say our machines, as good as they were in the spring of 1917, were still not up to the Huns. We usually had 1000 to 2000 feet ceiling clear above us. So even at 16,000 feet we were still liable to be jumped from on top. But that, of course, didn't have to worry us. And we were usually outnumbered too, 2 or 3 to 1. We were very rarely fighting on equal terms. In those sorts of engagements, when we spotted the enemy formations below us, we used to engage irrespective of whether there was anybody above us or not, we just used to chance it. And usually any enemy aircraft that were above us would come down and jump us as we went down. It's not really possible to describe the action of a fight like that because, having no communication with each other, we simply had to go in and take our man and chance our arm, and keep our eyes in the back of our heads to see if anybody was trying to get us as we went down. But there was always the point where you had to go down anyway, whether there was anybody on your tail or not. So the fight began at these altitudes and engaged and disengaged with bursts of perhaps 30 or

40 rounds, tracer ammunition, so that there was always some idea of where you were fighting. Because your sights were really no good in these quick dogfights. There wasn't time to focus anything. It was just snap shooting.

So the whole squadron would enter the fight like that in good formation. But in half a minute the whole formation had gone to hell. There was nothing left except chaps wheeling and zooming and diving on each other's tails. Perhaps four in a row, you know: a German going down, one of our chaps on his tail, another German on his tail and another Hun behind that. Extraordinary glimpses one got. People approaching head on, firing at each other as they came and just at the last moment turning and slipping away. A fight lasting ten minutes or quarter of an hour, would come down from 15,000 feet to almost ground level. By that time, ammunition exhausted, guns jammed and there'd be nothing left to do but to come back home again. Because you only had two hours' petrol anyway, so you couldn't stay up for very long.

In early 1917 a plan was formulated between Field Marshal Haig and the new commander-in-chief of the French forces, General Nivelle, that the French would attempt a large-scale attack along the Aisne, while the British would mount a diversionary attack at Arras. The French attack did not achieve its desired results, leaving its army, still suffering the effects of the previous year's struggle at Verdun, in mutinous disorder. The British were meanwhile committed to fighting the Battle of Arras, which began on 9 April. In support, the Royal Flying Corps was to carry out its usual reconnaissance, artillery spotting, bombing and contact patrol roles. On 11 April, Charles Smart, a BE2e pilot, recorded his impressions of the battlefield in his diary:

All the guns on both sides in the district were going away at full speed. The whole ground, particularly on the enemy's side, was simply seething with bursting shells, these together with the flares presented a wonderful sight, there seemed to be millions of spurts of flame spread all over the countryside and it must have been as near hell as possible for those down below. The air was just stiff with flying shells and we got no end of bumps from them as they passed under and over us. One 'C' Flight machine was struck by a passing shell, both pilot and observer being killed.

The fact that the British possessed inferior aircraft to the Germans did not prevent Trenchard's offensive aerial strategy from being carried out up to the hilt. The Germans had introduced a further refinement to the Albatros – the DIII, with an upgraded engine and V-strutted wings modelled on those of the French Nieuport. Yet the British continued to mount attacks day in, day out, flying deep into German territory, suffering terrible losses. During April 1917, the life expectancy of a pilot arriving at the front dropped to seventeen days. Experienced airmen were being replaced by barely trained young men. Tryggve Gran:

A striking example of a raw beginner's first sortie was a young lieutenant who had just arrived at the squadron. He was terribly eager to get behind the German lines – and soon he had his wish fulfilled. His formation was attacked by a greatly superior enemy force and a nasty and bloody fight ensued. Suddenly, the young lieutenant's plane moved right out of the dogfight and in the next minute disappeared over the horizon. Wounded, thought his comrades, and got on with the unequal battle. But it was no bullet that had driven him away. No, the confusion and noise of the combat had somehow frozen his nerve and like a drunkard who is not responsible for his actions, he fled the combat zone without plan or objective. Finally when he was down the coast near Boulogne, he must have fainted for his plane ran into the cliffs at a terrific pace and was destroyed.

One of the replacements to arrive in France at this time was Sergeant William Robinson Clarke of 4 Squadron, the first black West Indian to serve as a pilot in the Royal Flying Corps. Born in Kingston, Jamaica, Clarke had initially seen service as a driver, before being sent for pilot training. On 28 July, Clarke's RE8 was attacked by five enemy aircraft. Clarke was wounded and lost consciousness but his observer took the controls and managed to land the machine. Clarke survived his injuries, returning to Jamaica after the war.

During the Battle of Arras, Bernard Rice wrote regularly to his father from 8 Squadron at Soncamp. His letters are affecting for their general mood of optimism, with a tinge of something darker:

I looked back, and saw a wicked looking little scout spitting fire and coming down on us at a frightful speed. My observer fired like stink while he was manoeuvring to get behind us again (he was firing through his prop). Just as he was about to make another dive on us, I turned and we kept on firing. By the time he was ready to dive again, he was up to 30 yards from us so I went into a split arse spiral, which did him altogether, so he made off, and flattening out, we sent another shower of bullets after him, eventually regaining our own lines with 16 holes in our biplane. Even then they wouldn't let us alone but sprinkled us well with shrapnel from field guns. This sort of work is going on all day long, and everybody is sticking it well. The Hun does not attempt such work. He goes about in bunches, and a few of his scouts try and catch us napping from time to time, while

patrols of our own endeavour to catch him at it and
keep us pretty well protected. Don't get anxious about
me. I am taking risks of course, everyone is, but I am
coming back alright, never fear.

A second letter gives Rice's reaction to mounting casualties.
'Eddy' is Rice's brother, also an airman:

Eddy tells me rather ruefully that he hasn't heard from
you for over nine weeks. Of course I know you are jolly
busy, but you might dash him off a line instead of one
of mine sometimes. I told him you only wrote to me
about once a fortnight, and trusted Peggy to give him
news of you. Anyway, that cheered him up. You know,
any moment you might lose him. He is doing the most
wonderful work which I can never make anybody
at home understand because they live in a different
atmosphere. It is equivalent to flying from Coventry to
Manchester, photographing, or bombing there, and
coming back every day. You are being shelled all the
way and chivvied by fast scouts who belt lead at you all
the time. Every now and then your pals on either side of
you burst into sheets of flame, and pitching forward,
dive to earth at frightful speeds, attaining perhaps 500
miles per hour before striking the earth some five miles
below. What sort of nerve has the fellow got to stick
this sort of thing, and he's so devilish cheery, too? It
hasn't taken any effect on him at all. You bred a man
when you brought that old lad up, let me tell you.

Here's some news. About our casualties. I haven't
said much in this direction, have I? But we have had
some, and pretty heavy too. Somebody comes down an
hour before dark, and reports a good shoot. A couple of
Huns driven off etc. He also reports seeing a machine of
our squadron attacked, and shot down in flames. Off I
rush to the 'drome. 'How many have you got out, Jack?'
'Mine are all in, old man, but "C" Flight has one out

still.' I have one out myself, so I wait. Presently, the droning of an engine, and a machine goes by. One of 51s, says somebody. 'Get the flares out!' howls the 'orderly dog', and I keep myself quiet by firing Very lights and rockets to help one of these two home – the lucky one. At last when everything is becoming blotted out, the drone of an engine, and somebody sweeps down and lands.

Blue wheels. Mike's are red.

So poor old Bill and Mike are gone this time.

I order the empty waiting hangar to be closed down, and go in to a sad little mess with two vacant places. Somebody says he saw the scrap. 'Old Bill and Mike, they put up a damn fine fight but the Huns were too numerous and fast for them.' A message on the 'phone and we dispatch a party to bring them in. And next morning we go and salute at the graveside led by the C.O. himself. That's all.

This morning I was up, and watching some machines dodging Archie. Suddenly a flare, and something like a comet rushed earthward. I looked the other way and tried to draw my observer's attention to an imaginary machine in the other direction.

I won't say any more on that subject. I only broached it because it seems people at home are getting low spirited about things in general. Chiefly I suspect because they are getting their little luxuries cut off. But if we can keep cheerful out here, can't those at home do the same? If spirits drop at home now, after all these months of sacrifice and work, and they want to fix up a peace now that we have the end almost in sight, or perhaps I should say now that the beginning of the last stage has arrived, of what avail the huge loss of life in the past three years?

One man who was still in France three years on, was the first man to land at Amiens back in August 1914 – Hubert Harvey-Kelly. Harvey-Kelly was now the commanding officer of 19 Squadron, stationed at Vert Galant. On 29 April, he received orders to send aircraft on a patrol to engage with von Richthofen's Jasta over Douai. It was not Harvey-Kelly's job to go up himself – he was too senior and considered too valuable, but his old competitive instincts could not be denied, and he took to the air with a member of 'C' Flight. While he was up, Trenchard arrived at his aerodrome to pay him a visit, with Maurice Baring in tow. The two men waited in vain for Harvey-Kelly to return. He had encountered eleven Albatri on his patrol, and was shot down by German ace Kurt Wolff. The 'gayest of all gay pilots' died three days later in hospital.

In Lewis Carroll's poem, 'Jabberwocky', a monster is slain by a boy in a strange and sinister world. In April 1917, an Albatros was destroyed by a BE2c (or 'Quirk'), in the skies above Arras. William Bond of 40 Squadron, a pilot and parodist, made the connection:

'Twas brillig and the Slithy Quirk
Did drone and burble in the blue,
All floppy were his wing controls
(And his observer too)

'Beware the wicked Albatros',
The O.C. quirks' had told him flat;
'Beware the Hun-Hun bird and shun
The frumious Halberstadt'

But while through uffish bumps he ploughed,
The Albatros, with tail on high,
Came diving out the tulgey cloud
And let his bullets fly.

One, two; one, two, and through and through,
The Lewis gun went tick-a-tack,
The Hun was floored, the Quirk had scored,
And came 'split arsing' back.

'Oh hast thou slain the Albatros?
Split one, with me, my beamish boy,
Our RAF-ish scout has found them out',
The C.O. wept for joy.

Bond himself described the parody as 'cheap' but others disagreed – most notably Mick Mannock who pasted a copy of it inside his diary. In the copy that Bond sent home to his wife, he substituted the word 'galumpling' for the phrase 'split arsing'; the crude version was intended for gentlemen's eyes only. On 22 July, Bond, a *Daily Mail* journalist in peacetime, was shot down and killed by a direct Archie hit.

By the end of the Battle of Arras on 16 May, the British had made gains but no significant breakthrough on the ground, while in the air they had suffered appallingly. They had lost 245 aircraft, 211 airmen killed or missing and another 108 taken prisoner. The Germans lost 66 aircraft. The British losses may not seem large compared to army casualty figures, but over just one month, in just one area, they were serious: the month was to be remembered by the Royal Flying Corps as 'Bloody April'. Yet there was cause for hope. Despite the losses, the Flying Corps had managed to support the army effectively throughout the battle, and three important aircraft were arriving on the Western Front: the Bristol Fighter, the SE5 and the Sopwith Camel. Experience had shown that air superiority could transfer quickly between sides and the Albatros DIII could not be expected to remain supreme for long.

For one particular Royal Flying Corps officer, the war was coming to an end. Frederick Winterbotham, of 29 Squadron, the man who shared his pre-war world tour with us earlier in the book, was shot down in July, and became a prisoner-of-war:

> I'd been out on dawn patrol. We hadn't had a scrap, but everything was hotting up. I thought I'd have the day to rest and I sat down to breakfast, when in came my commanding officer, to say that I had to go up again. I told him that my engine wasn't going very well and I'd put it in to have it overhauled, ready for the evening. 'That doesn't matter,' he said, 'you'd better borrow an aeroplane. You're taking your flight up to escort some photographic machines. The army wants it.' So I went and found somebody who had a machine. But the machines were very personal things. You'd got your seat at just the right height, you'd got your rudder bar in just the right place, you'd got your gun sight just opposite your eye. If you were flying the machine of somebody a foot shorter than you, everything was wrong, but they didn't have time to alter this, so I had to go up in a machine where everything was in the wrong place for me. I was also minus my silk garter, which went round my compass, and was a great help to me.
>
> Off I went with my flight of five aircraft, to escort these machines. Our instructions were to fly over 8000 feet. As soon as you see the photographic machines going down – they had to dive down to take their pictures – dive down after them and look after their tails. The time came, and I was watching out for the photographic machines to go down, when all of a sudden, there was an enormous barrage of anti-aircraft fire between us and the photographic machines. This was a new trick by the Germans. I couldn't see what the machines were doing. And at the same moment the barrage went up we were attacked. A dozen German fighters came down, out of the sun. We had a hell of a

scrap. Within three minutes, the gun on the top of my plane jammed. So there I was, without a gun. You know what one was supposed to do in this situation? One was supposed to haul the gun down on its hinges, steer the aeroplane with your knees, put the gun right and put it back up again. In the middle of a dogfight. Quite impossible! It was during the time that I was trying to clear the stoppage in my gun, that somebody got on my tail. I didn't feel or hear anything, except that my engine went, 'Phut' just like that.

I now had no gun and no engine. I had to start going down. I looked around and saw that I was on my own and I turned my nose towards home, but somebody came along and shot at me, and so I had to go on down. We were so far over the German lines that it was absolutely hopeless to try and get back again. I was tremendously lucky because I was feeling rather cold around the legs and I looked down and found that my boots had been shot off my legs and I hadn't noticed it. The bullets that had stopped my engine, had missed my petrol tank by about an inch. And as I'd watched my left winger being shot down in flames less than a minute before, I was not in a bad way, really. So I went into a 'falling leaf' so I couldn't be shot at, and went down. It was a long way behind the German front lines, fortunately, because if you came down *in* the German front lines, they shot you, out of hand. I noticed a bit with some grass about, so I floated down onto it, sideslipping. As I landed, I went nose first into a shell hole and the aeroplane turned upside down. The only thing that was wrong with me was that I got my head jammed under the top wing and my nose was broken. I was terrified of fire and I crawled out from underneath this shattered aeroplane and I found myself surrounded by German soldiers all pointing their rifles at me. Fortunately, I'd come down near the German anti-aircraft guns and these were really part of the German air force.

There was a great rapport between airmen, British and German. We always used to take a German that we'd shot down back to the mess and give him dinner before he was taken off to the cage. Well, a German anti-aircraft officer pulled me up and took me back to his battery. My nose was bleeding rather badly and he got a doctor and fed me with coffee, until I was picked up. The curious thing was that, in 1974, I had a delightful letter from Mr. Weigers, a German living in Texas, who asked me if I was the young captain who he'd pulled out from beneath his aeroplane at a battery in France. And of course, I was, and I had the chance to thank him for looking after me.

But I was very annoyed at the fact that I'd lost my gun and engine in the middle of a fight, in which we were at a great disadvantage to start with, as they had guns firing through their propellers. We had them in the newer machines – the Sopwiths and SE5s. We were the only ones left who had a Lewis guns on the top – and very shortly after I was shot down, my squadron got replacements.

That evening, I was taken off to an intelligence centre not far behind the lines, and I was welcomed by a large jovial German officer, who welcomed us in. He said, 'Hello! How are you? I am a gentleman. You can talk to me, I am a sportsman!' I said, 'Oh, that's good fun. What sport?' He said, 'I have played polo in the Argentine. Now you tell me all about everything!' So I gave him my name and number. He said, 'I know all about your squadron. You come from 29 Squadron, and your commanding officer is Major De Crepiny, is that not so?' I said, 'Well, as long as you know it all, there's no need for me to tell you!' And that's how we went on. They knew everything about all the aeroplanes that flew over them because we did it all so regularly. So they could plan their operations much more carefully than we did. We just had to go and bash in.

However, that evening, they entertained us, and two of the German squadron came along to have drinks with myself and two other chaps who'd been shot down the same day. It was a Leutnant Dossler who had claimed me and he brought along the cushion out of my aeroplane. And do you know, it was riddled with bullets, and in his very halting English, he said 'Ah! One inch and you are a soprano!'

So I'd been pretty lucky, really, and I remember the most interesting thing they told me that night was that they'd just taken two men across Germany to Russia, people called Lenin and Trotsky, and one of the Germans said, 'You wait! The Russian war will soon be over. These men are going to stop it!' That was in July 1917, and of course, how right they were.

Then we went back to a little house on the edge of a German aerodrome, where we were collected until there were about twenty of us there. They were shooting down about three of us a day, at that time. We were very hungry and we were only given one slice of wurst and some sour bread. We could buy cigars, which are wonderful if you're hungry – you smoke one of these and it took your appetite away. The Germans must have been short of food, but they had a special ration for prisoners, imbeciles, and the very old. We were all on the brown bread and wurst diet. But it was the time when the harvest was ripening in Belgium, and they took us out for walks, so when we went walking through the fields we would pick the heads of corn, and rub it between our hands and then munch it. The cherries were out, and the officers would let us stop and pick them off the trees. We used to exercise in a barbed wire cage about thirty yards square, and the Belgian women, dressed in black – who were very short of food themselves at that time – would come up to the cage and poke crusts of bread for us through the barbed wire.

After that, we were taken by train in cattle trucks to Cologne. In those cattle trucks, were herded Russian prisoners, who were hardly alive. They had been brought from the Eastern Front to dig the trenches and do the dirty work. Some of them died overnight going to Cologne. They smelt and they were full of every sort of bug. They had a few tattered clothes and their eyes were staring out of their heads. It was the most pathetic sight I've ever seen. A bunch of dying Russians. At Cologne Station, we were taken out of these cattle trucks and marched along the platform to be shut up in a cell underneath the station, for the night. Fortunately, they didn't put the Russians in with us that night, but a poor misguided German woman spat at us all along the platform. The next day, we were taken up the Rhine by train to Karlsruhe. We couldn't escape – there were armed guards with us at all times.

For three weeks, my poor parents believed that I'd been killed. The artillery staff captain whose job it was to note all the fights above the battery had been in the Gloucester Yeomanry with me and he'd found out that I was in this particular squadron, and he'd watched our dogfight and he'd seen one of the leading planes go down in flames, and reported back that it was me. It wasn't for three weeks that my family discovered that I was alive. I still have their letters.

It was a funny thing. At Karlsruhe, you found that you were back amongst all the people that you'd learnt to fly with in England. All the people who were shot down were sent there. It was good in a way, because each new batch of prisoners was looked after, until their own food parcels arrived. So we stayed there until they took us off by train to a place called Trier, and it was coming winter time. Very cold. We had a little court-yard that we could move about in. We got hold of a football and kicked it around, but there was one French officer who objected to us playing football, and he put on his best uniform and walked around us and amongst us as we were playing, so we kicked our balls at him.

It wasn't so bad at Trier. There was an extraordinary camp commandant, a German officer, who'd been a military attaché in London before the war, and he loved the English and loathed the French. Soon after we arrived, it started to snow, and we piled up the snow in the courtyard, and filled it with water, and made a skat-ing rink. And we also started to dig a tunnel – we were rather naïve. Our building was very close to the outer fence and each night, we would take out the earth that we'd dug and hide it under the snow around the skating rink so that they wouldn't see it. Then, one evening, the commandant called all the English officers together. He spoke English very well. He said, 'Gentlemen, I regret to tell you that your tunnel has been discovered. I beg of you, do not try to go out of it, because if you do, you will be shot. But don't, on any account, tell the French.'

The French officers were very funny. They had their orderlies and servants with them, to look after them. I remember, there was a little courtyard outside one of our old dormitories and there was an old water pump, and one of the orderlies had to go and pump the drink-ing water for the French during the day. He was an opera singer, and he used to sing the most glorious arias as he was pumping away. It made quite a nice change. On one occasion, some of the French orderlies – whose food was rather meagre – drew their knives over a single lump of sugar. They were very emotional prisoners. The British were fairly calm in comparison.

I chummed up with two very nice Frenchmen. One was a Chasseur Alpin, and the other was an Algerian and they both played bridge. So we had a bridge four straight away. I don't know if you've ever played bridge with a Frenchman, but he likes to play at about eighty miles an hour, and he doesn't stop to think.

Our time at Trier came to an end in Spring 1918, and we were sent off to Schweidnitz in Silesia. It's a long way away and very cold and we were housed there in what had been an old lunatic asylum. I took on the job of being adjutant for the British force. I wanted to do that because I wanted to improve my German, and we were there right up until January 1919, before we were sent home. There were many nice people there. Mike Bowes-Lyon, the Queen Mother's brother was one. And a lot of pilots. We tried to dig a tunnel there, again, but the ground was so hard, and I was rather broad in the shoulders, so for me to get through it would have meant enlarging the tunnel by four inches on either side, so I was told to stay at home. Just as well, because when we did the 'get-out' they caught them all. They were walking down a street at night, when there shouldn't have been many Germans about, but some-body got suspicious and told the guards, and they went out and rounded them all up and put them in solitary confinement. The next day, we set up a sort of squabble outside the German Guards' camp. There was always one non-commissioned officer who carried all the keys, hanging from his belt. We started fighting, and they tried to pull us apart, and we had one fellow with a bit of soft soap and he got behind the officer and we took impressions of these keys, and then we stopped fighting, of course. It was all put on as a show, and we made a key by melting down some silver paper and wire and we were able to go in the middle of the night and pass food to these chaps in solitary confinement. We were never discovered.

One day, a Prussian general came to inspect the camp. We had managed to get, through Holland, a cricket net and a couple of bats and balls, and we used to practise cricket. It was something to do. This general came around, and immediately ordered that the bats and balls be gathered together and burned. That was the difference between the German adjutant, a very brave and charming man, who was easy to get on with, and the Prussian general. That was my first taste of Prussians, and they were all the same.

One learned a lot about people in the camp. The prisoners divided themselves into three groups. There were those of us who were young public schoolboys, and wanted to keep fit. We formed a keep fit brigade. There were those who gambled away their houses and their money – somebody set up a roulette table, but I don't know if people ever paid up. Finally, there were those who were almost permanently drunk. You could get plenty of cheap Moselle wine in Schweidnitz. It was quite extraordinary.

Some people went off their heads. We had one man who became very peculiar. He picked up a knife from the table and tried to stick people. He thought we were all his enemies. He had to be taken away quietly. There were some unstable people, who we tried to nurse along. They'd probably had some pretty bad experiences.

When the Kaiser abdicated, all the German guards came out and threw down their rifles, and came up to us offering iron crosses in exchange for a cake of soap, or anything we could give them. And then the population of the town, who were starving – I saw them hacking up a dead horse in the street – wanted to come and get our food, and the adjutant of the camp set up his machine gun opposite the gates and told the mob if they dared to come in and steal our food, he would shoot them. It was an extremely courageous thing to do because he was really no longer in command.

Eventually, we were told we could come home. We were packed into trains and we had a long trip back. On our way, we stopped one night at a station, some way west of Berlin. It was so cold, and there were eight of us in the carriage. One of us said, 'There's a funny smell in here!' We quickly opened the windows. Somebody in the station had purposely turned on the gas and attached it up to our carriages, attempting to gas the lot of us.

When we finally arrived at Edinburgh Station, a band played us off the platform into a great hall where we were received with great plates of food. And joy. That was our return. I went straight home and shortly afterwards, I received a letter from the air staff saying that they had forgiven me for being taken prisoner of war and that no further action would be taken.

I was twenty years old when I came back, but in some ways I was nearer thirty. I was a completely different person. I'd met Tom, Dick and Harry. I'd known danger. I was thankful for my life. I had aged beyond my years. It had been a tremendous experience.

During his time as a prisoner, Frederick Winterbotham became proficient in German, which he put to good use some years later, when he became a British agent in pre-war Nazi Germany. During the Second World War itself, Winterbotham was put in charge of the distribution of Ultra Intelligence, collected by the Enigma machines at Bletchley Park. The Imperial War Museum's sound archive holds a typed transcript of a 1984 interview given by Winterbotham in which he discusses his role at Bletchley. Parts of this transcript have been scored out. Thirty-nine years after the end of the war, the story of Winterbotham's involvement with Ultra was still deemed too sensitive to be fully revealed. Frederick Winterbotham's life as a Great War pilot may have come to an end in July 1917, but his adventures had certainly not.

9

Bombing and the Royal Air Force

In the opening chapter we read of the predictions made by H. G. Wells in his 1908 novel *The War in the Air*. It is worth looking again at his vision of the future so as to understand the fear generated by the invention of the flying machine, the fear that bombs dropped from the sky could inflict a holocaust on an enemy city:

> As the airships sailed along they smashed up the city as a child will scatter its cities of brick and card. Below, they left ruins and blazing conflagrations and heaped and scattered dead; men, women and children mixed together as though they had been no more than Moors, or Zulus, or Chinese. Lower New York was soon a furnace of crimson flames, from which there was no escape.

By end of the novel, German aggression has led to a world-wide conflict which causes civilization to cave in on itself:

> In five short years the world and the scope of human life have undergone a regressive change as great as that between the age of the Antonines and the Europe of the ninth century.

Wells was a socialist who feared Germany's desire to 'achieve its dream of imperial expansion, and to impose the German

269

language upon a forcibly united Europe'. This view might explain why another socialist, Mick Mannock, felt and expressed such anger towards Germans. Moreover, Wells was a utopian who was suggesting a 'fantasia of possibility' that might point the way to an alternative future. His novel was not so much a prophecy that bombing would bring about the end of civilization as an allegory highlighting the dangers of placing too much faith in progress and in the governments who encourage it. He is stressing that a future war may not be a simple matter of victory for one side or defeat for the other, but a more confused matter of physical devastation and social disharmony for both. The history of the twentieth century bore out his warning.

Wells was not proved right immediately, however. As the Great War began, doom-mongers on both sides predicted that bombing would deliver an aerial 'knock-out blow' that would cause such destruction and panic that the government of the bombed nation would be forced to accept peace on unfavourable terms. Such fears were unrealistic for two reasons: firstly, the physical and moral strength of citizens to resist an onslaught was greater than was commonly believed, and, secondly, the means to deliver a sufficiently diabolical onslaught did not and would not exist for some time. Royal Flying Corps airmen were throwing darts and grenades over the sides of lightweight aircraft in August 1914, and even though technological advances were rapidly made they were not rapid enough to deliver the sort of decisive blow that a different war and a different kind of bomb would deliver in 1945.

While the Royal Naval Air Service was carrying out daring bombing raids against Zeppelin sheds in enemy territory during the first months of the war, the Royal Flying Corps was carrying out less ambitious raids on localized military targets and ad hoc attacks on targets that happened to present themselves. The bombs carried were of two types: a larger

112-pound bomb and a smaller twenty-pound Hales bomb which, despite its weight, contained only 4.5 pounds of explosive. Cyril Gordon-Burge, an observer with 12 Squadron in 1915, remembers the nature and limitations of bombing at this early stage:

> The equipment for bombing operations was very rudimentary. The principal equipment was the BE2c. And at first the BE2c usually carried one 112-pound bomb. Sometimes, instead of the 112-pound bombs, we used to carry four twenty-pound bombs under each wing for anti-troop bombing. The only bombing that was done usefully was against lines of communication, such as railways and bridges. You used to try and get as low as you possibly could so that you could release your bombs practically over the target. The technique was to take a sight on your target as you glided down towards it. Then, when you thought you were low enough, you used to release your bombs. That was the only technique that we followed. You just used eyesight, that's all. We had no bombing sights. There was no accuracy at all, as a consequence.

The Royal Flying Corps' aggressive strategy and its role in support of the army were reflected in its bombing policy. In April 1915, the first Victoria Cross to be won by an airman was awarded to pre-war aviation pioneer William Rhodes-Moorhouse, for bravery while bombing a railway junction thirty-five miles behind German lines at Courtrai. German reinforcements had been reported moving through Courtrai towards the Ypres Salient in preparation for an attack, making the junction an important target. Rhodes-Moorhouse took off in the afternoon, carrying a single 112-pound bomb, and flew over the enemy lines at 1000 feet. Without any means of aiming, he came down to 300 feet as he approached the junction, and let go of the bomb, which struck its target. His attack was a success, but his problems were not over; at such a low altitude, he came under machine-gun and rifle fire from the ground and from an adjacent church tower. His aircraft was riddled with bullets, one of which struck him. He struggled back to his aerodrome at Merville, where, fatally wounded, he reported his success. 'If I must die, give me a drink', he is believed to have said. He died the following day and was awarded a posthumous Victoria Cross. Rhodes-Moorhouse was twenty-eight years old and married with a son – making him unusually mature for an airman – and that son, also called William, was shot down and killed twenty-five years later while flying a Hurricane with 601 Squadron during the Battle of Britain.

Rhodes-Moorhouse senior's bomb attack was notable not only for its daring, but also for the fact that it succeeded. The low altitudes at which aircraft jettisoned their bombs put airmen in danger without guaranteeing accuracy. In the middle of 1915, experiments carried out by two lieutenants attached to the Central Flying School led to the introduction of the CFS 4B bombsight, which allowed the pilot to predict the correct angle for the bomb's release. Sidney Attwater:

> The bombsights were a crude affair. You set the bombsight on your own aerodrome, for height, wind, speed on sliding graduations. You sighted your target through one sight, set a stopwatch going, and flew on until the target appeared in the next one. You stopped your watch and set the scale to the seconds, and that was it. I know I got frostbite and so did many others, setting that watch without gauntlets on.

Crude and hand-numbing it may have been, but the sight had an immediate effect on bombing accuracy, and it allowed aircraft to operate at safer altitudes.

In 1916, as the DH2 and FE2b won air superiority back from the Fokker Eindecker, and Trenchard intensified British offensive strategy, so bombing raids on railway stations, junctions, lines, supply dumps, troop billets, aerodromes and other points of tactical importance were stepped up. Alan Jackson, a BE2c pilot with 5 Squadron, remembers the increased emphasis on bombing:

Machines that flew up to the lines and across them now had to carry two twenty-pound bombs and drop them on any target that they thought worthwhile. And the object of this was to make quite sure that the pilots did cross the lines and go over enemy territory. Because very often, they rather shirked that, either through nerve tiredness, or because they preferred not to. But obviously they'd be reluctant to drop the bombs on their side of the lines so they had to do it. And they'd choose some railway station that they might have thought would be useful. And as often as not they didn't hit it, so it didn't much matter.

Larger formations of aircraft began to take to the skies, laden with bombs. Alan Jackson:

We started wing bombing. Three squadrons would bomb together. On one occasion I was in charge of one of these bombings, in which you had to go quite deep into the enemy territory. And as many fighters as could be got from the different squadrons were put up in the air to protect you – which, incidentally, you never saw, but they were there, high up in the air. We'd fly at different levels, each squadron at a certain level, rendezvousing on a certain mark. That was the beginning of the mass bombing that eventually developed.

Of course, it was not merely the Allies who carried out raids on points of tactical importance. The Germans, despite their more defensive overall strategy, were mounting similar raids. Robin Rowell was with 8 Squadron, stationed at Marieux:

> Late in January 1916, the Hun came over to do his utmost to destroy our aerodrome. He must have dropped nine to twelve bombs all round the hangars, and we must admit that we were all taken unawares as it was the first trick that he had played on our part of the line. Three machines appeared from the direction of the lines amongst clouds of our AA fire, which from the ground seemed to have little effect. As they drew nearer, we could see that they were of the Albatros biplane type, and were all heading for our aerodrome. They were flying in a good line, one behind the other, when suddenly we heard a weird shriek and Sholto Douglas shouted, 'Lie down on the ground, boys!' We all obeyed instantly. The fun had started. One by one, they dropped the damned things round us, until the last machine rounded up by dropping a full nest of three eggs right in front of 'D' Flight hangar. No one was hurt and no damage was done. We all set to, filling up the holes in the aerodrome, so that we would not do our machines any harm by running into them. It's a horrid experience, much worse than being shelled, because you can hear the bombs coming long before the explosion takes place.

While British aircraft dominated the skies throughout the Battle of the Somme, the heavy emphasis placed on bombing behind enemy lines inevitably took a toll on aircraft and airmen. In the build-up to the battle, Archibald James was a flight commander with 2 Squadron, who considered that, on one occasion at least, Trenchard was asking too much of his men:

> One day in the middle of June, I was shown into Trenchard's room on the first floor, a fairly big room in

a sort of villa residence. On the wall was a big map and Trenchard said, 'As you probably know a great battle is going to start on 1 July. A glance at the map will show you that this straight main road right in the centre of the battle area is the key to German supplies. The road runs from Albert to Bapaume. In order to deal with this situation I am forming a special squadron of eighteen machines by drawing two from each of the BE2c squadrons on the northern two army fronts that won't be involved in the battle. They will operate from an aerodrome here under my direct hand, with no brigade or wing between the squadron commander and myself. You are in charge and you are in charge of the timetable. The machines will fly single-seater unescorted at 3500 feet to get out of the reach of small arms fire and they will carry 112-pound bombs with which they will put the road out of action. It's my pet project. I've told Sir Douglas Haig what I'm going to do. I have made out an establishment for the operation and here it is.'

He handed me a typescript and said, 'Now, go for a walk. We lunch at one o'clock. And immediately after lunch you will come up to the room here and you will tell me if there's anything more needed to make the scheme a success.' So I said, 'Thank you, sir', and went out. It was a lovely summer's day and I hadn't gone very far before I came to a big fallen tree. I sat down and I read the paper and did a bit of thinking. I then went back. With Trenchard lunch lasted no more than twenty minutes, and we finished and Trenchard said, 'Come with me.' I went upstairs behind him.

Trenchard said, 'Have you read the paper?' I said, 'Yes.' He said, 'Is there anything more that I haven't put on the paper required for a success?' I said, 'No. I can see nothing required at all.' He said, 'Then you are satisfied?' I said, 'With one exception.' He said, 'What's that?' I said, 'I want to go back to my regiment.' 'What on earth do you mean?' said Trenchard. I said, 'Well, sir, several times over the last few years you ordered me not to argue with you, and I don't propose to do so now. I'm a seconded officer and I propose to go back to my regiment.' He said, 'I order you to argue with me!' I said, 'You are quite clear, you are ordering me to argue with you?' He said, 'Yes!'

'Well,' I said, 'the reason why I won't take on the assignment is that in my opinion it is doomed to failure. The machines are to fly single-seater unescorted, and they will be shot down one after the other. The Fokkers will see to that. And when the first six or eight have been shot down the others will run cunning. They'll jettison their cargoes. The whole thing is bound to be a failure. And I am not prepared to be associated with a failure, because you have to sack the commanding officer of a failure.' Trenchard said, 'You will not go back to your regiment! You will go back to your squadron!' And with that I was bundled out and went back to my squadron. Trenchard then appointed a fellow named Dowdeswell to command the squadron. Which he did. And the thing turned out exactly as I had predicted. It was a total failure.

Nevertheless, successes were achieved elsewhere; on 1 July a single bomb dropped from a BE2c onto the railway station at St Quentin landed in an ammunition shed. Fire from the shed spread to two hundred ammunition trucks waiting in the sidings, and from there to a train next to which stood the men of two battalions waiting to be moved to the front. The grisly chain of destruction can only be imagined.

As new advances and opportunities were sought, the advantages of bombing at night became clear; an aircraft could fly over enemy territory unobserved and unmolested. Archie could only be aimed hopefully at the sound of the intruder and enemy machines could have little chance of finding a bomber in the dark. No. 5 Squadron began to practise night flying at the end of 1915. Alan Jackson:

> We started in a very modest way. We had no special navigation lights either on the aircraft or landing lights on the ground. So we filled petrol tins – took the tops off, filled them with paraffin, and put rags inside and lit them. These made flares. We put them out in a line, in the form of a cross, with the long end of the cross pointing towards where the wind was coming from. And in this way we were able to mark the aerodromes. I remember the first time I went up – I found it much easier than I expected. Because as you were coming down low you could see the lines of flares, and it was perfectly simple to make a decent landing at night along these flares. Gradually we developed this technique.

As if to demonstrate how war hastens progress, Harold Satchell (the pilot of an FE2b, an aircraft which had become entirely outmoded for daytime operations) describes the advances that had been made by late 1917:

> We were flying FE2bs for night bombing. They were 160-horse-power pusher machines, with the pilot and observer sitting in front of the engine. We always used to say that in the event of a crash we would act as a cushion for the much more important engine. And we had no parachutes. If the plane came down, we came down with it. We carried 430-pound weight in bombs, and our targets were usually railway stations, aircraft depots, aerodromes and an occasional Zeppelin hangar. In winter, we took off just after dark, at about six o'clock in the evening. That meant we were home in time for dinner shortly after nine. There was always a mad rush to get off because the first aircraft over

the target area usually got less anti-aircraft fire and machine-gun fire than the aircraft that followed.

The usual procedure after taking off was to climb to about 1000 feet. After that, you plugged in your wireless transmitter, sent your identification signal, and, if they were receiving you, they fired up a white rocket. After you'd seen the rocket, you headed up to the lines. As you arrived over the lines, you'd see the Very lights going up below you, showing where the infantry were facing each other. Then you flew over into Hunland, taking a compass bearing for your target. Arriving over the target, you circled round to get the best possible view of whatever it was you were bombing. Then you dropped the bombs. Coming back from the raid, you probably went a bit off course. Behind our lines were lighthouses. Each one sent out a separate numeral in Morse code. You knew where the aerodrome lay in relation to each light, so, provided the weather was good, it was quite easy to find your way home.

One night, we had orders to send out two aircraft to patrol the Lille, Laventie and Douai triangle, to see if trains were moving, in which direction, and at what time. At ten o'clock the weather was very bad but the army rang up and said that the job must be done. So I rumbled off the ground, with my observer in front, at about eleven o'clock. At 1000 feet, I plugged in my transmitter, tapped out my recognition signal and waited for the rocket. It came up and we headed for the lines, which we crossed south of Armentières. There was an absence of anti-aircraft fire and we carried out a reconnaissance at 1000 feet. Then the weather improved, the moon started shining through, and I climbed up to 7000 feet to get a better view of the area we were covering. At about twelve o'clock I heard a resounding thump on the aircraft and felt a horrible vibration. I swung around to the west to head towards our side of the lines. I opened up the throttle to keep my height, but the vibration increased. The thermometer started going up and the altimeter started going down. I opened up the throttle still more and the vibration got even worse, but I felt that was worthwhile, if only to reduce the risk of having to land in Hunland. I'd always taken a very poor view of being taken prisoner.

We were now dropping down to 5000 feet. I was half stood up in my seat, looking back at the engine. There were sparks coming off the exhaust manifolds, the rocker arms and the tops of the cylinders. I tried to figure out what had happened but it was very difficult to come to a definite conclusion. Perhaps some part of the engine had come off and fallen back through the propeller and broken it. I looked ahead and far in the distance, about eighteen miles away, I could see Very lights going up on the front line. I saw one that was nearer than the rest and headed for it. We were now down to 4000 feet. I saw a German on the ground, signalling up to me with an Aldis lamp, in an effort to make me land on his airstrip. I didn't see the force of his argument at all, so I kept on. I looked back at the engine again. Everything was red-hot and I only hoped that we would reach the ground before anything caught fire because I was sitting on the main petrol tank. That was an uplifting thought.

By this time, we were down to 1500 feet. Below me on the starboard side, I saw a long white strip, which looked like a road. I wondered for a moment whether I should land on it, but I didn't dare lose valuable height circling round in order to check on it, and in any case there was always the danger of running up against poplar trees which line the roads in France. So I kept on. It was just as well I kept on, because it was actually a river. We were soon down to 500 feet. On the starboard side, I saw a row of trees go past, and I thought this is where we start to flatten out. I began to pull back the stick.

Everything stopped. The aircraft stopped, the vibration stopped and the jangle of what sounded like a thousand milk cans behind me stopped. The only things that didn't stop were my head and the observer's head. He knocked his on the gun mounting and he got knocked out briefly. My lower jaw met the sharp edge of the cowling. I could tell from the sharp crack that I'd broken it. At that moment, I was very glad of the second cushion that I always sat on. Without it, I'd have broken my top jaw and that's a much harder job to repair.

I didn't know if we were behind Hun lines, behind our own lines, or in no-man's-land, but at that moment rifle fire started opening up on us from both sides with glorious impartiality. We got into a shell hole. When the firing died down, I looked at the stars, found the pole star and headed due west. We crawled along, making as little noise as possible, and then fell into a big crater. We climbed up the opposite side, and ran into some barbed wire with tin cans hung on it. The cans gave out a jangle and immediately twelve rifles opened up on us from fifteen yards' range. Once again, I was the less lucky one. A bullet got me in the leg and I could feel the two ends of the sciatic nerve jumping where the bullet had severed it. I didn't think there was much use making any further progress and I shouted, 'Don't shoot! We're Royal Flying Corps!'

After that, I must have passed out for a short while. The next thing I remember is four or five fellows crawling along on their hands and knees with a stretcher to bring me in. I said, 'Why the hell did you bastards open fire without challenging?' They said, 'Sshhh! The enemy's fifty yards away!' I said I didn't care and I repeated the question. They said, 'Well, we know there's a German attack coming and we've got orders to fire without challenging.' I didn't feel fit enough to continue the argument and they took me in. After that, I was bumped along on a trench railway to a dressing station in Arras. And as far as I was concerned, that was the end of the 1914–18 war.

For all the developments that were being made, the bombing raids discussed so far have all related directly to the land battles being fought below. In the meantime, war was being brought home to the British people in an entirely new way. The first bomb of the war to fall on British soil fell harmlessly enough; in December 1914, a German bomb dropped from an aircraft over Dover broke a window. A more potent method of dropping bombs was waiting in the wings, however: a rigid hydrogen-filled airship constructed around an aluminium-lattice framework, designed by – and named after – Count Ferdinand von Zeppelin. The Zeppelin was the vessel that had prompted General von Moltke, Chief of the German General Staff, to declare before the war that Germany had the means to strike a first and telling blow whose 'practical and moral effect could be quite extraordinary' and which had provoked Wells to write The War in the Air.

The mere existence of the Zeppelin had caused the Royal Naval Air Service to build seaplane bases along the English coast to serve in defence of the mainland, and to mount its 1914 bombing raids on Dusseldorf, Cologne and Cuxhaven. An RNAS flight was established at Hendon charged with the defence of London, and searchlights and anti-aircraft guns were positioned within and on the outskirts of the capital in preparation for the coming attacks. Yet the German leadership hesitated before using its terrifying weapon. It was concerned about international reaction to a breach of

Article 25 of the 1907 Hague Conference which prohibited bombardment of undefended places by any means. In addition, the Kaiser did not wish to mount a direct attack on his cousin King George V, whose family name remained, until 1917, Saxe-Coburg-Gotha. Over time, however, internal resistance to the use of the Zeppelin crumbled, and on 19 January 1915 three Zeppelins mounted attacks on Great Yarmouth and King's Lynn. The pre-war cry of the *Daily Mail* that Britain was no longer an island seemed borne out, and public disquiet mounted.

The first British pilots to fly over home soil against the Zeppelins in 1915 were faced with a fairly hopeless task since the Zeppelins flew at night. Humphrey Leigh, an RNAS officer, was based at Chingford in Essex:

> On one occasion in 1915, two men went up from Chingford in a large Sopwith pusher with the idea of coping with a Zeppelin. Their armament consisted of a single Remington rifle. There were no arrangements for night flying at that time – no system of landing lights. They went up – and they crashed out towards Hatfield. The pilot was killed and the other got away with it. The orders to go up had come from the Admiralty – and a lot of people in the Admiralty didn't know what an aeroplane could and could not do. It was a complete waste of an aircraft and man-power.

As the raids became more regular, Conrad Mann, an air mechanic at Felixstowe RNAS station, was ordered to seek an unusual form of protection:

> The raids got so bad that we were losing sleep and therefore we had to have time off till midday the next day. When we heard the warning we were instructed to go to the beach and lay on our backs, extending our arms and touching the fingertips of the man on

either side of us. So that we wouldn't all get blown up together. To extend the risk, as it were.

During the spring of 1915, Hauptmann Erich Linnarz, captain of Zeppelin LZ38, dropped on Southend (along with his bombs) a placard on which he had written a cryptic greeting:

You English. We have come, and will come again soon. Kill or cure. German.

Linnarz was as good as his word. On the night of 31 May, LZ38 came again, and this time it dropped its bombs over London, killing seven people and injuring thirty-five. LZ38 flew at such a height that it was not seen from the ground. On 7 September, SL2 killed eighteen people and injured thirty-eight during a raid on south London. The following night, L13 peppered central London with bombs, killing twenty-two people. One of the bombs scored a direct hit on a London bus, killing nine passengers and the driver. Florence Williams was on board:

I boarded the No. 8 bus at Old Ford. When we reached the top of Bethnal Green Road, I heard a loud bang and screams. Looking up at the sky, I saw the searchlights all meet on a Zeppelin. As the bus went on, round Norton Folgate, I was very frightened and started to cry. A woman on a seat opposite came and sat by me and cuddled me up to her. Something told me to get off the bus and I broke away, though she made a grab at me to pull me back. There was an explosion and a blinding flash like lightning. The poor woman fell back with a terrible scream.

This is the sort of eyewitness account normally associated with the Blitz of twenty-five years later. Yet long before Hitler attempted to force Britain to sue for peace before the country fell victim to a popular uprising, the Great War

German leaders were pursuing a similar strategy. Might they succeed? While an element of panic may have existed among a British public unused to experiencing war at such close quarters, the prevalent mood seems to have been one of anger at a perceived lack of protection. During a parliamentary debate in early 1916, Evelyn Cecil, MP for Hertford, declared:

> I am quite convinced that, while there is no panic, there is a very strong feeling of want of confidence in the general management. What we want is vigour, guidance, courage and determination.

Sir Percy Scott, a naval gunnery expert, had recently been placed in charge of the defence of London, and he promptly sprang into action, abandoning the pom-pom guns that had been making little impact on the Zeppelins and requesting additional gun stations and searchlights. The London Mobile Section was formed, consisting of a 75-mm gun, brought over from Paris, which could be driven across London to counter the intruders wherever necessary.

At a cabinet meeting in February 1916 an agreement was reached concerning home defence that henceforth the Royal Naval Air Service would be responsible for preventing Zeppelins from reaching Britain, and the Royal Flying Corps would be responsible for destroying those that did. Numerous improvements were made, including the implementation of a system of observers across the country who would keep watch, and the formation of a Home Defence Wing, made up of squadrons distributed around the country, given training in night flying, and equipped with the latest incendiary bullets, which gave them a far better chance of bringing down a Zeppelin.

The effects of the changes were soon felt. Zeppelin L15 was commanded by Kapitanleutnant A. Breithaupt, who recorded his wartime experiences in 1919. Recalling a raid over London in 1916, Breithaupt wrote of the city's defences:

> When crossing the coast the batteries opened a lively fire on us and we were picked up by the searchlights . . . London was practically dark beneath us. The British understood how to screen lights. When we reached the suburbs, fire was so heavy that I decided to carry out the raid from another quarter . . . Suddenly, murderous fire again broke out from an unexpected quarter. Simultaneously through the searchlight beams enemy aeroplanes stole past and above us . . . The incendiary missiles dropped by the airmen were plainly visible, and these, had they hit the airship, would inevitably have set it on fire; finally, at the end of 40 minutes of tension, we were clear of the 'unfortified city'.

Breithaupt's words make clear that, once the changes were made, Britain was no longer toothless against aerial aggression. On 31 March, L15 was brought down. Breithaupt wrote:

> On this flight, we were met with heavy fire over the northern suburbs of London, where artillery and airmen combined to give us the fatal blow. It must be acknowledged that the enemy's aim was wonderful. For some inexplicable reason, the airship did not catch on fire and as soon as I knew the result of the fire, I turned about and tried to reach Ostend. The airship began to sink in a slow even curve from an altitude of 3000 metres over London to 800 metres over the coast. About 0100 hours, the L15, as a result of loss of gas, broke her back, and fell vertically into the sea about 25 kilometres from the coast. I was in the car, completely under water, and I was tossed about by the water streaming in, but marvellous to relate, suddenly rose to the surface, and was pulled, completely exhausted into

the airship by the crew . . . The elevator helmsman who was next to me was drowned, the rudder helmsman had all his teeth knocked out and I escaped with slight concussion and various minor injuries.

Cyril Gordon-Burge began flying in home defence with 36 Squadron in the middle of 1916:

At that time they were very anxious to get these home defence squadrons moving, and to get them operational against the Zepps. As far as I remember, quite a group of pilots arrived at about the same time. And the aeroplanes too. And from that point onwards we were training during the day and flying at night. Our day was taken up pretty well sixteen or eighteen hours out of the twenty-four. The amount of sleep we got was pretty negligible.

We used to sit on the aerodrome waiting for the Zepps to come over. We used to get pretty good information long before a Zepp came over the country – 2 or 3 hours notice. We required that in order to get up to the required height. In those days it took you an hour or more to get up to 10,000 feet. When we got the explosive bullets and the fire bullets, we could set a Zeppelin alight. Explosives used to release the gas from the gas bags, which would trail behind the Zepp, and if you put an explosive bullet into that it would catch it alight.

On the night of 3 September the mood of the country changed. William Leefe Robinson, flying a BE2c, became the first pilot to bring down an airship over Britain, and a national hero in the process. The airship – not actually an aluminium-framed Zeppelin, but a wooden-framed Schütte-Lanz – was watched by countless thousands of jubilant people as it came down in flames. Robinson had spotted Schütte-Lanz SL11 in the glare of two searchlights, and climbed to 12,000 feet to confront it. He initially lost it in cloud, but, forty-five minutes later, spotted it again and hurried towards it. Robinson positioned himself underneath the airship and emptied an entire magazine of incendiary ammunition into it from bow to stern, without any noticeable effect. He then flew towards the stern, and from 500 feet away he emptied another magazine into it. Again, no effect. Finally, he fired a third magazine into it. There was no searchlight on the Schütte-Lanz by now, and it hung, suspended in darkness. Suddenly, it turned into a falling tornado of fire, and the country had found a hero.

The belief that Robinson had personally freed Britain from the grip of a tyrant is clear from the diary entry of an Essex schoolgirl, Nell Tyrell, who lived in Brentwood:

> Nothing was done to stop them until the memorable evening of Sep 3rd 1916 when Lieut. Leefe Robinson brought down the first Zeppelin in flames over English soil – Frank was just in time to see it fall and the glow in the sky over towards London from our house. It fell at Cuffley near Enfield; the cheering was defeaning [sic] and cars started at once for the spot.

Three days after he brought SL11 down, Robinson was awarded the Victoria Cross. In a letter to his parents written several weeks later, a sense of disbelief, pride, and pleasure in the circus that now surrounded him, are all evident:

> I do feel really ashamed for not writing to you darling old people before, but still, there it is – you know what I am.
>
> Busy – !! Heavens, for the last seven weeks I have done enough to last anyone a lifetime. It has been a wonderful time for me!
>
> I won't say too much about 'straffing' the Zepp for two reasons; to begin with most of it is strictly secret and secondly I'm really so tired of the subject and

telling people about it, that I feel as if I never want to mention it again – so I will only say a very few words about it.

When the colossal thing actually burst into flames of course it was a <u>glorious</u> sight – wonderful! It literally lit up the all the sky around me as well of course – I saw my machine as in the fire light – and sat still half dazed staring at the wonderful sight before me, not realizing to the least degree the wonderful thing that had happened!

My feelings? <u>Can</u> I describe my feelings? I hardly know how I felt. As I watched the huge mass gradually turn on end, and – as it seemed to me – slowly sink, one glowing, blazing mass – I gradually realised what I had done and grew wild with excitement. When I had cooled down a bit, I did what I don't think many people would think I would do, and that was I thanked God with all my heart. You know darling old mother and father I'm not what is popularly known as a religious person, but on an occasion such as that one must realize a little how one does trust in providence. I felt an overpowering feeling of thankfulness, so it was strange that I should pause and think for a moment after the first 'blast' of excitement, as it were, was over, and thank from the bottom of my heart, that supreme power that rules and guides our destinies?

When I reached the ground once more, I was greeted with 'Was it you Robin?' etc, etc. 'Yes, I've straffed the beggar this time!' I said, whereupon the whole flight set up a yell and carried me out of my machine to the office – cheering like mad.

Talking of cheering, they say it was wonderful to hear all London cheering – people who have heard thousands of huge crowds cheering before, say they have heard nothing like it. When Sowey and Tempest brought down their Zepps I had an opportunity of hearing something like it, although they say it wasn't so grand as mine, which could be heard twenty and even thirty miles outside London.

It swelled and sank, first one quarter of London, then another. Thousands, one might say <u>millions</u> of throats, giving vent to thousands of feelings.

I would give anything for you dear people to have heard it. A moment before dead silence (for the guns had ceased to fire at it) then this outburst – the relief, the thanks, the gratitude of millions of people. All the sirens, hooters, and whistles of steam engines, boats on the river, and munition and other works all joined in and literally filled the air – and the cause of it all – little me sitting in my little aeroplane above 13,000 feet of darkness!! It's wonderful!

And to think that *I* should be chosen to be the recipient of the thanks of all England! (For that's what it amounts to!)

Dear old 'G' who will be with you when you receive this will tell you something of the letters and telegrams I have received. The day after I was awarded the V.C. I received 37 telegrams, which includes one from my colonel and one from General Henderson, who is of course boss of the whole RFC.

I have had tons of interviews too, amongst which are those I have had with – a Russian Grand Duke, Lord Curzon, General Sir David Henderson and heaps of others. When I went to Windsor to get the V.C., The King was awfully nice, asked me all about you dear people and Grandfather etc: and showed me some awfully interesting photographs taken from the air over the German lines.

Oh, I could go on telling you about what I have done and go on writing for a month of Sundays, but I must cut things short. I have, of course, had hundreds

of invitations most of which I have had to refuse owing
to duty.

I went up to Newcastle for a day and was entertained by the Lord Mayor who gave a dinner in my
honour, where I was presented with a cheque for £2000
by Colonel Cowen of Newcastle. They wanted to make
the whole thing a grand public function but H.Q.
wouldn't let them, for which I was very thankful.

I've had endless other small presents – some of the
nicest are paintings of the burning Zepp.

By the by, about five artists have offered to paint my
portrait for the R.A.

As I daresay you have seen in the papers – babies,
flowers and hats have been named after me, also poems
and prose have been dedicated to me. Oh, it's too
much!

I am recognized wherever I go about town, now,
whether in uniform or mufti. The city police salute
me, the waiters, hall porters and pages of hotels and
restaurants bow and scrape, visitors turn round and
stare. Oh, it's *too* thick!

Many of those flying in France watched these events back
at home with a jaundiced eye. In their view, Robinson
had done little to merit public adulation and the nation's
highest award for gallantry; the skill required to stay alive
on the Western Front far outweighed that needed to shoot
down an airship over Cuffley. Archibald James was a pilot
with 2 Squadron at Hesdigneul:

Anybody who shot down a Zeppelin was given a VC,
which was quite an absurd award because – given the
luck to find yourself above a Zeppelin – they were dead
easy to shoot down. Ridiculous VCs were given for that
accomplishment.

While it is hard to deny that the award of the Victoria Cross to Robinson was politically motivated, the fact remains that his action had lifted the morale of the nation at a time when a lift was quite desperately needed. Yet Robinson's apparent good fortune was to set in motion a sad series of events. In 1917, he was sent to train on the new Bristol Fighter, before going out to France with the newly formed 48 Squadron. The Bristol Fighter was a two-seater fighter-reconnaissance tractor mounted with a forward-firing synchronized Vickers machine gun for the pilot and a Lewis gun on a Scarff mounting for the observer seated behind him, facing the tail. Its Rolls-Royce Falcon engine gave it a top speed of 110 miles per hour at 10,000 feet, and a great deal was expected of it. Who therefore better to lead its first patrol over the lines than the hero of Cuffley? And why not mount the patrol near Douai where Robinson might come face to face with Manfred von Richthofen, the German talisman, whose Jasta operated in the area? On 5 April 1917, that is precisely what happened. Four of the six Bristols (including Robinson's) were shot down by a formation of Albatri led by Richthofen. A fifth Bristol was damaged but managed to limp home alongside the sixth. Robinson and his observer survived and were taken prisoner.

Richthofen gave a subsequent newspaper interview in which he claimed that the Bristol was an unimpressive aircraft and no match for the Albatros, a claim that would be proved false. Moreover, the incident gave fuel to the views of hardened Western Front airmen who denigrated Robinson's abilities; he was clearly unfit to lead a patrol at the front. Yet fault for the fiasco did not lie with Robinson. The fact was that the Bristol was a new type of aircraft – a two-seater with genuine fighting qualities – and nobody had yet worked out how to use it properly. H. N. Charles, an officer with 56 Squadron, explains the problem:

There was a great difference of opinion about whether you should aim the Vickers gun on the Bristol Fighter by aiming the aeroplane or whether you should use the aeroplane as a gun platform for the observer to fire the Lewis gun. At first, a group of Bristol Fighters flying together wouldn't bother to aim their Vickers guns.

This was a mistake. An older two-seater such as the FE2b had to be flown in tight formation, using the observer for defence, because of its limited performance. It became clear in time that the Bristol Fighter was a very different aircraft and ought to be flown aggressively. This knowledge came too late for Robinson, however. He was already in a German prisoner-of-war camp, where his reputation as British hero and destroyer of Zeppelins, and his repeated bids for freedom, ensured him harsh treatment. An old friend and fellow pilot, Tryggve Gran, wrote:

> We little realised what German captivity would mean for our friend. Robinson wasn't the man content to sit with folded arms behind the German barbed wire. No, from the first moment he sat on German soil, there was only one thought which preoccupied his mind: he must reach freedom again.
>
> Time after time he succeeded in escaping from his jailers but every time the goal was in sight, he was arrested again and taken back – to severe punishment. The guard over him became more and more strict and in the end even an attempt to flee became impossible. Even so, Robinson was not going to give up. No; now he began to help his comrades and more than one British officer gained his freedom with his help.
>
> Of Robinson's jailers, there was one in particular who tried to make life in the POW camp a hell on earth. He had many methods, and when in 1918 the food rations for the prisoners was so short that they literally starved, he played a devilish trick on Robinson.

The English officers took their meals in their quarters. One day when Robinson came to the normal eating room, he found on the door the inscription, 'Eintreten Verboten'. He took no notice of this and went in and ate his meal. An hour later, the Commandant of the camp came with some soldiers. Robinson was taken to a cell and for disobeying an 'order' – so say his comrades – whipped until he fell unconscious. Time passed and in November came the Armistice. Just before Christmas he was taken back to England but his strength had left him and soon he lay with an attack of raging influenza. In his delirium, Robinson returned to the torture inflicted on him in the POW camp. 'You're hitting me! You're hitting me!' he cried almost to the last.

William Leefe Robinson died of influenza on 31 December 1918.

Once Robinson had brought down the first airship, it was as though a psychological barrier had been removed. Zeppelins began to fall regularly from the skies. On 23 September 1916, two were brought down. Nell Tyrell watched the destruction of one and wrote an account in her diary:

Our Zeppelin was the most exciting of all. I call it ours because it fell so near Brentwood and we saw it from beginning to end. We were first warned by a policeman at 9.15 pm coming to say that our lights must be put out as Zeppelins were about. It was a Sunday evening, ideal in every way for a raid. We of course put out all lights and went upstairs to be in readiness to get the children up in case of Brentwood being bombed. We all watched the searchlights from our window, trying to find the raider or raiders.

She went up to the outskirts of London and we could hear bombs dropping and see shrapnel bursting in the distance and then quite suddenly we heard the loud throbbing of Zeppelin engines and knew that she was not a great way off. Then away in the distance, a searchlight found her and in a flash, searchlights from everywhere seemed to spring up and all converged on the spot. The Zeppelin looked like a large silver cigar shaped fish, which wriggled and twisted to get out of the lights – she flew along right in front of the windows until she seemed to be just getting out of range of the searchlights and we thought we had lost her, when suddenly our guns on the Shenfield Common fired twice and we saw the shells burst around her. At the same moment, in a shaft of light, we saw an aeroplane above the Zeppelin drop its little red signal light, to stop firing, and a moment after the airship showed a tiny red flame which spread wildly along the whole length and enveloped it in flames. Shouts of delight and cheers were heard everywhere and no one thought of the awful death of the crew of the doomed airship, in the delight of getting her down.

She took quite a long time to sink to earth, behind Wilson's stores opposite. We all saw her drop except Frances who slept through all the excitement. It is a sight never to be forgotten, and although awful, was the most exciting moment I have ever experienced. After it was all over, we tried to go to sleep – but the crowds of cars, cycles, carts and carriages made such a noise that we none of us got any sleep that night.

Next day we went over to see the wreck and had to stop about half a mile away and walk to the spot, where the huge carcass lay, of twisted aluminium framework. She had fallen in a British Oak which had broken her in half and she lay all along the side of a turnip field about 200 yards from a farm house. All the dead and burnt crew had been removed to a shed belonging to a farm and we were lucky enough to just miss the removal of the bodies. While we were there an aeroplane flew around and some people saw that Lt. Sowrey, the air-man who wrecked her was in it, but I didn't see him.

Within Nell's account is a fascinating snapshot of a moment in time; she describes 'cars, cycles, carts and carriages' shar-ing a street, as one era overlaps another. But the Zeppelins, dark heralds of the modern age, would never again pose a serious threat to Britain. Zeppelin attacks would continue intermittently throughout the remainder of the war, but the effective organization of the country's resources had snuffed out their threat. Yet even as one storm lifted, another was brewing. Since the start of the war, the Germans had been developing a long-range bomber aircraft, and in late spring 1917 it went into action.

On 25 May 1917, the first large-scale aircraft raid on Britain took place. Twenty-one Grosskampfflugzeug – or Gotha – bombers bombed Folkestone and Shorncliffe, killing ninety-five people and injuring 195 more. The Gothas, large machines carrying three airmen and driven by two 260-horse-power Mercedes engines, were able to carry a thousand pounds of bombs to a height of 12,000 feet. At greater altitude, they carried a lighter bomb load. These machines might carry fewer bombs than a Zeppelin, but they were much faster, less vulnerable, and they could attack in daylight.

On 13 June, fourteen Gothas, stationed at Ghent, flew over London and dropped their bombs on the East End docks and the City of London. Liverpool Street Station was hit, as was an infants' school in Poplar. In all, 162 people were killed. Although ninety-two British aircraft took off to tackle the intruders, every Gotha returned safely to its aero-drome. They proved to be difficult targets: the defenders had little warning of their arrival, and insufficient time to gain the height necessary to meet them. Anti-aircraft fire proved similarly ineffective. The aerial defences of London had been unprepared for this new menace, and public agitation that had subsided in the wake of the Zeppelin threat asserted itself once more. The *Daily Mail* published photographs of the child victims of the Poplar bomb, alongside a 'Reprisal Map' of German towns within 150 miles of the British front line. Other papers urged caution, suggesting that the bombing might merely be a strategy to lure British resources away from the Western Front.

In reaction, the government wanted to do precisely that by relocating aircraft from the Western Front to home defence. Trenchard was understandably resistant to such a move. As a compromise, 56 and 66 Squadrons were moved temporarily to Canterbury and Calais respectively to counter the Gothas, although they were both returned to the front before the next daylight raid on London, on 7 July, which killed fifty-four people. Measures were taken once again to fortify the capital's defences. A central body, known as the London Air Defence Area, was created to oversee anti-aircraft gunnery, searchlights and intelligence of approaching raiders. A system of air-raid warnings was set up, and a ring of anti-aircraft guns was installed around the city, capable of reaching high-flying aircraft.

As had been the case with the Zeppelin attacks, the British defences improved over time. In September, the Gothas began mounting night raids on London, and the populace began taking shelter in cellars, heavily constructed buildings and London Underground stations. Cecil Lewis recalls flying against the Gothas at night:

> I and another couple of chaps took off, you know – paraffin flares, misty night, bit of a moon, which, of course, I didn't realise made all the difference. And once the excitement and tension of taking off was over, one was up in this magical, magical landscape, with the Thames estuary and the plumes from the trains as they came into London, and the clouds, and a little bit of a

moon. A marvellous romantic *Midsummer Night's Dream* sort of atmosphere. And climbing up and up and up to 14,000 or 15,000 feet. Seeing nothing, of course. Looking, searching, probing the darkness with one's eyes, which got night-adapted in about 25 minutes or so, so that you could see a little. But in fact, of course, quite incapable of finding a Hun even 200 or 300 yards away. He would have been quite invisible. The only thing you could hope for would be to see the glow of the exhausts, and you'd have to be pretty close to see that. You might know roughly where the raid was coming; you might know the direction; you might even know the height. But you couldn't actually do anything unless you could close that last 300 yard gap. And so very few people ever managed to find Huns over London. One or two did. One chap went in so close that he singed his eyebrows when the German caught fire. He must have been within twenty or thirty feet of that aircraft before he opened fire.

A large raid on London was mounted on the night of 18 December. It was carried out by twenty Gotha machines, as well as one of the new and even larger 'Giant' bombers, carrying a 300-kilogram bomb which fell on Lyall Street in Chelsea. One Gotha was shot down in the sea off Folkestone, and, despite the extent of the raid, relatively few casualties were suffered: twelve dead and sixty-six wounded. Large numbers of small ten-pound incendiary bombs were dropped, which the Germans hoped would cause wide-scale fires across London. They did not – although incendiary bombs would be used with a great deal of success over the city during the next war. It is interesting to note the range of aircraft sent up to engage the attackers: fourteen BE machines shared duties with four Bristol Fighters and nine Sopwith Camels, a truly diverse welcoming committee. The raid was received with the usual high anxiety and nervous excitement among London's citizens. Bernard Rice, a man familiar with anxiety and excitement on the Western Front, witnessed it, and his account, in a letter to his father, drips with sarcasm:

> I was present at the raid. I was amused. Archie went mad and fired like hell. I never heard a bomb or Hun the whole evening. In fact, I wanted my money back. First came the 'bobbies', peddling round on bikes with a 'Take Cover' notice, and continuous ringing bell attached. The streets cleared instantly. The tubes were thronged. All the people in the hotels were in the Gentlemen's departments downstairs! When it was all over, I expressed my disappointment to the club secretary Major Morley and he was quite indignant – 'Biggest raid we've had yet!' he declared. 'But where were the Gothas and where were the bombs?' I asked. 'Didn't you hear them dropping all around? And I could see the machines hovering overhead!' said he. The place was sprinkled liberally with Archie bits, and thousands of children were picking about in the roads next day. But bomb raid wash out! Me poo! I saw none! Can't imagine what they are shouting about. All people have got to do is to shelter from Archie and not push and panic and there would be no casualties. Biggest fraud of the century, I should think. Nobody need bother about London raids. But they do look well in print, though, don't they?

It was easy for Rice to be cynical. He took far greater risks every time he crossed the lines. Nevertheless, his point about news value is a good one. The excitement of the raids gave civilians a lurid taste of the soldiers' experience in France, and a sense of their newly discovered importance. It also provided a rallying call for those who wanted to see bombing raids launched against Germany.

The last Gotha raid of the war was mounted on 19 May 1918, when forty-three bombers took off for London. Of these, three were knocked out by anti-aircraft fire, and four shot down by home defence aircraft. Just as the authorities had learnt to cope with the Zeppelins, so they had now come to terms with the Gothas.

And as Britain became used to the sight of German bombers, so Germany came under attack from British aircraft. The British raids were born out of the desire to strike back at the enemy, and the political machinations that saw them launched were also to lead to the formation of the Royal Air Force. Public pressure for retaliation against the Zeppelin raids had been passionate since 1916, stoked by the newspapers and by Noel Pemberton-Billing, former member of the RNAS, independent MP and single-issue agitator. As a result, a Joint War Air Committee was formed, which gave way to a more powerful Air Board, charged with advising on air policy issues while bridging the gap between the air services. Long-range strategic bombing was a particularly pressing issue for the Air Board, and Trenchard made no secret of his opposition; with the limited resources available, he believed that such raids would sap the strength of the Flying Corps and inhibit its ability to offer tactical support to the army. Nevertheless, in 1917 the President of the Air Board, Lord Cowdray, and his Controller of Aeronautical Supplies, Sir William Weir, vowed to increase aircraft production to such an extent, that by the following year, a 'surplus aircraft fleet' would exist, which could form the basis of a strategic bombing force.

South African lawyer, politician and soldier Jan Smuts, one-time enemy of the British, had been invited by Prime Minister David Lloyd George to join his War Cabinet, and in 1917 he was asked to produce a report into the direction of air operations. Specifically, Smuts was directed to consider the reorganization of the air services, and the best means of implementing bombing operations. In his report, Smuts noted the 'competition, friction, and waste' that arose from the existence of rival air services. He went on to stress the importance of strategic bombing:

> An air fleet can conduct extensive operations far from and independently of both Army and Navy. As far as can at present be foreseen, there is absolutely no limit to the scale of its future independent war use. And the day may not be far off when aerial operations with their devastation of enemy lands and destruction of industrial and populous centres on a vast scale may become the principal operations of war, to which the older forms of military and naval operations may become secondary and subordinate. The march of events has been very rapid during the war. In our opinion there is no reason why the Air Board should any longer continue in its present form as practically no more than a conference room between the older Services, and there is every reason why it should be raised to the status of an independent Ministry in control of its own war service.

Smuts' talk of devastation and destruction might seem to owe more to H. G. Wells than to actual experience but he was articulating the nation's fears. So far as reprisal raids were concerned, he doubted whether the army or navy could conduct a strategic bombing campaign without heed to their own interests and priorities, and, given their history of competition and antagonism, he concluded that the Royal Flying Corps and the Royal Naval Air Service should be amalgamated into a new air service. This amalgamated service would then be able to take advantage of the 'surplus aircraft fleet' to mount an effective strategic campaign on targets in Germany, while squadrons on the Western Front would be able to continue their tactical work as before.

Smuts' recommendations were accepted by the War Cabinet and a bill was duly presented to the House of Commons, proposing the formation of the new service. As a result, the Royal Air Force came into existence. Contrary to popular belief, however, it was not the world's first air force independent of army or navy control. Three weeks earlier, the fully independent Finnish Air Force, consisting of one aircraft and a man to fly it, had been formed.

It is probably true to say that, by the time of the amalgamation, the Royal Flying Corps and Royal Naval Air Service were working in greater harmony than at any time during the war. Nevertheless, the union was in keeping with the spirit of the early Royal Flying Corps, which had been created specifically to bring the army and navy together under a single roof. The Royal Air Force was returning British military aviation to its roots. Its creation may have seemed an unnecessary sideshow at a time of great difficulty for flyers on the Western Front. It might have hurt the pride of some airmen, proud to consider themselves soldiers or sailors. But in practice, it would have little tangible effect on the lives and work of the men of the former air services.

As the politicians and generals debated policy, British attacks on Germany began. In October 1917, the 41st Wing was quickly formed at Ochey in north-eastern France to fly reprisal raids against Germany. The wing was under the command of Lieutenant Colonel Cyril Newall, a quiet, unostentatious man who would subsequently hold the position of Chief of the Air Staff during the Battle of Britain. It consisted of only three squadrons: 55 Squadron, flying the DH4 (dubbed 'the flaming coffin' for its tendency to catch fire in the air), 100 Squadron, flying the old FE2b, and 16 Squadron RNAS, flying the Handley Page O/100 and later the larger O/400. The DH4 and FE2b could only carry two or three 112-pound bombs, but the much larger

Handley Page machines, true heavy bombers, could handle bomb loads in excess of 1800 pounds.

Second World War British raids on German towns and cities are well known and documented, yet the Great War raids are not so familiar. Orlando Lennox Beater flew with 55 Squadron. His diary records an attack on the city of Mannheim carried out by ten DH4s on Christmas Eve 1917:

> Very cold morning and the water in our basins was frozen solid. We stood to at 07.30 am and started out on a raid to Mannheim at 10.10 am. We got our first whiff of Archie at 11.00 am when we were over Saarburg at 11,000 feet, and a good deal more when we passed Zabern. Some of the Archie was very close. Three Hun scouts were nosing about and appeared interested in our movements, hanging onto our tails for miles and firing merrily. However they gradually lost distance and faded away into the mist.
>
> The Rhine was on our right and plainly visible and looking very nice indeed, very broad and peaceful with numerous barges crawling along. Presently, we caught sight of Mannheim and from that time until we dropped our bombs the time seemed to drag interminably. The big railway sidings just south of the town was crammed with rolling stock, thousands of trucks and boxcars. We sailed over the city at 12.20 pm, greeted warmly and enthusiastically by a cloud of Archies, and proceeded to drop our bombs in the most pretentious part of the town we could see. Then a graceful curve to the north-west and full speed ahead for home. Sped on our way by a perfectly frenzied Archie and six Hun scouts which swept down from the clouds. They were most tenacious and hung on our tails in the hope of picking up Turner and Castle who was last seen going down near Speyer. The rest of us got back just before 02.00 pm, very cold and hungry.

Lennox Beater was clearly not concerned with hitting – or for that matter avoiding – specific targets. An attack on 'the most pretentious part of the town we could see' does not suggest meticulous pre-planning. Of greater immediate concern to the bomber crews was the cold. Cold was a problem for airmen throughout the war in open cockpits, but for the bomber crews who were airborne for long periods and at great heights, it was a particular issue. William Wardrop of 7 Squadron RNAS would cover his face with Vaseline, put a silk stocking over his head, and then put his fur-lined helmet over the stocking. He wore a pair of silk gloves under his leather flying gloves, and sheepskin boots and leather clothing. Nevertheless, on one occasion, he suffered frostbite in the air:

> The bombs got jammed and I couldn't release them with my gloves on. So I took my gloves off and made certain that these bombs went, and unfortunately I couldn't get my glove on again, and I got in serious trouble with the medical officer for doing such a thing. Frostbite feels as though you had put your hand in a furnace. You just blistered up. My arm was blistered from the elbow to the wrist.

Wardrop remembers the Handley Page and the method of dropping bombs:

> There were three of us in the bomber. The pilot and the observer sat side by side in the front, and the gun-layer at the rear. The gun-layer had three Lewis guns, one below for firing back underneath the tail, and two above. The observer had two Lewis guns in the front cockpit, and he was also responsible for the bomb-dropping equipment. He would lie almost prone and he had five lights, two red, two green and one white, to guide the pilot to the left or right, to get him lined up on the target. The bombs were hanging tail downwards

on a hook, and you pulled a lever which released the hook, and a bomb would turn over and fall nose first. And if we had a big 1660-pound bomb, it was slung underneath the aircraft horizontally, held up in the centre, and when it was released, it turned over itself and came down nose first.

In December the 41st Wing was increased in size, and renamed VIII Brigade. In May 1918, once the Royal Air Force had come into being, it became known as the Independent Air Force. By this stage, it consisted of five squadrons. The Air Staff had great hopes for strategic bombing and it listed a number of key targets for the Independent Air Force to attack. Among these were the steel works of the Saar Valley, the Bayer Works at Cologne and the chemical factories in Mannheim. Then, in June, the Independent Air Force came under Trenchard's command. He had found himself without a job, having relinquished command of the Royal Flying Corps to take up the post of Chief of the Air Staff before resigning following a clash of personalities with Lord Rothermere, the Secretary of State for Air.

The majority of the bombing that came to be done by the IAF, under Trenchard, was tactical rather than strategic in nature. Attacks on factories fell, those on railways and aerodromes increased. This is understandable: the IAF was growing very slowly. The anticipated 'surplus aircraft fleet' which Smuts had counted upon, when he delivered his report, never materialized. By the armistice, the IAF consisted of only ten squadrons, and the machines available were prone to engine problems and susceptible to bad weather. In addition, bombers had difficulty locating specific targets and even greater difficulty hitting them, with bombsights that had not greatly improved since the days of the CFS 4B sight. Perhaps it is true to say that Trenchard attacked what targets he could, and these usually turned out to be tactical. All the same, it is rather convenient that a man who had confessed his opposition to strategic bombing was now at the head of a strategic bombing force, and using it to carry out primarily tactical operations. It can never be denied that Trenchard did his bit to assist the army on the ground.

Nevertheless, as the war came to an end, new technology was becoming available to the IAF. The DH17, a bomber with an enclosed cockpit, was about to come into production, and the Handley Page V/1500, a machine capable of carrying a bomb load of 2700 pounds, with a range of 1350 miles, had already been produced. Perhaps most significantly, a large-scale raid on Berlin, to be mounted by Handley Page V/1500s, was planned for 18 November – genuine retaliation for the attacks carried out on London over the previous three years. Had the war continued beyond 11 November 1918, it is likely that the numbers of casualties and the amount of damage caused by aerial bombing would have increased significantly.

Although the casualty figures caused by bombing were small compared with those in other arenas of war, the inconvenience wrought, and the fear and anger provoked, were all significant. H. G. Wells' fears that modern warfare would lead to an increase in confusion and social disharmony were clearly well founded. During the Zeppelin menace, social disharmony was plain to see; public discontent became a very genuine worry to the British government, until the populace was mollified by conspicuous defence measures. Then, when the Gotha attacks began, defences were further strengthened and retaliatory air strikes launched against Germany; all measures intended to reassure the people.

As the war ended, the world was still a long way from the nightmarish picture painted by Wells in the final chapter of his apocalyptic novel:

Everywhere there are ruins and unburied dead, and shrunken, yellow-faced survivors, in a mortal apathy. Here there are robbers, here vigilance committees, and here guerilla bands ruling patches of exhausted territory, strange federations and brotherhoods form and dissolve, and religious fanaticisms begotten of despair gleam in famine-bright eyes. It is a universal dissolution. The fine order and welfare of the earth have crumpled like an unexploded bladder.

Yet in 1945, a British prisoner of war, Geoffrey Sherring, witnessed something similar as he wandered around the Japanese city of Nagasaki in the wake of a nuclear explosion:

The heat must have been intense. Everything that was made of ordinary wood crisped and roasted before it actually caught fire. For instance, our camp fence turned a dark brown. The rice crop had been green in the fields – but by the end of the afternoon it had turned brown and ripened prematurely. All the trees went autumn-coloured, and the leaves fell off them, those that didn't actually catch fire. All these effects on the natural order of things about us were fascinating to see.

For example, kites were always hovering over Naga-saki – big brown birds of the buzzard type. A number of them must have been hovering when the bomb fell, because I came across two or three of them, walking about in the city with no feathers on. Their feathers had been burnt off them in mid-air, and they'd collapsed to the ground. They were wandering around on foot. Horrifying sight.

And the dead were lying everywhere. In the first few days after the bomb dropped, when we were actually sleeping in the city, my little corner of brickwork was also occupied by a Japanese woman whose husband's corpse was with her – and she'd covered it over with straw matting, but gradually it became distended and smelly. She didn't want to hand it over until the police more or less wrestled it from her. This problem of corpses became very severe, so we gathered all the timber we could find, that had been used in the construction of houses, and putting it in long rows down the middle of the concrete road and then we stacked the corpses neatly on top of this pile of timber. We were left with rows of corpses a hundred yards long.

The scene that Sherring witnessed had its origins in the Great War, when world powers took the aeroplane and attempted to turn it into a machine that could deliver a 'knock-out-blow'. In four years, progress was made. In another twenty-seven, the process would be complete.

10

A Fight to the End

Great War airmen of all nations flew in machines made of wood and fabric which carried tanks full of petrol, and they all shared a common anxiety. Hans Schröder witnessed a terrible sight in July 1917:

> It [the British aircraft] exploded in front of my window and burst into flames. The burning petrol greedily consumed the unlucky pilot, whose face was charred; his breeches were burnt away at the thighs, and the roasting flesh sizzled in the heat. From all sides came men with buckets, intending to throw water on the blaze.
>
> Then a car full of airmen came along, and my friend Klein jumped out. 'Not so bad!' he exclaimed. 'So it was your roof I sent him down onto! He was a really obstinate fellow; I shot his bus up over Lauwe, and he waved to me as if to say he'd land. I went down; I followed, and ceased fire. Then he suddenly pulled his nose up and put at least twenty bullets into my machine. Well, after that there was no mercy for him. We buzzed round and round this part of the world at a height of fifty metres, like two dogs chasing one another; he had no notion where he was, but he pulled his machine up, and I zoomed after him. I was hanging on my prop when I put a burst into him, and as I went

into a loop I saw him go down by one wing and crash into Wevelghem. In any case he was a bad lot; that sort spoils the chivalry one expects in flying. He deserved his fate.'

The blaze died down gradually, but there was a hiss from the burnt thighs when the spectators emptied their buckets of water on the body. There was a ghastly smell of grilled ham, but the legs below the knees were hardly touched by the fire. The fine new laced boots, reaching almost to the knees, proclaimed that this was the body of a human being who only a little while ago had been full of the warm life that pulsated in all our bodies.

When I returned late that night to my new quarters, I found two surprises. On dismounting from my car, I discovered two bottles of Bols in my overcoat pockets, and in my room there was a pair of brand new high-laced boots, which reached to the knees. I took them up, and they gave off an odour of smoked bacon. My good [batman] Paul meant it kindly with me, but I had a vision of their former owner. So I shoved those boots outside the door and braced myself with a Bols.

Arthur Gould Lee of 46 Squadron believed that 'there were few fliers who were not obsessed to some degree, though usually secretly, with the thought of being shot down in flames'. Mick Mannock was not the only man to carry a revolver into the air with which to shoot himself rather than burn. And one reason why this fear became an obsession with so many pilots and observers was because none of them – on the British side – was ever issued with parachutes. For Arthur Gould Lee, the failure of the flying services to provide parachutes was so unforgivable that he gave his war memoirs a simple and pointed title: *No Parachute*.

Speaking many years after the war, Archibald James attributed the lack of parachutes to practical limitations:

Refusal to issue parachutes: the answer's a very simple one. The development of parachutes was in its infancy and the only available parachutes were so cumbersome and big that there simply wasn't room for them in the cockpit. The harness would have affected the efficiency and mobility of the personnel in the aircraft – they'd have been jammed into their seats.

In fact a practical parachute – the Calthrop 'Guardian Angel' – *was* available for a substantial part of the war, and aircraft could have been modified to accommodate them. From early 1918, German aircraft were fitted with Heinecke parachutes, which saved the lives of more than sixty airmen before the war's end. One of these was Ernst Udet, the second highest-scoring German ace. The fact is that the British authorities believed that parachutes would impair fighting spirit, and encourage men to abandon their machines without putting up a concerted fight. These concerns were expressed by the Air Board in an unpublished wartime report, displaying a breathtaking lack of faith in, and lack of concern for, the men whose interests they were supposedly protecting. Eventually, in September 1918, an order was placed for five hundred Calthrop parachutes, of a type that had been available back in July 1916, yet none had been issued by the end of the war.

Gould Lee's diary entry for 3 January 1918 is chilling. It makes a mockery of the Air Board's complacent attitude:

> I'm terribly depressed this evening. Ferrie has been killed. He led his patrol out this afternoon, had a scrap, came back leading the others, then as they were flying along quite normally in formation, his right wing suddenly folded back, then the other, and the wreck plunged vertically down. A bullet must have gone through a main spar during the fight.
>
> The others went after him and steered close to him in vertical dives. They could see him, struggling to get

clear of his harness, then half standing up. They said it was terrible to watch him trying to decide whether to jump. He didn't, and the machine and he were smashed to nothingness.

I can't believe it. Little Ferrie, with his cheerful grin, one of the finest chaps in the squadron. God, imagine his last moments, seeing the ground rushing up at him, knowing he was a dead man, unable to move, unable to do anything but wait for it. A parachute could have saved him, there's no doubt about that. What the hell is wrong with those callous dolts at home that they won't give them to us?

One man for whom Gould Lee had the greatest respect was Albert Ball. In a diary entry written in June 1917, he considers how fine it would be to have Ball's guts, 'to be completely without fear, to attack regardless of the odds, not giving a damn whether you're killed or not'. The most eventful period of Ball's career had begun two months earlier. On 7 April he returned to France with Major Blomfield's 56 Squadron, where he was to fly the new SE5 Fighter. With a top speed of 120 miles per hour, a ceiling of 17,000 feet, a fixed synchronized Vickers gun on its central cowling and a Lewis gun on its top wing, much was expected of the new machine. Hubert Charles, an engineer with 56 Squadron, recalls the SE5's arrival at London Colney where the squadron was stationed before flying out to France:

We hadn't seen an SE5, and Albert Ball went and fetched the first one, and when he was flying it around, before he had landed, everybody simply couldn't believe that this was the new SE5 Fighter. The thing looked hopeless. It was hopelessly slow, it didn't want to do any aerobatics, when it landed it was boiling, and after it landed, the paint was sticky on the outside of the cylinder block. The very first thing I did was to take the radiator off and we fitted it with a wire mesh filter bag, in the header tank, so that if any more paint came out from the water jacket, it couldn't block the radiator. And we washed the water jackets of the engines out and put the radiator back, and from then on, the engine ran without boiling.

And one by one, we went through the obvious faults on the SE5. For example, in some circumstances, if you filled the oil tank to the top, it promptly bust! So we vented the thing into the crank case. Our aim was simply to get the aeroplanes to fly to France with their engines, controls, and Lewis guns working. We could leave the Vickers guns and interrupter gears until France.

Ball was, at first, hugely disappointed by the new machine. He had the factory-fitted windscreen removed, complaining that it obscured his forward vision, and on 8 April he visited Trenchard to ask him to be allowed to carry on flying his Nieuport 17. In the end, he agreed to fly the SE5 for squadron work, and the Nieuport for what Maurice Baring called 'individual enterprises'. This meant that Ball would lead patrols each day in the SE5, before climbing into his Nieuport to fly off alone in search of further fights. Royal Flying Corps pilots were not permitted to paint their aircraft in individual colours, but Ball streamlined the Nieuport's propeller hub by covering it with a large aluminium bowl, which he painted bright red. From then on he became the Flying Corps' most distinctive, as well as its most celebrated, pilot.

In time, the SE5's imperfections were resolved at squadron level and it became an extremely effective fighter. When it was fitted with a new 200-horse-power Hispano-Suiza engine, it became a truly formidable machine, with a top speed of 138 miles per hour. Ball, meanwhile, was pushing the SE5, and himself, to the limit. On one occasion, when attacked by five enemy machines, he shot four of them down in less than ten minutes. The other one scampered for home. By 2 May he had accounted for thirty-eight victims, and, three days later, he experienced a very narrow escape. Having already shot down one Albatros, he flew head-on at another. He described the encounter in a letter to his fiancée:

> Well, Bobs, I thought it was all up with us, and it was going to be a ramming job. But just as we were about to hit, my engine was hit by a bullet and all the oil came into my face. For a short time, I saw nothing, but when all got OK again, I looked down and saw the Hun going down out of control.

Ball had flown straight at the Albatros, with his trigger button pressed. He had prepared himself for death, but death had not come. On his return to Vert Galant, his nerves were shattered, and he could not concentrate on filing his flight report. The recording officer listened as he muttered, 'God is very good to me . . .' In the same letter to his fiancée, written that evening:

> Oh, won't it be nice when all this beastly killing is over, and we can just enjoy ourselves and not hurt anyone. I hate this game, but it is the only thing one must do just now.

He wrote a similarly reflective letter to his parents that evening, quite different in tone from the childlike correspondence that they were used to receiving:

> Am indeed looked after by God, but oh! I do get tired of always living to kill, and am really beginning to feel like a murderer. Shall be so pleased when I am finished.

Bad weather the next morning allowed Ball to spend time in his garden. In the meantime, his SE5 was undergoing repairs, after the battering it had received the previous day.

An engineering officer, C. K. Shaw, remembers speaking to Ball:

> My opinion of him had been of someone who was ... not exactly arrogant ... but brave. But that was completely different from the young man that I saw sitting in my office on that day when my mechanics were repairing his SE5. When I saw him, I said, 'Cheer up, old boy. What's wrong?' 'Oh,' said Ball, 'I've got a hunch.' 'A hunch?' I said. 'I don't think I'm going to last very long,' he said. 'Oh, that's absurd!' I said. 'You're here for a long time yet! Don't you worry!' 'No,' he said, 'I don't think so. I don't think so.'

This was not the nerveless hero of popular repute. On the evening of 7 May eleven SE5s of 56 Squadron set out on patrol over Douai. Ball led 'A' Flight. In a sky thick with cumulus cloud, the patrol met various German formations, and confused and scattered dogfights broke out. Ball seems to have engaged with an Albatros DIII flown by Lothar von Richthofen, the brother of the Red Baron, who was forced to make an emergency landing. It is possible that Ball and Richthofen brought each other down. All that is known for certain is that Ball crash-landed near the village of Annoeullin, where he was pulled from the wreckage of his SE5 by a young woman, who cradled him in her arms as he died.

A month later, the supplement to the *London Gazette* announced the award of his Victoria Cross. It was not awarded for a single action, but for his consistent acts of bravery over eleven days in April and May. At the time of his death, he had reached a point of nervous exhaustion from which he could no longer summon up the strength to fight as he had been doing. As was the case with so many pilots, he knew when his time on earth was up; having reached the limits of human endurance, he understood the consequences. His death would bring tributes from the King and from General Haig among many others. It was reported in newspapers across the world, from Japan, whose press praised his 'glorious record', to South America, where he was considered a 'heroic pilot'. Albert Ball was a recognizable hero in a faceless war.

In June 1917, another new British fighter arrived on the Western Front. Its technical name was the Sopwith Biplane F.1, but, thanks to a hump in front of the pilot, it became much better known as the Sopwith Camel. The Camel had a maximum speed of 117 miles per hour, a ceiling of 19,000 feet and it was armed with twin Vickers guns firing through the propeller. It was a descendant of the Pup, and a complete contrast to the SE5. Where the SE5 was robust and stable, the Camel was sensitive and unpredictable. It had to be held in flying position continually to prevent its nose from rearing up, and the powerful torque of its rotary engine gave it a violent right turn which had to be carefully balanced with left rudder to prevent a spinning nosedive. Yet these quirks made it extremely manoeuvrable, and its knife-edge personality made it a wonderful combat machine. The Camel would become the most successful fighter aeroplane of the war, destroying around 1500 enemy aircraft. From *Winged Victory*:

> Camels were wonderful fliers when you got used to them, which took about three months of hard flying. At the end of that time you were either dead, a nervous wreck, or a hell of a pilot and a terror to Huns.

As larger and larger formations of fighters began to meet in the skies, it made sense to organize them into larger groups on the ground. In June, the first German Jagdgeschwader was formed. This was a mobile fighter wing, made up of four Jasta, with transportable ground back-up that could be moved up and down the front to provide localized air superiority wherever it was needed. Manfred von Richthofen was placed in command of Jagdgeschwader 1, and its pilots promptly copied the example of his distinctive red Albatros by painting their own machines in bright colours and swanky patterns. This – and the fact that it travelled the country before unloading at its next venue – led to Jagdgeschwader 1 being dubbed first 'Richthofen's Circus' and later the 'Flying Circus' by mocking opponents. Friedrich Lubbert was a member of the Flying Circus, and a man who plainly idolized his leader:

> When I came for the first time to the wing formation of Baron von Richthofen, he invited me to lunch and he was very friendly and a very agreeable officer. Of course it was a great honour to be in the troop of Richthofen. And it was very interesting to see how Baron von Richthofen made an air fight. He was a very good shooter and he saw all. That was his success. He had a very good influence on us, and in the day we had much practice in shooting, and otherwise we played together hockey, billiards, table tennis, and in the evening we played poker and we loved him very, very much.

In June 1917, a large-scale Allied offensive was launched in Flanders. Haig's intention was to break through on the Ypres Salient, before moving north to the coast, but, prior to launching the main advance, he had to capture the Messines Ridge, which overlooked the entire area. On 7 June, as the German lines came under fierce bombardment from more than two thousand British guns, nineteen vast mines were simultaneously detonated below ground. The German defenders were taken by surprise and the attack proved successful; the village of Messines was quickly captured by advancing British troops. This preparatory advance was followed on 31 July by the Third Battle of Ypres (otherwise known as Passchendaele), an attack along a seven-mile front by the British Fifth and Second Armies, and the French First Army. The Royal Flying Corps had its usual crucial role to play in the battle: aerial photography, artillery observation, contact patrols, tactical bombing and the clearing from the skies of enemy aircraft that attempted to interfere with these tasks. According to Archibald James, the work of the squadrons was similar to their work on the Somme – but more intense; as aircraft became more successful in their allotted tasks, so more was expected from them in return.

The conditions which infantrymen had to endure at Passchendaele were appalling. Persistent rain created mud that was churned into liquid by relentless artillery fire. The bad weather persisted throughout August – infantrymen risked drowning if they slipped off duckboards which traversed the pools of glutinous muck. T. E. Rogers of 6 Squadron felt fortunate to be spared the hell on earth:

> While I was sleeping in a nice warm camp-bed, having dinner in a nice mess, sitting in front of a good warm fire, all the time I was thinking of the infantry, in that terrible weather. I nearly wept, for the PBI – the poor bloody infantry.

While the conditions in the air were not as bad as they were on the ground, airmen still had to contend with heavy rain, low cloud and mist. Archibald James:

> One of the problems at Passchendaele was visibility. 1917 was a deplorably wet autumn, almost continuous rains right through. That meant that you got a fearful amount of mist. And there was one particular sort of mist which was called ground mist which was quite unapparent on the ground but very, very apparent in the air. It was a sort of brown haze which went up to approximately 3500 feet. And if you were flying at 3500 feet, you would see the almost flat top.

Poor conditions below combined with poor visibility above made contact patrols difficult. T. E. Rogers flew an RE8 over the battlefield:

> The infantry were supposed to light Very lights in succession along the front to the point where they had advanced. The observer would plot the spots where the lights appeared, and he would seldom get very many. Well, usually the infantry couldn't get any distance at all. They were in mud and slush. In fact, throughout the three months that I was over Passchendaele, there were very few occasions when I had a whole string of lights recorded on my map.

Norman Macmillan of 45 Squadron flew a Sopwith Camel over Passchendaele:

> Passchendaele brought new responsibilities to the fighters. We had a variety of tasks to perform. They were detailed for us. We were not freelance. We were sent out on distant offensive patrols, or close offensive patrols, at stated heights above the ground. Their object being to attack any enemy aircraft that we might see. And they involved us in combats. Sometimes we were sent to escort artillery observation machines carrying out shoots for the gunners. And at other times we were sent out on ground-attack patrols.

Ground-attack patrols were a new idea. Aircraft flew at low level, using their machine guns to strafe ground targets. Norman Macmillan flew his Camel on a ground-attack patrol during a British bombardment. He had instructions to fly through a 'tunnel' created by the arc of the shells, and the experience proved quite outlandish:

> We were told that the height of flight of the field gun shells was 600 feet above the ground. The guns were ranged practically wheel to wheel along the front on

which we were engaged. Our task was to fly into the tunnel, below the flight of field gun shells, look for any target we could see, any Germans in trenches, any machine-gun posts, anything at all. Shoot it up, fly through the tunnel and come out the other end. We were warned that we must not try to fly out sideways. If we did, we would almost certainly meet our own shells in flight and be brought down by them. That would apply whether we turned right or left. Once we entered the tunnel there was nothing for it but to carry on and go through to the very end. .

We flew in pairs, and I and my companion flew to the south of the tunnel, turned left, entered it, and instantly we were in an inferno. The air was boiling with the turmoil of the shells flying through it. We were thrown about in the aircraft, rocking from side to side, being thrown up and down. Below us was mud, filth, smashed trenches, broken wire, broken machine-gun posts, broken limbers, rubbish, wreckage of aeroplanes, bits of men – and then, in the midst of it all, when we were flying at 400 feet, I spotted a German machine-gun post and went down. My companion came behind me and, as we dived, we fired four machine guns straight into the post. We saw the Germans throw themselves onto the ground. We dived at them, sprayed them. Whether we hit them, we didn't know. There was no time to see. There was only time to dive and fire, climb and zoom, and onto the next target. There we saw a number of the grey-green German troops, lying in what had been trenches but were now shell holes. We dived on them, fired, and again we were diving on a target which we could not assess. We dived on another target and then our ammunition was finished. We flew out of that inferno, out of the tunnel, and escaped.

And as we came out of it, having taken not more than ten minutes in the passage through that tunnel,

I felt that we had escaped from one of the most evil things that I had ever seen. We were shut in by a cloud of shells, over a heap of rubble, mud, filth, destruction, and damnation – and in the midst of that inferno, we were shooting at men who'd cast themselves into the mud to escape our bullets.

The dangers of flying through a barrage were clear. Jerry Pentland, an Australian ace flying a Spad with 19 Squadron, was lucky to escape from his ground-strafing patrol alive:

I was flying through our barrage and you could see the howitzer shells landing and you were underneath them, and then one of these shells took my controls away and I crashed in no-man's-land. My leg was bust up, I was cut on the head. They brought me back on a stretcher, and we got a shell underneath us on the duckboards and one of my stretcher-bearers was killed, the other was wounded, and I got a big bit of shrapnel in the backside. Little bits of it were working their way out for years, but I only had the big piece removed in 1978.

After three months of fierce fighting, the village of Passchendaele was taken by the Canadian Corps, bringing the battle to an end, but enormous casualties had been suffered and no breakthrough achieved, and stalemate continued on the Western Front.

Towards the end of the battle, William Barker, a Canadian flight commander with 28 Squadron, had planned an ambitious early morning attack on a German aerodrome, hoping to encounter Jagdgeschwader 1. Flying alongside Barker that day was Harditt Singh Malik, the first Indian to fly with the Royal Flying Corps. Malik, a Sikh who wore a specially fitted leather helmet over his turban while flying, had applied for a commission in the RFC on completion of his history course at Oxford University. He had been rejected, before being accepted by the French flying service.

When Malik's Oxford tutor heard that a suitable subject of the British Empire had been turned down for a commission, presumably on racial grounds, he wrote to Sir David Henderson, a friend of his, asking him to intervene. Strings were pulled, bigotry was forgotten, and Malik was commissioned into 28 Squadron. He recalls the morning of 27 October:

It was rather a bad day, with low clouds, and Barker came up with the idea of flying and shooting up von Richthofen's squadron, who were relatively far from us. Our commanding officer was one of these old regulars and he said it was a stupid idea and he didn't approve at all. Barker was a very independent sort of fellow, and he knew the General commanding the area, and he approached him, for special permission. He obtained that permission and our CO could do nothing. Barker then asked for volunteers and three of us volunteered to go with him. We were flying Camels, single-seater machines.

So on that very bad day, we started out, and we ran into a very big formation of Germans. There was quite a dogfight, and a German pilot dived on me, and shot me through the right leg. On the Camel, you sat on the main petrol tank. The bullets that hit me came through the tank itself – fortunately not through the empty part but through the liquid, and that's why I didn't catch fire. If it had gone through the vapour, it would have caught fire. But I was disabled, because my tank was finished and I only had the gravity tank up on the wing. With the gravity tank you couldn't climb, and if you couldn't climb, you couldn't fight. So I was completely at the mercy of the German pilots.

But then I shot down the man who shot me, because instead of turning back, he dived straight in front of me, and I could shoot him down. But all I could do then was get as low as possible and get home – and home was forty miles away. Three German fighters followed me and shot all they had at me, point blank. Later, when my plane was found and examined by my squadron, they found over four hundred bullet holes in it. But after those first bullets had entered my leg, not one more hit me or any vital part of the plane. It was the greatest luck.

At first, I thought I would be shot down and killed, but after a bit, when they seemed to be unable to hit me again, I somehow lost the fear and I got the feeling that I'd be all right. I didn't panic. I kept flying. In due course, they left me. They must have run out of ammunition, but then I was shot at from the ground until I got to the lines, and then I looked for somewhere where I could land. But there was no flat ground, because that part of the line had been shot up for so many years. It was nothing but shell holes full of water. But finally, I got down – and fainted.

The next I remember was being in a stretcher taken to the Casualty Clearing Station. My squadron got to know about this and my mechanic was sent across to recover the plane. He wrote to me, months later, saying that he was quite amazed that I landed on that terrain. He said it was a miracle. I spent several months in hospital. An interesting thing was that when Barker got back to the squadron, his report was almost word for word the same as mine. My report ended, 'The last I saw of Captain Barker, he was surrounded by Huns fighting but I don't think there's any hope of his coming back.' And he said exactly the same thing about me.

Barker had escaped from the initial dogfight, and he flew on in search of prey. He came across a formation of Albatri and shot two of them down, before landing in a field forty miles from his aerodrome. He was to win the Victoria Cross in

October 1918, and he died in a flying accident in Canada in 1930. Malik was the only Indian airman to survive the war. After a career in the civil service, he was appointed to serve as Indian ambassador to France.

Manfred von Richthofen had been shot down on 6 July 1917 during what ought to have been the routine destruction of an FE2d of 20 Squadron. Richthofen's Albatros and the FE2d flew directly at each other, machine guns blazing. Richthofen was struck a glancing blow on the head by a bullet fired by the observer of the FE2d, which fractured his skull, yet he managed to land his aircraft before fainting. Six weeks later, he was flying again, and on 3 September he encountered Algernon Bird, a Sopwith Pup pilot of 46 Squadron. Bird remembers:

'A' Flight of No. 46 Squadron, of which I was a member, had received orders to carry out the first offensive patrol of the morning. I had attained a height of about 14,000 feet in my Pup, and I proceeded over the lines to a point about ten miles on the German side and commenced the patrol. Normally we were treated to a liberal dose of Archie but on the morning in question, everything appeared more than usually calm – an ominous calm as it proved.

Suddenly an enemy machine was seen some way away, and our flight commander indicated his intention of diving. I followed suit, but by this time, another enemy machine had appeared and I attacked him. It then became clear that we were involved in a scrap with a large number of the enemy. While chasing my particular opponent, I took a glance over my shoulder to find myself being followed by two triplanes that I took to belong to an RNAS squadron with whom we occasionally cooperated.

The next thing I knew, I was under a fusillade from machine guns at very close quarters. My engine cut out, and I got one under my right arm, which momentarily knocked me out. On recovering, I found that I had got to do all I knew if I was going to stand a chance of reaching our lines. The two enemy triplanes were making wonderful shooting practice at me, and my machine was being hit times without number. Splinters were flying from the two small struts just in front of the cockpit, and from the instrument board.

It was impossible to fly straight for more than a few moments at a time when they got their guns on me, and my progress towards our lines was very slow compared with the height I was losing, for my engine was a passenger only. I was now a few hundred feet off the ground and looking for a place to put my machine down. I found a field in which a German fatigue party was digging trenches, where I landed, hitting a tree in the process. All the while, my assailants had kept up a heavy fire whenever they could get their guns on me. Upon my machine coming to rest, it looked as if the trench digging party were going to finish the work that their airmen had begun, but fortunately for me, an officer drove up in a horse and cart and took charge of taking me back to his HQ where I was searched, my flying kit removed, and my wound dressed.

Richthofen's own report of the fight is flattering to Bird's abilities, but he includes a couple of details which – if true – are unsurprisingly missing from Bird's own recollections:

I was absolutely convinced that I had a very capable opponent, because he refused to surrender even after I had forced him down as low as fifty yards above the ground. Even then he kept on shooting. Before he landed, he emptied his machine gun into a column of our infantry, and then, when on the ground, deliberately steered his plane into a tree and smashed it.

Algernon Bird was Richthofen's sixty-first victim and his last until 23 November. Richthofen had still not properly recovered from the head wound sustained in July and, suffering headaches and nausea, he agreed to take a period of extended leave.

The machine that Richthofen was flying against Bird, and which had tricked Bird into thinking he was being assisted by the Royal Naval Air Service, was the new Fokker Dr.1, better known as the Fokker Triplane. It was not particularly quick, but its rate of climb and speed in the turn were excellent: according to Richthofen it 'climbed like a monkey and manoeuvred like the devil'. Even though the great majority of Richthofen's victories were achieved in Albatri, the image of the man that has engraved itself in the popular imagination is of a pitiless assassin in a blood-red, three-tiered killing machine. The Triplane did not initially have such a menacing reputation, however. In early September 1917, James McCudden wrote to a friend:

> The Triplane is an awfully comic old thing and I am awfully keen to see one out of control. I reckon it will be like a Venetian blind with a stone tied to it.

The first two Triplanes had been delivered on 28 August. Apart from Richthofen, the next man to receive one was Werner Voss, a gifted pilot with a fighting style similar to that of Albert Ball, aggressive and direct, happy to dive in among large enemy formations. Voss painted his Triplane silvery blue with a large mustachioed face on its nose, and he always flew in a silk shirt, explaining that, should he be taken prisoner, he wanted to look his best for the ladies. By 23 September, this dandy had accounted for forty-eight enemy aircraft.

On that day, Voss came up against seven SE5as of 56 Squadron, all flown by expert pilots. James McCudden and Arthur Rhys Davids dived on him, but Voss whipped his

Triplane round to face them in a manoeuvre that McCudden had never seen before. Voss's movements were so quick that he seemed to be firing at all seven of his opponents at once. He had such control of his machine that nobody could get a sight on him. The fight continued for ten minutes. At one brief moment, Voss was at the apex of a cone of bullets fired by five machines simultaneously – ten guns in all – but nobody could hit him, and he made no attempt to escape. In the whirling chaos, Voss managed to force down two of the SE5as before he spent a fraction of a second too long firing at another, allowing Rhys Davids, the boy with a copy of Blake in his pocket, to fire into him from behind. For once, Voss did not turn to confront his attacker. Rhys Davids continued to fire before shooting past Voss in a dive. McCudden saw the Triplane hit the ground where it disappeared into a thousand fragments. 'It seemed to me,' he wrote, 'that it literally turned to powder.'

Hubert Charles was on the 56 Squadron aerodrome at Estrée Blanche when the pilots landed:

> Everybody was talking about the Voss fight in the mess. Rhys Davids was so excited that he was stammering. He always was after a fight. Keith Muspratt said that this chap they'd fought had put up the finest fight that he'd ever seen anywhere. He was fighting them all at once, and they'd all got the wind up. It was the final dive by Rhys Davids while the other two chaps were engaging his attention that did it. It was a wonderful fight by a wonderful fighter pilot.

A month later, Rhys Davids was himself killed. His place at Balliol would never be taken up.

At the beginning of 1918 it was clear to German High Command that an opportunity to mount an offensive had arisen – the collapse of Russia had freed up troops and matériel from the Eastern Front – but it was one that might not last long. The Allied naval blockade was taking its toll, and American forces would soon be arriving in numbers on the Western Front. Ludendorff, the German Commander-in-Chief, began drawing up plans for a breakthrough on the Somme. The British knew that an attack was coming, but they did not know where, and they did not know when.

And while British troops on the ground would soon be forced to defend, so the Royal Flying Corps, accustomed to flying offensively over enemy lines, would have to formulate a new strategy in order to support them. Trenchard, in a pamphlet issued shortly before he relinquished command, made it clear that the RFC would defend through attack: before an enemy advance, aircraft would have to watch for signs of hostile concentration. When it was clear that preparations were in progress, bombing raids and artillery fire must be brought to bear on those preparations. And once the advance was underway, aeroplanes must be used to attack forward troops, reinforcements and lines of communication. Major General John Salmond replaced Trenchard in February, but this strategy would remain in place.

As the British had to adapt their thinking, so did the Germans. They had to begin venturing over the British lines to bring back reconnaissance reports. German two-seater machines such as the LVG and the Rumpler were capable of flying above the ceilings of British fighters, and one man – James McCudden (who had been an engine fitter when he arrived in France in 1914 with 3 Squadron) modified his SE5a so that it could attain the heights necessary to counter them. McCudden wrote of one fight:

> The visibility was good and I knew I should not have to wait long before an enemy came over our line to take photos. The Hun usually take the photos about the hours of eleven and twelve, for the sun is then at its brightest and the ground shadows are small ... At

17,000 feet, on looking west I saw a Hun very high over Péronne, and so I remained east of him, climbing steadily. After 15 minutes I got up to his level at 18,200 feet ... and he tried to run for it. I fought him down from 18,000 to 8000 feet and he tried hard to save his life, but after a final burst from both my machine guns, his right hand wings fell off and I nearly flew into them.

McCudden was a thinking pilot. Unlike Ball or Voss, he did not rush headlong into a fight, trusting to skill to extricate himself. He weighed up the situation, and chose only to attack if he had the tactical advantage. Otherwise, he would break off:

On 3 January I encountered a Rumpler at 19,500 feet over Bullecourt and fought him a long way east of his lines, but he was an old hand, and saved his height instead of losing it, and at last I had to leave him, for we had now got over Douai at 18,000 feet. Here I turned back, because a lucky shot from him might have disabled my engine and have caused me to come down in Hunland, and I did not want that to happen.

But while McCudden used his brain to give himself every chance of survival, he had striking physical attributes as well. Hubert Charles:

McCudden had incredible touch, eyesight, and he had conscious control over his Eustachian tubes. He could come down from 18,000 feet as fast as he liked and just indulge in ordinary conversation. If anyone else did that, he'd have been deaf for a quarter of an hour. Not more than one human being in 100,000 can do what McCudden did. He was like a bird. And he was a shooting genius. Geoffrey Bowman said that if you gave McCudden a box of a thousand rounds of ammunition, he would shoot down as many enemy aircraft as the rest of the squadron would with a Leyland truck load.

In April 1918, McCudden received the Victoria Cross from the King in person at Buckingham Palace. The award was made for 'most conspicuous bravery, exceptional persever-ance, keenness, and very high devotion to duty'. On 9 July, with fifty-seven victories recorded, he was on his way to the front to take command of 60 Squadron after a period of leave. After taking off on the final leg of his journey, his engine failed and he crashed into a wood. Hubert Charles, in a new role as accident investigator, was sent to the aerodrome. He discovered the following:

> That was the whole cause of the crash – the engine cut-ting in and out. The most likely cause of that was the air intake drains, and when I saw the wreckage, I saw his aircraft wasn't fitted with the right type of air intake drain. If you opened the throttle, and a great lot of stuff was suddenly sucked out of the air intake, you'd have black smoke coming from the exhaust and the engine would be cutting out – I think that was the most likely reason for his crash.

Three weeks after McCudden's death, his brother Maurice wrote to his sister Kathleen. The letter is unsettling. It juggles Maurice's reaction to his sister's engagement with an abrupt analysis of his brother's death.

> I have just received your welcome letter and wish to send you my congratulations. I should be glad of any magazines or any cheap literature. I received a letter from Mother by the same post as yours telling me all about your engagement and about Jim's end. Jim's internal injuries would be caused by the safety belt round his waist. As the machine hit the ground, the sudden impact of hitting would tend to throw the pilot

forward, but the safety belt would prevent this, hence causing internal injuries. If Jim had not been strapped in, he would have been thrown forward on the front of the seat and his head and face would have been an awful sight.

Since the advent of the SE5a, the Sopwith Camel and the Bristol Fighter, air superiority had rested in the hands of the British. Despite the odd teething troubles, they had all proved to be effective aircraft. The Germans had produced machines such as the Fokker Triplane and the latest Albatros, the DV, which, though they had their qualities, suffered from poor endurance. It did not matter particularly how long an aircraft could remain in the air when it was fighting over friendly territory, but German aircraft were soon to be faced with the prospect of flying repeatedly over British lines. The pattern of the war was changing and a new aircraft was needed. In fact, a new German machine was to arrive in the shape of the Fokker D.VII. Responsive and easy to fly, with a maximum speed of 124 miles per hour and a ceiling of 23,000 feet, the D.VII was an impressive machine. More than one thousand would be produced before the end of the war – but none would arrive in time for the push.

On 21 March, the offensive began with a massive artillery bombardment, followed by a stream of troops heading towards the British positions. William Butler, a pilot with 8 Squadron at Nurlu, ten miles east of Albert, wrote in his diary:

> Awakened at 2 am by a most appalling noise. Laid and listened to it for some time before I could realise what it was. It sounded like all the furies on earth let loose or a colossal and continuous thunder clap. The morning was totally unfit for flying owing to thick ground mist.

The mist may have prevented British aircraft from making a useful start, but even once it had begun to clear, aircraft attempting to bring down 'zone calls' from appropriate batteries were received with silence; partly because of the severance of telephone lines, partly because the batteries already had plenty of pre-assigned targets to occupy them. Some aircraft found themselves being sent out to report on the movements and strength of enemy troops – the kind of work that the Royal Flying Corps had not carried out since September 1914. However, the most pressing work that airmen were called upon to carry out was ground attacks. British aircraft were sent out to bomb and strafe enemy troops all over the battlefield. And it was not just the small, nimble scouts that were called upon. Frank Ransley of 48 Squadron was called into action, even though his two-seater Bristol Fighter hardly seemed ideal for the job:

> Our orders were to go as low as possible and concentrate on shooting up German troops or any other worthwhile ground targets. The 'Brisfit' being a two-seater was much larger than a scout machine and had a bigger wing spread and was not built for low flying. I cannot remember how many machines I flew that were put out of action by fire from ground troops. The mechanics and riggers worked non-stop at this time to put us in the air again. Major Keith Park inspired us all with his calm certainty that we should win through although he hated sending us out on these near suicide missions. So we soldiered on.

The same day, Horace Cole, a signaller with the Rifle Brigade, was taken prisoner by the advancing Germans. As he was being escorted back to a first aid post, he witnessed a British aircraft carrying out a strafing attack:

> We had to cross part of the River Somme and when we reached a particular spot, there was a pontoon

bridge strung across the river ahead of us. We had to halt because there was a battalion of Germans coming across – and suddenly a plane appeared on the scene. And the pilot was flying at roof height and firing at the Germans, and they were just falling dead. They didn't have a snowball's chance in hell. They had nothing to protect themselves with. They were exposed on a rickety old bridge. This went on for over a minute, until somebody on the opposite bank of the river mounted a machine gun, and because the plane was flying so low, they couldn't miss it. The plane was shot down. In that time, the plane must have killed hundreds. When we got to the first aid post, I saw the pilot and the observer of the plane. The pilot had been hit in the head. And the strange thing was that the observer was searching the pilot's balaclava helmet, looking all over it to find the bullet hole. I don't know why.

The following day, William Butler was sent on a reconnaissance patrol:

Went on patrol at 2 pm with Kendal. Our job was to find out how far the Hun had got. This was no easy task as there was no particular barrage on one line. The shelling was general. We tootled about at 2000 feet for an hour without seeing much except smoke and fire but we gradually were able to pick out small attacking parties of Huns between Nurlu and Sincourt and from this we concluded that we had retired to the Green line of defence – our last line before Péronne and the Somme battlefield. This meant the Hun had advanced nearly 9 miles in two days.

As the Germans surged forward, Gustav Lachman, the pilot of a German two-seater, was given orders to destroy a bridge ahead of the advancing troops:

I was caught by five fighters. It was a very brisk and short encounter and I was really a dead duck because my machine was much less manoeuvrable and my observer was soon put out of action by a shot to his chest. When I tried to turn, the very manoeuvrable single-seaters flew rings around me. Although this was my first really sharp encounter in the air, I wasn't really scared. It was this feeling of almost detachment. And I believe when one is near to death, the second ego steps out and observes one. I had the feeling that I was observing myself, and I was quite satisfied that I took the whole situation so calmly.

I had been wounded in the leg and it was like a sledgehammer blow. Then I did something that was totally against the rules. I went into a straight, sharp nosedive. But it saved me because I dived into a layer of cloud which made visibility oblique. With tremendous speed, I approached the ground. My engineering instincts told me that if I pull up the machine too sharply then the wings would go, so I pulled up very, very slowly, and the machine recovered.

Apathy came over me, which is a typical characteristic of the shock after being wounded. My first instinct was to land, to be out of it. I had my packet. I wanted to be out of it. And there I saw in front of me a mound completely covered with barbed wire and I was gliding straight towards it and I didn't give a damn. I wanted to be out. Then suddenly somebody knocked me on the head and yelled into my ear, 'Gas!' so I opened the throttle again and I carried on, and then my calm decision returned. And of course it struck me as ridiculous to crash into barbed wire and the right decision was, of course, to fly straight on until a town appeared on the horizon and to land on a field in order to get to a field hospital as quickly as possible because we were both very severely wounded. And that I did.

The German advance continued. From William Butler's diary for 23 March:

> Went up on patrol with Redmayne at 10.30. Flew up Somme to Péronne. Péronne was in flames. The smoke was terrific. The whole country seemed to be burning. It was almost impossible to find out how far the Hun had got. Two bridges over the Somme at Péronne had been blown up by our people so that we concluded all our artillery had retired over the Somme which proved afterwards to be correct. The two main roads from the battlefield were choked with traffic. 6″ guns hitched onto steam rollers, tenders or anything that could pull them out of reach of the Huns. All kinds of M.T. and remnants of what had been going west. It was a heartbreaking sight from the air to see an army in such retirement.

It is worth noting that while the Royal Flying Corps was heavily engaged in bombing and strafing attacks on German targets, the Germans carried out far fewer similar attacks. The opportunity arose for the German Air Service to deal a significant blow to the retreating British forces, but it was not taken. German machines continued to fly against British aircraft, however. Whilst William Butler was engaged in reconnaissance, artillery observation and bombing, all in the course of a single patrol, he received a fright, or a 'gust' as he puts it:

> We were uncertain which was Hunland and where to drop our bombs, so decided to go well over and not risk dropping them on our own chaps. Getting well on the way when a formation of Huns came on the scene. They were a fair way away so did not take much notice except to keep an eye on them. Good job we did as three of the blighters headed for us, noses well down. I right reversed without any further argument and they

saw us well into our own lines before they rejoined their formation.

We gave bomb dropping a rest and tootled about over our own lines and picked up a 'zone call' on a Hun battery. Sent a couple of corrections down and then had another try to get over. This time we nearly finished our little bomb droppings for good. We had one eye on a formation a long way away and only gave an occasional glance to the other side. I just caught sight of a machine out of the corner of my eye, and I looked round, and it was a Hun diving on us. Never had such a gust in my life. Did half a flat turn to get out of his sights and went into a vertical side slip. He drove us right down to 400 feet over our own lines. Shall not forget that descent in a hurry. Had no thought of the machine folding up or about stunting. In a case like this, it is remarkable what you can do with a machine. The Hun put a couple of bursts at us but he had all his work cut out to keep us in his sights. By the time he sheered off, I was completely lost so flew due west and then saw Amiens and found our way home. It was a lucky escape.

For several days, the Germans continued to make further territorial gains. Many squadrons were forced to retreat as they surged forward, and William Butler's was one of them; 8 Squadron had retreated from Nurlu to Chipilly on the 22nd, and from Chipilly to Poulainville two days later:

Huns now in possession of Chipilly. Went up on patrol with Redmayne. Tootled about over Chipilly, until we discovered the Huns had got there. They put several holes in the plane to let us know. We acknowledged by loosing off all our bombs. Rather funny bombing one's old aerodrome two days after leaving it.

As fierce fighting took place on the ground, ground-strafing aircraft played a crucial role in preventing German troops from entering a gap that was developing in the British lines near Albert. As the Germans poured their strength into this vulnerable part of the line, more than half of the squadrons on the Western Front were involved in defending the area, including squadrons operating to the north. John Baker was an RE8 observer with 4 Squadron at Chocques, two miles west of Béthune. His squadron was one of many called upon on 25 March to carry out the orders of RFC Commander-in-Chief, John Salmond, to bomb and shoot up everything on the enemy side of a line running north–south near Albert. 'Very low flying is essential,' Salmond ordered. 'All risks to be taken. Urgent.' Baker wrote of the show in a letter to his brother:

> We had a priceless evening yesterday. We suddenly had orders to send every available machine to bomb and machine gun a few thousand Huns who were massing to attack. The sky was simply filled with our machines, and No. 4 Squadron were over first, and I was flying with the formation leader in the first machine of all. I think he must have put the vertical gust up the Germans all right – 200 aeroplanes suddenly appearing and opening up on him just as he was massing to attack.

J. C. F. Hopkins was an FE2b pilot with 83 Squadron, carrying out tactical night-bombing operations, intended to stall the German advance. His principal target was the Bapaume–Albert road. He remembers:

> Looking at it from up in the air, the road showed up almost white in the moonlight. And you'd see an obvious column of troops marching along – it would show up as a black blob along the road. And it was so bright, you could pick out the individual vehicles from about 1500 feet. We were dropping small twenty-five pound anti-personnel bombs mostly – they were aimed at destroying troops on the move. Even before

we started bombing sometimes, you'd see the troops scatter to the side of the road. It was almost impossible to evaluate what damage we did to actual columns of troops. One thing – the road was very badly damaged. We must have frustrated them tremendously.

Despite all these efforts, the Germans took Albert on the evening of the 26th. Yet they were to make little further progress north of the Somme, and emphasis was shifted to an attack on Amiens, south of the Somme. By 30 March, German troops had reached the outskirts of Amiens, but the attack made little further headway against a stiffened British defence. That defence included a large number of exhausted airmen. John Baker, in a letter home:

> I am very jubilant today: it has been raining like anything and if it lasts till evening now, it will mean a whole day without a flight. You can't think how we long for a rest now. I can't get the blinking hum of the old machine out of my ears.

On 5 April, the Somme offensive was at an end. The Germans might have broken the stalemate on the Western Front for the first time since 1914, achieving tactical victories in the process, but these were not matched by strategic success. The intention of breaking through the British lines and pushing north to the coast had come to nothing. So far as the war in the air was concerned, the Royal Flying Corps had stepped once more into the breach during a retreat – just when the army was most in need of help. Ground-strafing, an unpleasant but highly effective activity, had made a substantial difference to the battle on the ground.

So it seems fitting that as the aeroplane was proving its worth yet again, it should be given its own independent service. On 1 April 1918, the Royal Flying Corps and the Royal Naval Air Service came together to form the Royal Air Force. The RFC squadrons retained their numbers, while the

RNAS squadrons had 200 added to theirs, turning 5 (Naval) Squadron RNAS into 205 Squadron RAF. The reaction to the union amongst service personnel varied. Some of the prouder naval types, such as Thomas Thomson of the new 217 Squadron, refused to see the point:

> When they formed the Royal Air Force from the Royal Naval Air Service and the Royal Flying Corps – all that happened was a complete hotch-potch. They were trying to join together two disparate services. The Navy tradition was very firmly embedded and the Army had a regimental tradition. The ex-RNAS rating would take off his hat to receive his pay, the Army man would keep his hat on. Where the ex-RNAS man would double across the parade ground, the ex-RFC man would march across it. It was absolutely terrible – the biggest pot-mess that I ever came across. In the officers' mess, ex-naval squadrons still sat down to toast the King, whereas the army people got up, and where you had a combination in one mess, it was absolutely ludicrous! Fred Karno's army! Nothing less! Whoever thought Jan Smuts was the fount of all knowledge in recommending this, beats me!

Others, such as Aubrey Ellwood, objected initially, but came to appreciate the benefits:

> None of us in the RNAS wanted to be amalgamated. Nor do I expect did the RFC want to be amalgamated. We were accustomed to our own traditions and customs and I think we were all rather sorry. But I think we saw the point. By that time, we'd learnt that the air had a definite function of its own to perform, apart from just supporting the army or navy, so the obvious thing was to get together and make a service of it. So we very soon got over our regrets. It was easier for me, as a member of RNAS in France to take the change than it

was for some people who'd been completely separated from the RFC. Not only did we understand what we were doing for the army, but we made very good friends with them, and we were exactly the same as them except we wore different uniforms.

For those more interested in flying than in being soldiers or sailors, the day passed like any other. No. 10 Squadron's diary for 1 April 1918:

> The beginnings of the R.A.F. resulted in some fairly intelligent conversation at breakfast. Wing Medical Officer thinks he will look well in the uniform, and is glad about the belt. Weather uncertain. Little work done. Some tennis.

Some were worried that they might not look well in the new grey-blue uniform. Frank Burslem of 73 Squadron:

> We heard that the mills in Yorkshire had a lot of this colour wool in their warehouses. They'd bought it to make uniforms for the Hungarian army, but they hadn't been able to use it because of the war, so somebody in Whitehall got the idea to use it up on us. It caused a lot of ridicule at the time, because people thought that it was a comic opera style uniform and a lot of letters appeared in the press about that.

On 20 April 1918, Manfred von Richthofen claimed his seventy-ninth and eightieth victories. The eightieth was Second Lieutenant David Lewis of 3 Squadron, who did all he could to escape the Baron:

> I twisted and turned in an endeavour to avoid his line of fire but he was too experienced a fighter, and only once did I manage to have him at a disadvantage, and then only for a few seconds. In those few ticks of the clock, I shot a number of bullets into his machine

and thought I would have the honour of bringing him down, but in a trice the positions were reversed and he had set my emergency tank alight, and I was hurtling earthwards in flames. I hit the ground four miles north-east of Villers-Bretonneux at a speed of sixty miles an hour. I was thrown clear of my machine, and except for minor burns, was unhurt.

On 10 March, Richthofen had prepared a last will and testament, much of which was devoted to passing on the benefits of his combat experience. In the document, Richt-hofen warned against blindly chasing an opponent over enemy lines, a caution which reflected the fact that German machines did most of their fighting over friendly territory. On 21 April, however, the day after he brought down Lewis, Richthofen broke his own rule. On that day, three flights of Sopwith Camels of 209 Squadron flew an offensive patrol over the Somme area, where they were attacked by a for-mation of Fokker Triplanes and Albatri. Thirty aircraft were suddenly rolling, diving, turning, banking and firing bullets at each other. In the midst of the fight was Wilfred May, known as 'Wop', a young Canadian on his first patrol, under orders not to take part in the general dogfight, but to stay on the sidelines, and head for home at the first sign of danger. Before long, May became sucked into the fight. He put his Camel into a tight vertical turn, firing both his guns. He held them open too long, and they jammed; at which point, he broke off from the fight.

May flew home, congratulating himself on getting out of the scrape, unaware that a red Fokker Triplane was easing itself into position behind him. The Baron's eighty-first kill seemed only seconds away. Jolted awake by Richthofen's guns, May tried to dodge and spin clear. He came down from 12,000 feet to almost ground level. Touchingly honest, he has admitted:

The only thing that saved me was my poor flying. I didn't know what I was doing myself and I don't suppose Richthofen knew what I was going to do.

As the chase continued, Roy Brown, a flight commander in 209 Squadron, dived onto the Triplane's tail and sent a long burst of fire into it, before continuing his dive. When he pulled up, May and Richthofen had both moved off. Richthofen continued to follow May along the Somme Valley, where the Triplane came under ground fire from at least two Australian machine-gun posts, and from countless infantry rifles. Had Richthofen followed the advice of his last will and testament, he would have broken off the fight before he became vulnerable either to Roy Brown's Camel, or to the ground fire. But for some reason, the highest scoring ace of the war, unable to kill off the least experienced of opponents, chose to fly low for a mile and a half over enemy territory. His machine was seen to hit the ground near the Bray–Corbie road. Richthofen was dead, killed by a single bullet. As soon as the men on the ground discovered the identity of the downed pilot, they descended on the aircraft and picked it clean. One man was seen trying to slice Richthofen's finger away to get hold of his ring. From his scarf to his boots to the bits of his propeller, the Red Baron's relics were carried away. Many of the goods scavenged from his corpse continue to appear in auction rooms to this day, nicely rebranded as 'memorabilia'.

And debate still rages as to who killed Richthofen. Brown was credited with the victory, but more than one Australian machine gunner was convinced that he had fired the fatal bullet. The body was cursorily examined, but no autopsy was performed, and the question will never be satisfactorily answered. It begs, however, a better question; why did Richthofen – a man for whom air fighting was an extension of hunting, a cold-blooded and clear-headed exercise – allow himself to be lured to his death by a complete novice? Roy Brown wrote a letter to his father:

> What I saw that day shook me up quite a lot as it was the first time I have seen a man whom I know I had killed. If you don't shoot them they will shoot you so it has to be done.

Richthofen was buried by the British authorities with full military honours. As the body was lowered into the ground, twelve soldiers fired three volleys over the grave. The death was not treated with respect by all on the British side, however. Mick Mannock, never a man to withhold an opinion, replied to a request to toast Richthofen, with the words, 'I won't drink to that bastard.' Even today, so many decades after his death, he remains the most celebrated – and sometimes the most reviled – flyer in the history of aviation.

Whilst it had become clear in April that the Germans would not achieve the breakthrough that they had hoped for from their spring offensive, they continued to make advances until mid-July. But in August, an Allied victory at the Battle of Amiens led to a series of counter-successes, culminating in a breach of the Hindenberg Line in late September. From that point, an end to the war, and an Allied victory were assured. As the Allies began their final advance, and lines of communication became stretched, so Frank Burslem, a bomber pilot with 218 Squadron, began to fly with a new sort of payload:

> During the last push, we moved to Dunkirk, nearer the lines. The Allied troops had advanced so fast and so far that they could no longer advance. Supplies had to be brought to them, and our squadron was given the job of dropping food. We were given a map, told where they were, and told to drop bags of bully beef. The observer had three sandbags, each filled with about fifty tins of bully beef, in his cockpit, and when we

arrived at the destination, he lifted them over the side, and dropped them. There was no parachute attached to them, and the aeroplane was down at about 100 feet and the ground was all muddy beneath.

It may have become clear that the Germans could not win the war, but that did not mean that German pilots stopped fighting. Ralph Silk was an observer with 6 Squadron:

I'd been briefed with five other machines to ground strafe, bomb and take photographs of the retreating Germans. Everything was in chaos – the roads were chock-a-block with troops and guns. I was flying above the crossroads of Le Cateau, with four bombs on board. I was at about 3200 feet. The sky was clear, except for some cumulus clouds, and I was waiting for the signal from our leading machine to dive in and release our bombs, when, out of the clouds, like a flash of lightning, came a Fokker machine. I didn't see him until he was almost on my tail, because the frontal area was so small that he was on you before you had a chance to fire your gun. He flew out of the sun, which made it more difficult. Anyway, he was on my tail. I fired two bursts of twenty rounds at him, but he seemed to be encased in a cast-iron shirt, because I knew that the shots were good but still he came on, and hung on my tail, until, because his speed was greater than mine, he passed me. As he passed me, he was so near that I could see the rims of his goggles. Then, in a flash, another followed, and he was sitting on my tail, and again I fired a short burst at him. Suddenly, I could feel the lead whizzing past my head. 'Tac, tac, tac . . .' was the tell-tale noise. I felt the machine lurch, I turned my head round, and I saw that my pilot was slumped over the controls. Then I realised the engine had stopped. There was I, suspended in the air, with a dead pilot, Huns and bullets and wings all around me. I looked up to the heavens, and I said, 'Oh God. Help me!' And the next thing I remember was having a sledgehammer blow on my head and I put my hand to my helmet, and I felt it jagged and torn, and there was blood, and I had a blackout. The aircraft was falling through the air like a leaf, and I think it was the upward rush of air that brought me to my senses. By the grace of God, I had the presence of mind to pull on the joystick to break the fall. The machine staggered, stalled and fell into some trees. I can just about remember some Germans letting me down by a rope. Then I lost consciousness again, and when I woke up, I found that I was lying in a little French church, behind the lines, with a lot of other prisoners.

Just as ground-strafing had brought misery to attacking troops during the spring offensive, so now it would do the same to retreating troops. James Gascoyne of 92 Squadron chose not to kill one particular German. Better to humiliate him:

I flew over a big fat German on a horse. They were walking across a ploughed field. There was plenty of mud and dirt about. It suddenly appealed to me to see what I could do about it. I didn't want to hurt the horse so I dived down and flew very close over them. Before I got there he saw me coming down and jumped off the horse and got underneath its neck, holding the reins. Well, I frightened this poor horse so much that he started to gallop across the field and the fat German hung on to the reins and he was dragged him all through this muck and mire. He looked a proper sight when I had finished with him. The horse ran off and he was left standing in the middle of the field.

Strafing remained a dangerous activity to the very end. Gascoyne:

I had no idea that the war was about to finish. Two days before the Armistice, I was out ground strafing. I came across a village where the German troops were retreating. A whole line of transport was moving down a straight road and at the bottom of the road was a church tower. I started to fly down the street to have a look at it, before turning round to shoot it. Suddenly there was a burst of machine gun right into my machine. One bullet came through the windscreen, made a little hole in my helmet, and a little mark on my head – it felt just like being hit with a brick. My head fell over the side but I regained consciousness very quickly. I put my hand up and I found there was blood on it. Still, I went back to have a second run and I discovered where the firing was coming from. It was coming from a church tower at the bottom end of the village. He was at about the same height I was flying, and I was flying straight towards him. That was how I finished the war off.

Germany requested an armistice on 3 November, thus averting an Allied offensive across the German frontier. The Kaiser abdicated on 9 November, and the armistice came into effect at the eleventh hour of the eleventh day of the eleventh month. The war was over. On that day, the King sent the following message to the Royal Air Force:

The birth of the Royal Air Force, with its wonderful expansion and development, will ever remain one of the most remarkable achievements of the Great War.

Epilogue

On the day that war came to an end Phil Guard arrived in London to celebrate his birthday with his brother Fred:

> I stepped onto the platform before the train had stopped – into a crowd of people running and shouting 'It's over, it's over!' The good news seemed hard to believe. I met Fred at the Savoy and we set about the business of celebrating. In the wee small hours, by the time it was my birthday, I was wearing his brigadier's uniform, and he was wearing my humble lieutenant's.

James Colvin had survived the war and now had the chance of building a life with his girl – something that would have seemed unlikely just a week before:

> My dear little Sweetheart,
>
> You seem to have been having some high times at home. From all accounts, everybody at home seems to have gone mad when the news became known. You couldn't notice any difference here. Everybody was in high spirits, of course, but apart from that, there was nothing else. You see there was no possibility of celebrating it. There were a good many drunks that night, but that is a regular occurrence, but down the line, in the towns, there was plenty doing, I believe. I shall be

quite satisfied to get home and out of it all well, and hold a little celebration on our own, dear. We'll find a nice quiet place, somewhere all to ourselves, and then I can give you all these promised Xs. There will be quite a number by the time I get home, but I expect we shall get through them all right, what do you say Sweetheart? It is very nice of you to call me that dear. I wish you were whispering it in my ear, instead of writing it, but perhaps you will be before long. I hope so at any rate.

    Yours with heaps of love,

    Jimmy

These airmen had been doing a job of importance and responsibility. They had lived with the expectation of an early death. Suddenly, they were young again, with their entire lives to look forward to, and often little idea how to fill them. Some airmen, like Philip Townsend, of 12 Squadron, tried to hold on to what they knew best:

> After I was demobilized, I went with a friendly officer to a sale of government stock in Hendon. We were amazed by the offers – there were literally hundreds of aircraft, engines and parts. Anything pertaining to air-warfare was for sale at give-away prices. He had been a pilot of a DH4, I'd been the pilot of a Bristol Fighter and we both thought it would be lovely to buy an SE5a, which were up for sale for £5. We agreed to the price, he bought one, I bought one. We had them filled up with petrol and oil, tested them there and then for engine efficiency, then took them up and flew around Hendon for about half an hour. We landed within five minutes of one another, stopped our props, climbed out and shouted out at joy having enjoyed such a wonderful flight. At the time, the SE5a was the 'honey' machine of the war. We discussed things, reckoned up how much it would cost us – neither of us had a job to go to. I was twenty, he was twenty-one, and we were told that

it would cost us £10 to have the certificate of air-worthiness. Therefore, both of us became very dejected at realizing that we couldn't possibly afford them. We'd no hangar, no place at home where we could even house the aircraft. So we talked to the mechanics and they agreed to buy them back for £4 10s. It took us, I should think, half an hour in silent tears to walk away from Hendon aerodrome, realizing that we had been defeated in our objective of being civil flyers.

As airmen considered the future, their machines embarked on new and exciting endeavours. Marie Agazarian was a child in Surrey:

My mother went to Croydon airport immediately after the war and she bought a Sopwith Pup for £2. She had it towed to our garden in Carshalton, and it was placed on the rubbish dump for the five of us children to play on.

Many airmen remained within the Royal Air Force. Philip Joubert de la Ferté, the man who flew one of the first two reconnaissances of the war, was to take charge of Coastal Command during the Second World War. Louis Strange, welcoming the opportunity to place his life in danger, spent much of 1940 pestering the Air Ministry to be allowed to return to flying duties. And in spite of his age (forty-nine) and his medical condition (sciatica), he was posted to 24 Squadron. During the Battle of France, he fought off six Messerschmitt 109s as he flew a Hawker Hurricane across the English channel – despite the fact that he had never set foot in a Hurricane before that day. Bernard Rice, the author of such engaging letters to his father, remained in the Air Force for several years, until he set up in business, running a garage and hotel in Amersham. The man who talked us so vividly through a flight over enemy lines, who survived so many reconnaissance flights over the Western

Front, died in a car accident in 1934, crushed to death by a lorry.

Other men moved into other areas. Archibald James, a man of uncompromising opinions, was elected Conservative Member of Parliament for Wellingborough in 1931. A year later, another ex-member of the RFC formed his own political party; Oswald Mosley, observer, pilot, and leader of the British Union of Fascists, would be better remembered for his politics than for his flying, yet he carried a life-long limp thanks to the crash which invalided him out of the Flying Corps.

Robert Loraine, commanding officer of 41 Squadron, returned to the stage as an actor/manager after the war, but not before facing a court martial in 1917 on a charge of drunkenness. He was acquitted. Loraine's post-war successes included the part of Bluntschli in Shaw's *Arms and the Man* at the Haymarket Theatre, and appearances in a number of 'talkies' during the 1930s, including *Marie Galant* and *Father Brown, Detective*. But of all the airmen who served in the Great War, few can have had more varied subsequent lives than Cecil Lewis of 56 Squadron. Lewis was one of the four founder members of the BBC, a performer on radio's *Children's Hour*, a *Daily Mail* journalist, a winner of an Oscar for best screenplay, and a dedicated follower of Gurdjieff, an Armenian mystic and teacher of sacred dances.

Before these men went their separate ways, they had shared in the most exciting aspect of wartime flying: the fact that progress in an uncharted world depended on their own initiative. Robert Loraine's old friend George Bernard Shaw once remarked: 'The reasonable man adapts himself to the world: the unreasonable one persists in trying to adapt the world to himself. Therefore all progress depends on the unreasonable man.' But the men of the air services were not unreasonable men: they were modern men. In an age, unlike our own, in which people were not encouraged to pursue an individual path, or to follow their dreams, they swapped traditional lives for something new, and they found a haven for those willing to think for themselves. But this new world was also a dangerous world, and many modern men were to die as pupils, pilots, and observers. From an anonymous diary:

> Noon. 31st January 1919. Standing forward on upper deck, grasping the rail, the deck below full of troops, around me, other officers. All silent, all looking forward to the approaching white cliffs of Dover, gleaming in the clear but cold sunlight, over the sharp end of the boat. All is over. I am untouched by scratch or bruise, the mind unable to grasp all this, and around me, not these, but the many, so many, who were never to return.

And because they never returned, they never fulfilled their promise. Mick Mannock never became a Labour MP, Arthur Rhys Davids never taught classics at Oxford University, and Albert Ball did not retire to Nottingham to tend a garden where the flowers took their time to grow. Nor did Mannock become embittered by the treatment of war veterans, Rhys Davids never stammered with excitement at the Christmas dinner table, as he told the story of Werner Voss to bored relatives, and no midwife ever presented Ball and his girl with a brood of smaller Balls. None of these men ever picked a child up from school, joined the Home Guard or watched a film in Technicolor. None ever cared for a sick wife, cried at night over a lost love, or drifted into senility. Would they have sneered at The Beatles, laughed at footballers' hair, and voted for Margaret Thatcher? Would they have eaten an Indian meal, forgiven the Germans, and learnt to use a video recorder? It hardly matters. Like the silhouettes of 6 Squadron, they remain as they were:

When old age shall this generation waste,
Thou shalt remain, in midst of other woe
Than ours, a friend to man, to whom thou say'st,
'Beauty is truth, truth beauty' – that is all
Ye know on earth, and all ye need to know.

Acknowledgements

There are many people whom I ought to thank. First of all, the staff of various excellent research facilities: the Sound, Document, and Photographic Archives at the Imperial War Museum, the Department of Research and Information Services at the Royal Air Force Museum, the National Archive, and the London Library. I have used the Imperial War Museum archives before, and am well aware of the willingness of the staff to assist. The knowledgeable help that I received at the Royal Air Force Museum was greatly appreciated, and it was a genuine thrill to sit reading the diaries of Mick Mannock, Philip Joubert de la Ferté, Gilbert Mapplebeck, and others. I would encourage readers to discover these treasures for themselves.

I would like to thank Louise Stanley at HarperCollins who has administered both carrot and stick to coax a book out of me, and Jim Gill at United Agents who has put up with any number of strange phone calls.

I would like to send warmest thanks to: Charlotte Allibone, Max Arthur (a source of constant encouragement), Margaret Brooks, Will Brooks, Richard Collins, Victoria Coren (who set the ball rolling and edits better than any editor), Simon Frumkin, Meekal Hashmi, Oliver Harris, Peter Hart (who doesn't seem to mind me muscling in), Richard Hughes, Suzy Klein (an admirer of Werner Voss),

352

ACKNOWLEDGEMENTS

Lionel Levine (who *first* set the ball rolling), Richard McDonough, Harry Mount (who glanced at a page when the mood took him), Duncan Neale (a fine accountant), Helena Nicholls (who almost kept the book free of nudity), John Stopford-Pickering, Soulla Pourgourides, Claire Price (who provided many perceptive suggestions), Orlando Wells (who watched me smoke too many cigarettes). I am grateful to you all.

Whilst researching this book, I have discovered the best and the worst of the internet. To the members of Cross and Cockade, and the Aerodrome forum, I would like to express my appreciation. The breadth of knowledge displayed by members of both of these organizations is extraordinary. They are invaluable resources for anyone seeking greater understanding of an enthralling subject.

I would like to thank all those who have allowed me to quote from letters, diaries and interviews. I have done my best to ascertain and contact all copyright holders. I would like to acknowledge the use of quotes from the following books:

Maurice Baring, *Flying Corps Headquarters 1914–1918*, Heinemann Ltd, 1930

Duncan Grinnell-Milne, *Wind in the Wires*, Mayflower-Dell, 1966

Ira Jones, *King of the Air Fighters*, Ivor Nicholson & Watson Ltd, 1934

Arthur Gould Lee, *No Parachute*, The Adventurers Club, 1968

James McCudden, *Flying Fury*, Aviation Book Club, 1939

Hans Schröder, *A German Airman Remembers*, Greenhill Books, 1986

Victor Yeates, *Winged Victory*, Grub Street, 2004

I would like to thank the Royal Aero Club for permission to use the photograph of William Robinson Clarke.

Finally, I owe a huge debt to Alex Revell, surely *the* authority on Great War flying, who read the text with a critical eye. Having said that, any mistakes or omissions in this book are my fault, and nobody else's.

Index

Abeele 210
Aces High (film) 197
Admiralty 19, 20, 23, 26, 117,
    236, 282
Affaire de Coeur 201
Agazarian, Marie 348
Air Board 299, 300, 310
Air Ministry 76, 137–8, 348
Air Staff 304
Airco DH2 175, 176–7, 178,
    179, 230, 272
Airco DH4 301, 302
aircraft, military interest in
    16–17
aircraft disposal after war ends
    347–8
aircraft markings 105
airmen, deaths of, advising next
    of kin 213–14
airmen, first wounded by enemy
    activity 104
airmen as new breed 181–2
airmen lost in Great War 63,
    350–1
airmen's lives after Great War
    223–4, 346–50

airships 11, 16, 18, 91, 286–8
    see also Zeppelin airships
    Schütte-Lanz SL2 283
    Schütte-Lanz SL11 286–7
Aisne, Battle of the (1914) 103
Alainville 140, 141
Albatros aircraft 3, 101, 247–8,
    250, 257–8, 274, 291, 313,
    316, 322, 323, 325, 340
    DI 240–1
    DII 243–4
    DIII 253, 258, 314
    DV 330
Albert 337
alcohol consumption 191, 192,
    193–4, 195–6
Aldershot 37, 52, 84
Allen, Dermot 100, 102
Alston, 2Lt C. R. 220
Amersham 348
Amiens 92, 94, 96, 199–200,
    257, 337
Amiens, Battle of (1917) 342
Amiens Cathedral 164
Andrew, John 176–7
Andrews, Howard 90

anti-aircraft fire, German
('Archie') 105–6, 128–9,
133, 153
Antwerp 118–19
Armistice 345, 346
armoured cars 117–18
Arras 198, 257
Arras, Battle of (1917) 252–3,
254–6, 258
artillery observation 138–40,
141, 142–4, 145–7, 148,
167, 226–9
'clock code' 143–4
observer 226–9
'zone calls' 144, 147, 335
Atkins (Royal West Kent
Regiment) 46
Attwater, Sgt Sidney 173–4,
272
Auchel 35
Auckland 39
Australia 29
Australian Flying Corps, 2
Squadron 217–18
Aviatik aircraft 110, 111, 161
Avro 504 92, 110–11
Avro 504K 76–7
Avro company 14

Bagatelle, near Paris 9
Baird, 2Lt 219–20
Baker, John 336, 337
Ball, Albert, VC, MC, DSO** 27,
28, 183, 184, 225, 238–40,
311, 312–15, 350
Bangkok 37–8
banks, vertical 77–8
Baring, Maurice 94, 117, 121,
170–1, 190, 257, 312

Barker, Capt William, VC 320,
321, 322–3
Barking 13–14
Barlow, Air Mechanic R. Keith 93
Barton (6 Sqn airman) 189–90
Baxter, 2Lt James 219
Beater, Orlando Lennox 196,
302–3
Beaufort, Duke of 28–9
Beaumont, S. 219
Beeton, Arthur 118
Begbie (74 Sqn airman) 152,
153, 154
Bell, Gordon 104
Berry, William 48–50, 83, 84
Béthune 35
Bill (8 Sqn airman) 256
billets 202–4
Bird, Algernon 323–5
Bishop, William 'Billy' 205
Blaxland, Lionel 212
Blencome, 2Lt F. P. 218–19
Blériot, Louis 12–13, 32
Bleriot aircraft 92, 96, 97, 99,
100, 130
monoplane 12, 13, 32, 63–4
Blériot Aviation Company 32–4
Bletchley 59, 60, 61
Bletchley Park 59, 267
Blomfield, Maj Richard 202, 203
Boelcke, Oswald 167, 169, 240,
241, 242–3
Bolt, Edward 12, 22, 95–6
bomb, atom 306–7
bomb chutes 115–16
bombing, development of 113
bombing raids 116–17, 118–19,
269, 270–3, 275, 276, 281,
299, 301, 302–5

German 59, 61, 273–4, 281–6, 290, 293–9, 305
  night 276–81
bombsight, CFS 4B 272, 304
Bond, William 257–8
Boon, John 82
Borton, Lt Amyas 'Biffy' 106
Bott, Alan 151–2
Bottomley, Horatio 48
Boulogne 95
Bowes-Lyon, Mike 265
Bowman, Geoffrey 328–9
Boxer, 2Lt Edward Maurice 222–3
Bradshaw railway guide 80
Breithaupt, Kaptlt A. 284–6
Bremner, Donald 58, 67–8, 69
Briggs, Leslie 144–5, 146, 147–8
Brighton 80–1
Brisks, 2Lt L. W. 221
Bristol Boxkite 67–8, 69
Bristol Bullet 78
Bristol Fighter 258, 291–2, 297, 330, 331
Britain
  bombing raids on 282–6, 293–9, 305
  first British man to fly aircraft in 12
  first powered flight in 11
  patriotic fervour in 91
  society in (1914) 31
Britain, Battle of (1940) 149, 235, 272
British Army see also British Expeditionary Force
  Ace of Spades Concert Party 198
  Army, Second 316–17

Army, Third 230
  Army, Fourth 133, 230, 231
  Army, Fifth 316–17
  Artists' Rifles 46, 53–4
  Glamorgan Yeomanry 62
  Gloucestershire Yeomanry 30, 31, 263
  Guards, Brigade of 83, 86
  Inns of Court Officers Training Corps 45, 46
  King's Royal Rifles 50
    7th 49
  Lancers, 16th 44
  London, 20th 46–8
  London Mobile Section 284
  London Scottish territorial battalion 34–5
  manoeuvres (1912) 22–3
  Middlesex Regiment, 11th 198
  Norfolks, 7th 50, 51
  Royal Artillery 234
  Royal Engineers, Air Battalion 18
  Royal Engineers, Balloon Section 12
  Royal West Kent Regiment 46–8
  Scottish Rifles, 3rd 229–30
  Siege Battery, No. 6: 140, 141
  Siege Battery, No. 82: 147–8
British Expeditionary Force 98, 99, 100 see also British Army
Brokensha, Howard 1–6
Brooklands, Blue Boar pub 73
Brooklands Aerodrome 25, 34, 56, 63–4, 68, 71–2
  Wireless School 144–5
brothels 200–1

Brown, 2Lt Bertram 221
Brown, Roy 341, 342
Brownwell, Raymond 158–9
Bullen, Sgt 100
Bullock, John 100–1
Burne, Charles 38
Burslem, Frank 53–4, 77, 339, 342–3
Busk, Edward 17, 120
Butler, William 330, 332, 334–5
Butler (74 Sqn batman) 152

Cairns (74 Sqn airman) 152, 153, 154, 155, 157
Calais 296
Callaghan (airman) 178–9
Calthrop 'Guardian Angel' parachute 310
Cambrai, battle of (1917) 1
camera, 'A'-type 132, 137
camera, 'C'-type 133, 134, 135, 137
camera, 'L'-type 136, 137
Campbell, Archie 40
Canadian Corps 320
Canadian Rockies 28
Canterbury 296
captain, flying pupil 74–5
Carden, Capt 96
Carroll, Lewis 23, 257
Castle (55 Sqn airman) 302
Caudron aircraft 65–6
Cecil, Evelyn, MP 284
Chabot, Charles 37–8, 73–4, 80, 119–20, 125, 159
Chamberlain, Robin Hughes 163
Chanter School of Flying, Hendon 32

Charles, Hubert N. 202–3, 291–2, 311–12, 326, 328–9
Charlton, Lionel 99–100
Charterhouse 28, 30
Chingford 67, 282
Chinnery (6 Sqn airman) 189–90
Chipilly 335
Chocques 336
Cholmondley, Lt 116
Christmas festivities 191–3
Churchill, Winston 23
Clappen, Donald 31–6, 65, 74
Clarke, Sgt William Robinson 254
Clarke (6 Sqn observer) 81–2
Clifton Court, Mrs. Mulliner's Hospital 221
Clifton Suspension Bridge 64
Cody, Leon 21, 22
Cody, Samuel 11–12, 14, 20, 21, 22
Cody aircraft 12
  'Cathedral' 20–1
cold, protection from 303
Cole, Horace 331–2
Collett (55 Sqn airman) 196
Cologne 263, 281
Colvin, James 346–7
combat, aerial, perception of 149–50
combat tactics 237–8
commanding officers, influence of 205–8
Committee of Imperial Defence 16, 19
Compiègne 101
concert parties 198

Connaught Club 61
Coombs, Vernon 58–9, 72
Cooper, Gladys 15
Cooper (13 Sqn airman) 168–9
Cooper (observer) 143
Cornwall 38, 39, 40
Courtrai 97, 271
Coverdale (74 Sqn airman) 152
Cowdray, Lord 299
Cowen, Col 290
Craiglockhart War Hospital 209, 219–20
Croydon 48–9
Croydon airport 348
Crystal Palace Depot, RNAS 87
Cuffley 287, 290
Curzon, Lord 289
Cuxhaven 119, 281
Cyril (Handley-Page's carpenter) 14

Daily Mail 12, 13, 282, 296
Dartmouth Naval College 23
Davis, Lt 89, 125, 126
Dawes, George 165
Day (flying pupil) 73
De Crepiny, Maj 261
de Havilland, Geoffrey 14, 17, 18, 20–1, 120, 175
de Havilland aircraft *see also* Airco DH2/DH4
  Comet 14
  DH17 305
  Mosquito 14
death, escaping 214–15
death, fear of 184–5, 207, 213, 314 *see also* nerves, problems with
deaths of airmen, advising next

of kin 213–14
deaths of friends 210–11, 213, 214
Delta dirigible 91
Denham 61–2
Dimmock (46 Sqn airman) 212
Donald, Graham 65, 79–80
Dormer, Lt 247–8, 249
Dossler, Ltn 262
Douai 118
Douglas, Sholto 107, 274
Douglas (8 Sqn airman) 169
Dougville, New Zealand 39
Dover 91, 93, 281
Dover School of Boys 91
Dowdeswell (squadron commander) 276
Duce, R. J. 45–8
Dugdale, Rev. R. W. 214
Dunkirk 117, 342
Düsseldorf 119, 281
DWF aircraft 101

Eastchurch, Isle of Sheppey 18–19, 23, 31–2
Eastern Daily Press 50
Eastern Evening Press 51
Eddington, George 53, 59, 83–4, 95, 102, 211, 247–50
Edin, near St Pol 48
Edinburgh Station 267
Ellins, Cpl 214, 215
Elliot, Col Charles 56
Ellwood, Aubrey 338–9
English Channel 12–13, 92, 93–4
Estrée Blanche 326
Eyles, Jim 207, 208, 224

Farman aircraft 92, 110, 166–7
Farman (Henri) aircraft 94
Farman (Maurice) Longhorn 69, 70, 74
Farman (Maurice) Shorthorn 69
Farnborough 12, 16, 17, 37, 49–50, 85
 Laffan's Plain 22
Felixstowe RNAS station 282–3
female company 201–2
Ferrie (46 Sqn airman) 310–11
Festubert, Battle of (1915) 172, 233
Field, Laurie 71
fighter aircraft, development of 149, 159, 165
Filton 213
Finch-Noyes, Lt 101
Finnish Air Force 301
fire, fear of 308–9
First World War see Great War entries
Flanders 42–4, 316
flight, first powered 8–9
flight, wonder of 7–8
flying training 63, 64, 65, 67–72, 215
 cross-country flights 80–1
 first 'solo' 72–4
 'French School' 65–7
 night flying 81
 Royal Aero Club pilot certificate test 74–5
 spin recovery 76, 77
Fokker, Anthony 166–7
Fokker aircraft 343
 D.VII 149, 330
 Dr.1 Triplane 153, 154–6, 323, 324, 325–6, 330, 340, 341

E.I Eindecker 166–8, 176, 177, 243, 272
E.III Eindecker 167–8, 176, 177, 272
'Fokker Scourge' 167–9, 175, 176, 177, 179, 230
Folkestone 295
food drops 342–3
Foot, Isaac 40
formation patrols 250–2
Forster, E. M. 208–9
Forward Observation Posts 138
France, arrival in 94–6
France, first powered flight in 9
French, Sir John 98–9, 100, 103, 174
French air force at outbreak of war 92
French army 230–1
 Army, First 316–17
 Army, Fifth and Sixth 102
 officers and orderlies 264–5
 Territorials 42, 43
'friendly fire' 104–5
Fulljames, Reginald 71, 75, 76, 196
Furlong, Eric 15, 65–7, 70

Garros, Roland 165–6
Gascoyne, James 22, 77, 116, 344–5
Gaskell, Lt Penn 110
Gembloux 96, 97
George V, King 282, 289, 315, 345
German Air Service 92, 334
 Jagdgeschwader 1 (Richthofen's Flying Circus) 2–5, 315–16
 Jagdstaffel (Jasta), first 240–1

German Army
  Army, First 99, 100, 102
  camp commandant 264
  intelligence officer 261
  retreat 342–5
  Signal Corps 166
  Uhlans (cavalry) 118
German High Command 96,
  326
German Spring offensive (1917)
  330–7, 342, 344
Gheluvelt 117
Gidea Park 53–4
Giles (74 Sqn airman) 152, 153,
  154
Gladstone, Lt 216–17
Glasgow 95
Gloucester Station 30
Gnôme rotary engine 14, 36, 67,
  87, 160, 175
Go-Between, The 184
Goddard, Victor 23
Goodson, Col James 10
Gordon Bennett Cup 31–2
Gordon-Burge, Cyril 271, 286
'Gosport tube' 75
Gotha (Grosskampfflugzeug)
  bomber 295–7, 298, 299,
  305
Gould Lee, Arthur 205, 211–12,
  213, 309, 310–11
Grahame-White, Claude 14,
  25–6
Gran, Tryggve 181, 182, 215–17,
  253–4, 292–3
Gray, Thomas 8
Great War begins 30, 34, 37–8,
  91, 93
Great War ends 345, 346–8

Great Yarmouth 282
Green, Sgt 89
Greig, Capt 89, 125
Grey, Capt D. S. 241–2
Grey (No. 3 Sqn airman) 102
Grierson, Sir James 22–3
Grinnell-Milne, Duncan 7, 8,
  105, 181
Grosvenor, Lord Edward 26
ground-attack (strafing) patrols
  318–20, 344–5
Guard, Brig Fred 346
Guard, Lt Phil 346
gunnery training 89
Gurdjieff 349

Hague Conference (1902) 281–2
Haig, Gen (later Field Marshal)
  Sir Douglas 22, 171, 174,
  230, 252, 275, 315, 316
Haldane, Gen 130
Hall, A. M. 101
Hall School of Flying, Hendon
  34, 65–7
Hamel, Gustav 32, 36, 64
Hampshire Downs 14
Handley-Page, Frederick 13–14,
  15–16
Handley Page aircraft company
  13–14, 20
  Halifax 13
  O/100 and O/400 301–2,
    303–4
  V/1500 305
  Yellow Peril 13–14, 15, 25
hares, hunting 185–6
Harlaxton 70
Harris, Arthur 56
Hartley, L. P. 184

Harvey-Kelly, Maj Hubert 94, 114, 122, 257
Hastings 90
Hawker, Lanoe 150–1, 176, 242
Hawker Hurricane 272, 348
Hawkins, William 87
Heales, Sgt Horace 191–3
Heinecke parachute 310
Hell's Angels (film) 149
Henderson, Brig Gen Sir David 19–20, 96, 103, 121, 289, 321
Hendon Aerodrome 14–16, 32–4, 36, 49, 65, 66, 68, 69, 281, 347–8
Hesdigneul 290
Higgins, Gen 187
Higgins, Josh 110
Hindenburg Line 342
Hitler, Adolf 283
Hong Kong 29
Hopkins, J. C. F. 336–7
hospitals 209, 219–21
Hughes, Howard 149
Hume, Ross 81
Humphries (No. 4 Sqn airman) 106–7
Hunaudières, near Le Mans 9–10
'Huns', origin of 157–8

Immelmann, Max 167, 168, 169
'Immelmann turn' 168
Inca of Perusalem, The 188
India 45

'Jabberwocky' 257
Jackson, Alan 138–9, 273, 277

James, Archibald 104, 127, 132, 143, 148, 201–2, 239, 290, 317, 349
in 3rd Hussars 42–4
and Callaghan (FE2b pilot) 178–9
and 'contact' patrols 172, 233
and parachutes 309–10
on patrol 162–3
and Lord Trenchard 170, 274–6
and weapons 108–9, 113, 146
James, Baron 139–40, 143
James, Frederick 185–6
James, Maj 249–50
Japan 29
Jeanne (Amiens restaurateur) 199, 200
Jillings, Sgt-Maj David 104
Joffre, Gen Joseph 174, 230
John Bull 188
Johns, W. E. 201
Joint War Air Committee 299
Jones, George 217–18
Jones, Ira 152–7, 158, 184–5, 203, 210, 223–4
Jones (55 Sqn airman) 196
Jones (74 Sqn airman) 152, 153, 154
Joubert de la Ferté, Philip 19–20, 23, 96, 97, 100, 102, 130, 348
Juilly 101

Karachi 45
Karlsruhe 263–4
Keele, Tommy 198
Kemp, Leslie 38
Kendal (8 Sqn pilot) 332
Kiel Canal 119

King, Cecil 36–7, 52, 83, 84,
      87–8, 101, 114
King's Lynn 282
Kingston, Surrey 36
Kingston Barracks 36–7
Kitchener, Lord 48
kites, man-lifting 11, 12
Kitty Hawk, N. Carolina 9
Klein (German pilot) 308
Kluck, Gen von 99, 100, 102
Knowles (officer) 55–6

La Boiselle 232, 233, 234
La Fère 100–1, 117
Lachman, Gustav 332–3
Land Steffen Castle 54
Lawrence, Ikey 102
Laws, Flt Sgt (later WO1)
      Frederick 22, 131–2, 136–7
Le Cateau 100, 343
Léalvillers 187–8, 204–5
Leigh, Humphrey 68, 74–5, 282
Leighton (airman) 130
leisure pursuits 183, 184,
      185–94, 196–202 *see also*
      life, squadron
Lenin, V. I. 262
Leon, Lady 59, 60
Leon, Sir Herbert 60
Lewis, Cecil 82, 134–6, 145–6,
      196–7, 231–4, 235, 250–2,
      296–7, 349
Lewis, 2Lt David 339–40
Lewis, Donald 139–40, 143
Lewis, Gwilym 177, 204–5, 235,
      243
life, squadron 202–5 *see also*
      leisure pursuits
Lille 118

Linnarz, Hptm Erich 283
Livock, Gerald 69
Lloyd George, David 299
London
   Alexandra Palace 12
   after Armistice 346
   Connaught Club, Oxford Street
      61
   defence of 281, 284, 285
   Euston Station 61
   Fulham Road 14
   Liverpool Street Station 52, 61,
      295
   Lyall Street, Chelsea 297
   Marylebone Station 222, 223
   New Scotland Yard 53
   Poplar infants' school 295,
      296
   raids on 283, 284–6, 293–6,
      297–9
   St Bartholomew's Hospital 61
   Tottenham Court Road YMCA
      40
   Trafalgar Square 38, 48
London Air Defence Area 296
London Colney 311–12
London County Council 40
London Gazette 314
London General Hospital, 4th
      220
London Polytechnic 42
loneliness 211–12
Longmore, Lt Arthur 22
loops 77, 78–80
Loos, Battle of (1915) 35, 174
Loraine, Robert 122, 187–9,
      204, 349
Lubbert, Friedrich 316
Ludendorff, Erich 327

Lunde, Brig Gen 130
LVG aircraft 178, 327

McCudden, James, VC 93, 95,
    210, 325–6, 327–30
McCudden, Maurice 329–30
McFall (fitter) 214
Macmillan, Norman 180–1, 210,
    318–20
Maeterlinck, Maurice 190
Maghull Military Hospital
    218–19
Malik, Harditt Singh 320–2, 323
Mann, Conrad 282–3
Mannheim 302
Mannock, Edward 'Mick', VC
    205–6, 207–8, 212–13,
    224–5, 258, 270, 342
  death 309, 350
  Ira Jones' memories of 152,
    153, 154, 156, 158, 210
Mapplebeck, Gilbert 96–7,
    99–100, 105, 109–10,
    113–14
Marie Louise (Merville girl) 202
Marieux 120, 274
Marix, Flt Lt Reginald 119
Marne, Battle of the (1914)
    102–3
Marne, River, retreat to 100–2
Martinsyde company 20
Martinsyde Scout 122–3
Maubeuge 92, 96, 97, 98, 100,
    101, 110
May, Wilfred 'Wop' 340–1
Melun 101
Merville 201–2, 272
Messines 130, 316
Messines Ridge 316

Mike (8 Sqn airman) 256
Moltke, Gen Helmuth von 18,
    96, 281
Mons 99, 104
Mons, Battle of (1914) and
    retreat 100–2
Moore-Brabazon, John 12, 96,
    131, 132
Morane-Saulnier Type L 165
Morgan, Capt Tom W. M. 172–3
Morley, Maj 298
Morris, Lionel 241, 242
Morse code 139–40, 141, 142–3,
    146
Mosley, Oswald 349
Mulcahy-Morgan, Capt Tom W.
    172–3
Murton, Bertie 50
Murton, Leslie 50–2
Murton, Sidney 50
music 196–7
Muspratt, Keith 326

Nagasaki 306–7
Nancy 200–1
naval aviators 18–19 see also
    Royal Naval Air Service
nerves, problems with 209–10,
    215, 217–23 see also death,
    fear of
Netheravon 93
Neuve Chapelle, Battle of (1915)
    132, 171–2
New Theology, The 40
New Zealand 29, 38–9
Newall, Lt Col Cyril 301
Newbolt, Cpl 84
Newcastle 290
Newton (pilot) 148

Nieppe, Forest of 156
Nieuport 17: 236, 238–9, 312
Nivelle, Gen 252
Nivelles 96, 97
No Parachute 309
Nordholz Zeppelin station 119
Northcliffe, Lord 12–13
Norwich 50
  Britannia barracks 51
Notes on an English Character
    208–9
Nurlu 330

observation flights *see* artillery
    observation; reconnaissance
    entries
observers' training 88–90
Ochey 301
O'Flaherty VC 188
O'Gorman, Supt Mervyn 17
'Only Way, The' 197
Ostend 117
Ostler, Walter 44
Oyeghem 172

Page, K. P. 143–4
parachutes 309–11
Paris 99, 102
Park, Maj Keith 331
Parrott, Florence 59–62
Passchendaele, Battle of (1917)
    316–20
Pégoud, Adolphe 63–4
Pemberton-Billing, Noel 299
Penn Gaskell, Lt 110
Pentland, Jerry 320
Péronne 334
Peter, Edward 25
Pezarches 101

Pharos, The 91
photographic reconnaissance
    131, 132–8
Pigot, Robert 16
pilots, inexperienced 253–4 *see
    also* airmen *entries*
Piper, N. V. 21
Pissy 164, 165
Plumer, Gen 203
Porri (observer) 162, 163
Porter, Cpl 178
Powell, Maj Frederick 55–6, 70,
    78–9, 142, 160–1, 175,
    203–4, 213–14
  and leisure pursuits 186–7,
    188–9, 194, 200–1
Pozières 232
Pretyman, Lt George 131
Price, Professor 42
Prince, Maj C. E. 144
prisoner-of-war experiences
    260–7, 292–3
propeller interrupter gear 166–7
  Ross system 236
public school attitudes 208–10

Quénault, Louis 110

Rabagliati, Lt Cuthbert 97–9,
    101–2, 109, 115–16
radio transmitter, Sterling
    142–3
Raleigh, Maj 21
Ransley, Frank 126–7, 331
Read, Lt William 105–6
reconnaissance, photographic
    131, 132–8
reconnaissance flights 96–100,
    101, 102, 103, 167, 231–2

reconnaissance flights – *cont.*
  'contact patrols' 171–2, 233–4,
    235
reconnaissance role of aircraft
    22, 24, 124–5, 126–8,
    130–1
Rees, Thomas 241, 242
Remuera, New Zealand 29
Rhodesia 54
Rhodes-Moorhouse Jnr, William
    272
Rhodes-Moorhouse, William,
    VC 271–2
Rhys Davids, Arthur 190, 325–6,
    350
Rice, Bernard 226–9, 254–6,
    298, 348–9
Rice, 'Eddy' 255
Richards, William 38–42,
    140–1
  father 38–40
  mother 38–9
Richthofen, Lothar von 314
Richthofen, Baron Manfred von
    76, 150–1, 240, 242–3, 257,
    291, 316, 323, 324–5,
    339–42 *see also* German Air
    Service: Jagdgeschwader 1
Rickenbacker, Eddie 10
Rivers, W. H. R. 209–10
Robey, George 106
Robinson, Lt William Leefe, VC
    286–90, 291, 292–3
Robinson, Cadet 23
Rockefeller Foundation 54
Roe, A. V. 14, 20
Rogers, T. E. 44–5, 210–11, 317,
    318
roller-skating 186–7

Rothermere, Lord 304
Rowell, Robin 120, 133–4, 169,
    199–200, 274
Royal Aero Club, pilot certificate
    test 74–5
Royal Air Force
  Coastal Command 348
  formation of 299, 300, 301,
    337–9, 345
  Independent Air Force 304–5
  squadrons *see also* Royal Flying
    Corps
  No. 3: 339–40
  No. 6: 343–4
  No. 10: 339
  No. 12: 347
  No. 24: 348
  No. 73: 339
  No. 92: 344–5
  No. 209: 340–1
  No. 217: 338
  No. 218: 342–3
  post-Great War service in 348
  uniform 339
Royal Air Force Museum 14
Royal Aircraft Factory (formerly
    Army Aircraft Factory)
    17–18, 20, 236
  BE1 (Blériot Experimental 1)
    17, 18
  BE2 21–2, 94, 297
  BE2a 92
  BE2c 7, 17, 82, 119–20, 133,
    134–5, 138–9, 168–9, 247,
    257–8, 271, 273, 275,
    276, 286–7
  BE2e 128–9, 252–3
  FE (Farman Experimental) 18
  FE2b 89, 177–8, 179, 241, 242,

272, 277–81, 292, 301,
336–7
FE2d 323
RE (Reconnaissance
Experimental) 18
RE8 247–9, 250, 254, 318, 336
SE (Santos-Dumont
Experimental) 18
SE5 152–7, 258, 261, 311–13,
314, 315
SE5a 149, 224–5, 325, 326,
327–8, 330, 347–8
Royal Flying Corps 25, 26, 244,
258, 270–1, 284, 317, 327,
337
air superiority strategy 174–5,
229–30
aircraft at outbreak of war 92
Aircraft Park 94–6
Aldershot barracks 37
Awkward Squad 86–7
boys' section 51
Central Flying School, Upavon
19, 68, 88, 92, 272
combined into Royal Air Force
300, 301, 337, 338
discipline 83–7
enlistment 31, 36–7, 42, 44,
48, 49–50, 51–2, 54, 55,
70
medical examination 58–9
Farnborough HQ 85 see also
Farnborough
fatalities, first 92–3
and 'Fokker Scourge' 167–9,
175, 176, 177, 179
formation of 18–19, 20, 34, 36
Home Defence Wing 284
HQ 85, 94–5, 120–1

Military Aeroplane Trials
(1912) 20–1, 119
pilots, new, assigned to
squadrons 81–2
recruits, rank and file 82–3,
84–5, 87–8
role of 124–5
St Omer HQ 120–1
squadrons
No. 1: 91–2
No. 2: 42, 56, 91–2, 94, 95,
104, 107, 274–6, 290
No. 3: 1–6, 82, 91–2, 93, 94,
95, 96, 99–100, 102, 105–6,
131, 231–3,
339–40
No. 4: 94, 95, 96–7, 106–7,
110, 125, 139–40, 336
No. 5: 88, 94, 95, 100–1, 106,
160–1, 273, 277
No. 6: 81–2, 189–90, 210–11,
317, 343–4, 350–1
No. 8: 133–4, 169, 226–9,
254–6, 274, 330, 332,
334–5
No. 11: 163–5
No. 12: 271, 347
No. 13: 168–9
No. 16: 128–9
No. 19: 257, 320
No. 20: 323
No. 24: 176–7, 191–3, 348
No. 25: 202
No. 28: 320, 321–2
No. 29: 258–61
No. 32: 177, 235, 243
No. 36: 286
No. 40: 212–13, 257–8
No. 41: 186–9

Royal Flying Corps – *cont.*
  No. 45: 158–9, 180–1,
    318–20
  No. 46: 194, 211–12, 309,
    310–11, 323–4
  No. 48: 126–7, 291, 331
  No. 53: 196
  No. 54: 244–6
  No. 55: 196, 301, 302
  No. 56: 190, 202–3, 291–2,
    296, 311–12, 314, 325–6
  No. 66: 296
  No. 70: 181
  No. 74: 152–7, 184–5, 203,
    208
  No. 80: 194
  No. 83: 336–7
  No. 85: 205–6, 207
  No. 98: 48
  No. 100: 301
  No. 101: 215–17
  training manual 24
  Trenchard as commander
    170–1, 174
  Wing, First 170, 171
  Wing, 41st (later VIII Brigade)
    301–2, 304
  wings 121
  women in 59, 61–2
Royal Naval Air Service 19, 23,
    25, 26, 64, 119, 246, 270,
    281, 282–3
  7 Squadron 303–4
  8 Squadron 243–4
  16 Squadron 301–2
  Advanced School of Flying,
    Gosport 75, 76–7
  combined into Royal Air Force
    300, 301, 337–9

defence of Britain 24, 117, 281,
    284
  Eastchurch Squadron 117,
    118–19
  enlistment 38, 58
  recreation in 87
  recruits, rank and file 82–3,
    84–5
Royal Navy 23–4
Rumpler aircraft 327, 328
  Taube 110, 113–14
Russell (6 Sqn airman) 190
Russian PoWs 263

St Neot, Cornwall 39
St Omer 120–1, 163, 200
St Quentin 100, 276
Salisbury Plain 19, 20–1
Salmet, Monsieur 33
Salmond, Geoffrey 131
Salmond, Maj Gen John 131,
    327, 336
Samson, Cmdr Charles Rumney
    'Sammy' 58, 117–18
Sanctuary Wood 43
Santos-Dumont, Alberto 9
Satchell, Harold 277–81
Saulnier, Raymond 165
Saunders, S. S. 71–2, 86–7, 108,
    109, 111–13, 142–3
Schatzmann (chateau owner)
    203–4
Schlieffen Plan 96
Schröder, Ltn Hans 193–4,
    308–9
Schweidnitz, Silesia 265–6
Scott, Sir Percy 284
Senlis 101
Serris 101

Shanghai 29
Shaw, C. K. 314
Shaw, George Bernard 188–9, 349
Sheerness 31
Shenfield Common 294
Shepherd, Dolly 11–12
Sheppey, Isle of 18–19, 23, 31–2
Sherring, Geoffrey 306–7
Shorncliffe 295
Sieveking, Lance 26
Silk, Ralph 343–4
Silver Queen dirigible 91
Silwood, F. D. 72–3
Simpson, Capt J. H. 237
Skeddon (74 Sqn observer) 152, 153, 154
Skene, Lt Robert 93
Small, Frederick 111
Smart, Charles 128–9, 252–3
Smith, Russell 244–6
Smith-Barry, Maj Robert 75, 76–7, 111
Smuts, Jan 299–300, 304, 338
Smuts Report 229, 300–1
Somme front 133–5
Somme, Battle of the (1916) 47–8, 230–4, 238, 274
Somme, River 331–2, 334
Soncamp 254
songs 197
Sopwith, Tommy 236
Sopwith aircraft
  1½ Strutter 236
  Camel 1–2, 3–5, 79–80, 194, 217, 258, 261, 297, 315, 318, 321, 330, 340, 341
  Pup 244–5, 250, 323–4, 348

pusher aircraft 282
Scout 119
  Triplane 243–4, 246, 250
Southend-on-Sea 283
Sowrey, Lt 295
Spad aircraft 320
Spencer, William 62
spin recovery 75–6, 77
Spuy, Kenneth van der 93, 94, 107
spy drops 172–4
Star Wars (film) 149
Stephen (46 Sqn airman) 211–12
Stewart, Alexander 229–30
Strange, Capt Louis 94, 110–11, 115, 116, 122–3, 348
Stroud 28
Studd (airman) 178
Sueter, Murray 19
Swann (13th Wing airman) 214
Swingate Downs Aerodrome 91, 92–3
Sykes, Ronald 64, 76, 77–8

tanks 30, 235
Taylor, George 88–9, 125–6, 128, 177, 202
Taylor, Raynor 62
technical training 87–8
theatrical pursuits 187–9, 191–2
Thompson, Herbert 243–4, 246
Thomson, Thomas 338
Tomkins, Ernest 57, 64–5
Tonight's the Night (musical comedy) 197
Toul 200–1

Tournai 97
Townsend, Philip 347–8
Trenchard, Maj Hugh (later
    Lord) 22, 26, 35, 121,
    170–1, 174, 231, 257,
    274–5, 296
  and bombing 299, 304–5
  offensive strategy 175, 240,
    253, 272–3, 327
Trier 264–5
Trinidad 53, 54
Trotsky, Leon 262
Turner (55 Sqn airman) 302
Tye, Charles 13–14, 15–16,
    20–1, 25
Tyrell, Nell 287, 293–5

Udet, Ernst 310
Ultra Intelligence 267–8
Union Castle Company 54
Upavon 19, 68, 88

Van de Leene 172
Van der Riet, E. F. 196
van der Spuy, Kenneth 93, 94,
    107
Vancouver 28–9
veneral diseases 201
Verdun 168, 252
Vert Galant 163, 204, 257, 313
Vickers FB5 'Gunbus' 159–61,
    162–5
Victor, Monsieur 173–4
Victoria, Queen 28
Voisin pusher aircraft 110
Voss, Werner 325–6, 350

Waddington, Sgt Maj 86
Wadham, Vivian 99–100

Walters, Stanley 54, 73, 124,
    184
War Cabinet 299, 301
War in the Air, The 8, 269, 270,
    281, 305–6
War Office 16, 19, 20, 30–1, 35,
    51, 56, 57, 140
Ward, Simon 197
Wardrop, William 303–4
Warley Barracks 59
Wassigny 97
weapons 107–8, 109
  artillery shells 145–8
  bombs 270–2
  bombs, shrapnel 115–16
  darts ('flechettes') 113, 270
  grenades, hand 113, 114,
    270
  gun, sixty-pounder 147, 148
  howitzer, twelve-inch 147–8
  machine gun, Lewis 110–13
  machine gun, Maxim 122
  machine gun interrupter gear,
    Ross system 236
  machine guns firing through
    propeller 165–7
Weigers, Mr. 261
Weir, Sir William 299
Wells, H. G. 8, 269–70, 281,
    300, 305–6
Wervicq 128
Westcliff-on-Sea 31
Western Front 103, 138, 167,
    258, 290
Whitehead (Handley Page pilot)
    15, 16
Wilhelm II, Kaiser 29, 117,
    157–8, 266, 282, 345
Williams, Florence 283

Winchester, Clarence 15
Winged Victory 194–5, 209–10, 315
Winterbotham, Capt Frederick 28–36, 258–68
wireless telegraphy 139–44, 146, 148
wireless telephony 144–5
Wolff, Kurt 257
Women's Auxiliary Army Corps 61
Wooley, Frank 84–5
World War One *see* Great War *entries*
Wright, Orville 8–9, 10–11
Wright, Wilbur 8–11
Wright Biplane 65
Wright *Flyer* 9–10
Wyllie, Harold 81–2, 106–7, 128, 130, 168–9, 178, 189, 206–7

Yeates, Victor 194–5 see also *Winged Victory*
YMCA, Tottenham Court Road, London 40
Ypres, Third Battle of (1917) 316–20
Yuille, Archibald 80–1

Zeppelin, Count Ferdinand von 281
Zeppelin airships 11, 18, 23, 119, 281, 282 *see also* airships
L13 283
L15 284–6
LZ38 283
raids by 59, 61, 282–3, 284–6, 290, 293–5, 299, 305
Zeppelin 'Giant' biplane 297
Zeppelin sheds, raids against 270